T0365263

BEYOND
THE
SHORES

CROWN
NEW YORK

BEYOND
THE
SHORES

A HISTORY

OF

AFRICAN

AMERICANS

ABROAD

TAMARA J. WALKER

Published in the United States by Crown,
an imprint of Random House, a division of
Penguin Random House LLC, New York.

CROWN and the Crown colophon are registered
trademarks of Penguin Random House LLC.

LIBRARY OF CONGRESS CATALOGING-IN-PUBLICATION DATA
NAMES: Walker, Tamara J., author.
TITLE: Beyond the shores / Tamara J. Walker.
DESCRIPTION: First edition. | New York: Crown, 2023. | Includes index.
IDENTIFIERS: LCCN 2022056996 (print) | LCCN 2022056997 (ebook) |
ISBN 9780593139073 (paperback) | ISBN 9780593139066 (ebook)
SUBJECTS: LCSH: African Americans—Travel—History. |
African Americans—Foreign countries. | Americans—Foreign countries. |
African Americans—Biography.
CLASSIFICATION: LCC E185 .W237 2023 (print) | LCC E185 (ebook) |
DDC 910.89/96073—dc23/eng/20221214
LC record available at https://lccn.loc.gov/2022056996
LC ebook record available at https://lccn.loc.gov/2022056997

crownpublishing.com

Book design by Barbara M. Bachman

151204861

To John and Willie Mae

CONTENTS

BEYOND
THE
SHORES

PROLOGUE

MY MATERNAL GRANDPARENTS, the only ones I ever knew, were born five years apart in Montgomery, Alabama. First came my grandpa, John, in 1921, followed by my grandma, Willie Mae, in 1926. Both took their first steps in the shadows of the cotton plantations where their own grandparents had been enslaved, and came of age in the post-Reconstruction, "New South" era that promised the opportunities of urban industrialization but kept my family, like other Black Alabamians, tied to sharecropping, tenant farming, and menial service.

These were the forces that combined with legal segregation, voter disenfranchisement, and racial terrorism to make Alabama a place worth leaving and a starting point for the Great Migration, which saw African Americans (that is, the descendants of men and women once enslaved in what is now the United States) from the South fan out in search of safer, more promising destinations across the country. My grandparents, though, were part of a more circuitous and expansive trajectory.

When he was twenty years old, my grandpa worked at

A.J. Jones Grocery. The store was located at 604 Highland Avenue, just a few blocks south of where Jefferson Davis lived when he was president of the Confederate States of America during the Civil War, in what was known as the First White House of the Confederacy. Davis's home later served as a boardinghouse in the postwar era and in 1921 underwent an extensive, state-financed restoration of its nineteenth-century, Italianate features before opening as a museum. To white Alabamians, the house stood as a gleaming monument to what might have been; to my grandpa and other Black Alabamians, it was a constant, formidable reminder of the war their home state had fought to keep them in bondage.

By 1941, another war was under way, this time in Europe, and my grandpa was drafted to serve. The same country that relentlessly pushed his people down was now demanding that he put his young life on the line to defend it. The irony of the situation was perfectly captured in a letter in *The Pittsburgh Courier* by a twenty-six-year-old from Wichita, Kansas, named James G. Thompson, who asked: "Is the kind of America I know worth defending? Will America be a true and pure democracy after this war?" Ultimately, Thompson decided, "Let we colored Americans adopt the double VV for a double victory. The first V for victory over our enemies from without, the second V for victory over our enemies from within." By fighting for their country against foreign enemies, Thompson, my grandpa, and many other African Americans hoped that their bravery on the battlefield would be rewarded with equal opportunity back home.

My grandpa's exit from Alabama, then, was also an exit from the United States, taking him around the European theater and eventually to the beaches of Normandy. What label do we give the route he traveled, not only within Europe but back to Alabama, out west to Washington State, and over to Europe again, several times—including a three-year military post in Austria with my grandma and their children that became the stuff of family legend—before finally settling as a family of eleven in Colorado? Calling it part of the Great Migration feels incomplete, since that story doesn't account for the experience of crisscrossing oceans, of navigating language barriers, of venturing into new social systems where being American sometimes mattered more than being Black, or of accessing privileges and opportunities that were unheard of back home.

Indeed, while we are all familiar by now with the Great Migration thanks in large part to Isabel Wilkerson's magisterial *The Warmth of Other Suns,* we are generally less familiar with the journeys undertaken by soldiers like my grandfather who spent time abroad for military service; by entertainers, writers, scientists, and teachers who left this nation in pursuit of professional opportunities that were denied them at home; and by countless men and women who left simply to put distance between themselves and the country of their birth.

Wilkerson drew on the words of one of the more famous of those sojourners to title her book. In his 1945 memoir, *Black Boy,* Richard Wright recalled his move from Mississippi to Chicago as stemming from a powerful need to "respond to the warmth of other suns. And, perhaps, to bloom." Her telling leaves Wright in Chicago, among the fanned-out dreamers in hopeful pursuit of something more. But if we pick up just two years after *Black Boy*'s publication, we learn that, to his mind at least, the northern sun was never going to be warm enough—nor was any that shone on American soil. By 1947, Wright was living with his wife Ellen in Paris, having decided, he later wrote, "to live beyond the shores of my native land."

Wright is part of the story I tell in these pages, about the many and varied reasons African Americans left the United States, what they found when they reached their destinations, and how they felt upon returning home, if they ever did so at all. But for so long he, along with James Baldwin and Josephine Baker, has been made to shoulder nearly every chapter of that story. I spent a lot of my young life thinking that the history of African Americans abroad started and ended with these three, in Paris. That it started with Baker making her debut at the famed Théâtre des Champs-Élysées in the 1920s, continued with Wright and Baldwin holding forth at literary cafés near the banks of the Seine two decades later, and ended where they themselves did, each being laid to rest in (or near) the City of Light.

Their stories loomed large for good reason. In interviews, speeches, essays, books, and letters, these three gave firsthand insight into the sense of humanity, opportunity, and possibility that Paris offered African Americans during the exact moments when those things were under steady attack in the United States (and, ironically, during the exact same time that the United States stood as a beacon of freedom and welcome to European immigrants). Wright's fiery unpublished essay, "I Choose Exile," put it plainly: "There is more freedom in one square block of Paris than there is in the entire United States of America!"

This freedom, in turn, fueled the imaginations of film-makers, playwrights, poets, and novelists. I remember watching HBO's *The Josephine Baker Story* (starring Lynn Whitfield) with my family when it premiered in 1991. I was thirteen years old and sat in rapt horror through the film's first act, which opens with a scene from Baker's own youth in East St. Louis, Illinois, in 1917, when a white mob—angry over the rising numbers of Black employees in local factories—descended on the city's "African Quarter." On-screen, the camera pans across a sea of white men and women setting houses on fire, dragging Black people out of streetcars, beating them with pipes, and shooting at them as they try to flee. Then it zooms in on the dark corner of an empty theater, where a little girl is hunched over, trembling in fear. Amid the piercing cries of her neighbors, the girl makes a promise to herself: If she makes it out of this alive, she'll leave town and never look back.

The film's breathless second act shows Baker stepping off the RMS *Berengaria** from New York in 1925, twirling through the streets of Montmartre, dancing onstage in front of ador-ing crowds, taking romantic boat rides along the Seine, mov-ing into a rambling apartment, and, years later, marrying a Frenchman in a glamorous ceremony on the grounds of her

---

* The ship was originally a German ocean liner built for the Hamburg Amer-ica Line named the *SS Imperator,* briefly commissioned into the U.S. Navy after World War I, and eventually handed over to the Cunard Line, where it was re-named the RMS *Berengaria.*

very own château. The contrast between the horrors she left behind on one side of the ocean and the joys she found on the other left an indelible mark on me.

I did not yet know that Paris had its own history of racism, that Wright, Baldwin, and Baker were shielded from the worst of it because of their American citizenship, and that, even so, nothing could protect them from the racism of the white Americans who made their way to Paris during the same era. I did not yet know that Paris and three of its most famous residents were just a small part of a much bigger story of African Americans leaving their home country to see what lay beyond its shores. I did not yet know that my own family was part of that story, too.

Of course, African Americans have been leaving this land ever since first arriving on it in chains. They stowed away on vessels docked in the Chesapeake before sailing to Europe and the West Indies in the seventeenth century, fought for the British during the Revolutionary War to gain passage to Canada, emigrated to Haiti in the decades following its emergence as an independent Black republic in 1804, escaped Southern plantations to cross into Mexico after it abolished slavery in 1821, and founded towns for freed people in Liberia (at the behest of the white-led American Colonization Society, whose founders saw returning to Africa as the only condition under which enslaved people should be released from American bondage). What these few examples all had in common was the search for freedom from slavery during a time when it was available only to a small minority, either through emigration or through escape. Things changed, somewhat, with the Emancipation Proclamation, which made it possible for African Americans to live free in the country of their birth. But if they wanted a shot at experiencing meaningful citizenship or their full humanity, they still needed to say their goodbyes.

The modern history of African Americans going abroad in large numbers began in earnest during World War I. Barred from the marine corps and most of the navy, the majority of African American enlistees joined the army and were sent to Europe to provide support to the Allied forces. Among them were the members of the all-Black 369th Infantry, known as the Harlem Hellfighters, who helped to introduce jazz to the Continent. But it was not until the 1920s that a true phenomenon started taking shape. It was the decade when entertainers like Josephine Baker crossed the Atlantic to break out of the confines of the minstrel and vaudeville circuit and headline shows that used a wider range of their talents. Reports of their successes made their way back home thanks largely to Black newspapers like the *Atlanta Daily World,* Baltimore's *Afro-American, The Chicago Defender,* the *Cleveland Call and Post, The Pittsburgh Courier,* the *New York Amsterdam News,* and the *Norfolk Journal and Guide,* which commented on the warm reception the performers received both onstage and off. The papers' coverage, in turn, fueled a wave of new sojourners, including those in show business who wanted to try their own luck overseas, and ordinary citizens who wanted to take in a good show and have a good time among friendlier hosts than could be found in the United States. Continuing the cycle, Black newspapers (and later, magazines and guidebooks) across the country began sending editors over to spotlight Europe as a tourist destination with a wealth of daytime offerings, too, including museums, restaurants, and shopping districts.

We have now witnessed a century of people on the move. The task of writing any book covering such a long period always involves difficult choices about structure and content, and the choices are even more fraught when layering together two expansive topics like African Americans' relationships to the United States and their experiences of going to other countries. But it turns out that the arc of our country's history provides a useful narrative framework: In each decade from the 1920s to the present, the United States has presented African Americans with a defining set of challenges—Jim Crow, the Great Depression, the World War II era, the civil rights movement, and more—that made leaving the country seem, for many, like the best way forward.

Choosing from the long and diverse list of African Americans who left the United States for various corners of the world presented another challenge. This one offered no easy solutions: I imagined one version of this book taking, in each decade-focused chapter, an expansive look at an assortment of different people and places. But I decided it would be more meaningful to center the chapters on just one or two people whose stories best embodied what was at stake for African Americans in each decade. The choice also meant grounding each chapter in just one or two places where we could linger for a while and get a sense of how, during different points in history, countries outside of the

United States thought about African Americans, Blackness, and race more generally.

These were tremendously personal decisions, too. In some cases, I chose to write about people whose experiences helped me understand things about my own family, since my grandpa John, my grandma Willie Mae, and so many of my older relatives are no longer alive to tell their own stories or answer any of my questions about them. After all, they are the reason I wanted to write this book in the first place. In other cases, I chose to write about people whose experiences resonated with my own in some way, either because they traveled to places that made an impact on my own itinerant life, because they traveled at the same formative stages as I had, or because travel introduced them, as it did me, to new ways of being that would otherwise never have been unlocked.

Still, this book would have felt incomplete if I had insisted on such a tight focus from start to finish, and so I found different strategies along the way to make one point as clear as possible: Regardless of the specific names and places I chose or for various reasons had to set aside, every page of this book is about all of them. All of us.

CHAPTER 1

THE TRANSATLANTIC SENSATION

Florence Mills,

PARIS AND LONDON,
1920S

B Y THE TIME SHE FACED out into the crowd for her Paris debut, Florence Mills was already a stage veteran. Though barely thirty years old, she had a lifetime of performances under her belt, from the neighborhood juke joints where she'd belted out ballads as a toddler to the Broadway theater where she first performed *Blackbirds,* a musical revue that made her a star. That same show had brought her to the Café des Ambassadeurs on the Champs-Élysées (a combination nightclub and restaurant with a large dance floor separating the stage and dining area) on this night in May 1926. Now the beautiful young woman with the face-framing spit curls was poised for something even bigger. She stood backed by a hundred-person chorus and orchestra and flashed a dazzling smile at the audience, awaiting the drumroll that was her cue. Then she took over with the song, dance, and comedy routines that were as familiar to her at this point as her own heartbeat. "Une artiste véritable," one paper enthused the next day.

The comparisons were inevitable. "Here is Florence Mills, who right away makes us think about Josephine Baker," wrote the Parisian weekly *Le plaisir de vivre*. One reason for the association was the circumstances of both women's arrival in Paris: Florence's *Blackbirds* revue had opened in the city less than a year after Baker headlined *La revue nègre* at the Théâtre des Champs-Élysées, which kick-started her own French ascent. Both women also had signature hairstyles that made them easily identifiable, both were fountains of youthful charisma who entranced scores of admirers, and both were generating buzz for their energetic performances onstage. For all their similarities, though, the Parisian paper seemed intent on fetishizing their differences: Florence's complexion was "*café au lait*" (with more *lait,* the paper insisted to male readers, than *café,* as if to give them permission to lust after her without needing to interrogate their racial preferences) in contrast to Baker's "*café noir*"; Florence was "*civilisée*" while Baker was "*sauvage*"; and Florence's singing and stage persona called to mind the French actress and singer Alice Cocéa and the Hungarian American Dolly Sisters duo, whereas when it came to Baker, "On ne la voit pas blanche. Négresse elle est, négresse elle restera." (One cannot see her as white. Black she is, Black she will stay.)

As far as the paper was concerned, the verdict was in: "Si Florence Mills était un visage pâle, elle serait le plus formidable numéro de le Amérique." (If Florence Mills had a paler face, she would be the hottest number in America.)

The United States didn't know what a good thing they had in her.

Regardless of Florence's perceived advantages over Baker (which were themselves a product of French racist thinking and a sign that, compared with white Americans, locals weren't quite as evolved as they wanted to believe), it was the latter who would eventually become synonymous with Paris in the 1920s, while Florence wound up little more than a relative footnote. Bringing Florence back into the mainstream spotlight does more than simply renew attention to her remarkable life and career. It's an opportunity to remember that Baker was just one of countless African American performers who made their way to the City of Light, left indelible marks on its cultural landscape, and turned it into a destination for new forms of music, dancing, and cross-cultural mingling in ways that would be felt for decades to come.

Florence and her *Blackbirds* crew also responded to calls to take their talents beyond Paris, as word spread via audience members and European newspapers about the arresting new show. It wasn't long before the floodgates opened, with African American performers accepting invitations to grace cabaret and theater stages in London, Vienna, Berlin, and beyond. As the French German poet Ivan Goll put it in a 1926 essay titled "The Negroes Are Conquering Europe," in response to the force of the moment: "The Negroes are conquering Paris. They are conquering Berlin. They have already filled the whole continent with their howls, with their laughter. And we are not shocked, we are not amazed:

on the contrary, the old world calls on its failing strength to applaud them."

BORN FLORENCE WINFREY IN 1896 to formerly enslaved parents, she was one of eight children who all crowded into a small apartment in a wood-framed row house on Goat Alley in Washington, D.C. A notoriously poor and densely populated "hidden community"—one of hundreds carved out of alley-facing rear lots to accommodate the city's growing population after the Civil War—Goat Alley was tucked into the square formed by Sixth, Seventh, L, and M streets in northwest D.C. (today's Shaw neighborhood). As recently as the 1880s, the community was home to white immigrants from Germany, Ireland, and elsewhere in Europe, but by the early 1900s, nearly all of its four hundred residents were Black, including the Winfrey family.

Like the other alley communities in D.C., Goat Alley was cut off from the rest of the city in nearly every way. Neither sunlight nor streetlights penetrated its dark corners, and because there was usually only one way in and one way out, it saw no casual pedestrian traffic. The only people who crossed Goat Alley's threshold were its residents and those who preyed on them, like the mercenary landlords who ruled the neighborhood despite living in other parts of town. They came through at regular intervals to demand exorbitant rents for tiny units in cramped row houses that lacked water and sewage and were plagued by "leaky roofs, broken and filthy ceilings, [and] dilapidated floors," all of which made the homes there generally "unfit for human habitation."

Another source of trouble for the residents of Goat Alley was the constant intervention of white police officers and reformers who saw the community and others like it as breeding grounds for "vice, crime, and immorality." The Gerry Society, an organization that was co-founded by the lawyer Elbridge Thomas Gerry for the ostensible purpose of preventing cruelty to children and that operated in East Coast cities, posed a particular threat. Agents, known as Gerry men, made it their mission to keep children away from supposedly immoral environments like dance halls, theaters, and the poor neighborhoods that tended to surround such establishments. The Gerry men treated poverty itself as an immoral act, separating poor children from their families in ways that often caused more suffering than even the worst financial hardships.

Before they became marquee names, Buster Keaton, Milton Berle, and Al Jolson (who would later make a career painting his face coal black and depicting Black people as hapless minstrels) were all caught in the Gerry men's crosshairs, pulled from the stages of local performance venues, held in the organization's custody, and eventually placed in Catholic institutions (even if they had no connections to the faith, like Jolson, who was Jewish). The same fate would soon befall young Florence.

Growing up on Goat Alley, Florence earned the nickname "Baby Flo" when, at just three years old, she accompanied her mother to pick up laundry around the neighborhood and captured attention for singing Irish ballads like "Mother Machree" and "Little Grey Home in the West" in a high-pitched voice that would become her trademark. She learned the lyrics from her older sisters Olivia and Maude, who for their part likely learned the songs from the white immigrants who once lived in their neighborhood. Baby Flo soon found early success singing and dancing onstage at northwest D.C.'s popular Bijou Theater; that is, until the Gerry men came along when she was nine years old. They arrested her for underage performing and shipped her off to an institution run by local nuns. All this occurred against the wishes of Florence's family, who knew little about where she was being held and had no way of being able to visit her.

The experience conspired with the more quotidian hardships of life on Goat Alley to sour the Winfreys on living in Washington. When Florence was released from the institution after about a year, the family packed up and moved to New York. There was perhaps another draw to the city: It was a much bigger market for the sisters to try their luck as stage performers. Indeed, while living in New York, Florence, Olivia, and Maude became known as "the Mills Sisters," adopting the last name Florence had used since the beginning of her career after borrowing it from the doctor listed on her birth certificate. They began singing and dancing in venues throughout Harlem, which in the early decades of the twentieth century was becoming a hub for African Americans from the South and Black people from across the Caribbean, who all came together to create a neighborhood filled with diverse traditions and a destination for live music and cultural events. The crowds loved all three Mills sisters, but Florence was the clear standout. By the time she was twenty, she decided, in classic American fashion, to try to make her fortune out west.

Florence first set her sights on Chicago, where the World's Columbian Exposition of 1893 helped draw musicians from all over the globe. Ragtime performers from the South were among the first to arrive, setting up shop in dance halls, cabarets, and speakeasies. Along with fellow up-and-comers Cora Green and Ada Smith, Florence formed a group that regularly took the stage at the Panama Café. From 1916 to 1917, they performed as the Panama Trio; one critic described them as "the cleverest dancing and singing three in Chicago."

Chicago was also where Florence met Ulysses "Slow Kid" Thompson. Originally from Arkansas, Thompson left home at an early age to make a living as a performer. He started out in the Mighty Haag Railroad Shows, in Louisiana, at age sixteen, making his way around the South as part of various circus, minstrel, and vaudeville troupes, including the Ringling Bros. circus and Prof. Gentry's Famous Dog and Pony Show. He could tap-dance and do acrobatics, but his stock-in-trade was a slow, seemingly time-freezing dance routine that earned him his nickname. By 1916, Thompson was part of a touring group called the Tennessee Ten, which Florence joined after leaving the Panama Trio. If the two shared anything other than onstage chemistry, it was hampered by the fact that Thompson was married to a former performer named Letepha Rogers. The marriage was troubled from the start thanks in part to the mismatch between Thompson's commitment to the touring lifestyle and Rogers's preference to remain in Chicago, where they shared a home. Still, Thompson remained financially committed to Rogers, even sending her money while he was on the road.

Then, in 1918, Thompson was drafted into World War I. Barred from the marines and most of the navy, the African American soldiers who enlisted or were drafted to serve were relegated to noncombatant support roles, in which they generally undertook tasks like unloading flour and pipefitting. His involved performing in an army band in France, where he played jazz and ragtime for troops and locals. Doing so allowed him to keep his performance skills sharp enough that, when the war ended, he found his way back to Chicago and stepped right back onstage.

Florence had left the Tennessee Ten shortly after Thompson shipped off to Europe. She reunited with Cora Green as part of a new Panama Trio that included Carolyn Williams, who replaced Ada Smith when she decided to pursue a solo career, and the group went on tour to the West Coast and up to Canada. They returned to Chicago around the same time as Thompson, who was back with the Tennessee Ten after a brief stint performing in a duo called the Jazzerinos. Florence and Thompson's time in the city was short-lived, as their groups ended up touring Greek club owner Alexander Pantages's eponymous vaudeville circuit that included more than eighty clubs across North America, but the shared itinerary allowed the pair's romance to blossom. It didn't hurt that Thompson had discovered that his wife took up with a Pullman porter while he was away for the war, which provided an opening for him to pursue his own extramarital entanglement.

The relationship marked the beginning of a new phase in Florence and Thompson's life, in which their professional and romantic worlds would become intimately connected:

first, when they joined the Pantages circuit, and second, when Florence's career-defining break came about thanks to Thompson's advocacy.

It was the spring of 1921. Thompson had finally gotten divorced, and he and Florence were now free to get married and build their lives together. Their time as touring musicians had kept them on the road for forty weeks out of the year and left little room to try out new material or experiment. Both saw it as a waste of Florence's formidable talents in particular. She was proving to be the real star, and at this point Thompson began to promote his wife's career. Thompson still had a taste for performing, but he saw Florence as the draw who would bring opportunities to both of them. Harlem made perfect sense as their next destination; it was the country's new center of gravity for Black creatives in the 1920s, home to upstarts and established figures alike.

Florence and Thompson regularly dined out on Strivers' Row, where they ran into folks like Noble Sissle and his vaudeville partner Eubie Blake, two luminaries in the performance world who had co-written the songbook for a scrappy new Broadway musical called *Shuffle Along*. The show, whose script was penned by Flournoy Miller and Aubrey Lyles, another Black duo with vaudeville roots, opened on May 23, 1921, at the 63rd Street Music Hall, a venue that just barely counted as Broadway, since it was so far uptown from the central theater district. The show made hits out of songs like "Love Will Find a Way" and "Gypsy Blues," and an instant star out of a young comedic talent from North Carolina named Gertrude Saunders. Saunders was quickly snapped up to headline another show, for higher pay, leaving a gap in the cast. One night at dinner, Thompson approached Sissle to tell him that Florence wanted to step in for Saunders and play the supporting part of Ruth Little.

The casualness of the conversation belied Thompson and Mills's desperation to steer her career in a more sustainable, more satisfying, and hopefully more successful direction. They saw what *Shuffle Along* had done for Saunders and wanted the same for Florence. For his part, Sissle was intrigued, if somewhat skeptical. Even though he knew Florence's work, she was one of the last people he'd had in mind for the role. He wanted someone sensual, someone who could comfortably shimmy around while singing the blues and pull audience members to the edges of their seats in rapt adulation. For her part, Florence was easily and frequently mistaken for a teenager. Sissle needed convincing that she could shed her girlish qualities and transform into a grown woman in full command of her powers. Thompson did his part to make the case, and Florence also got an assist from her old Chicago pal Ada Smith, who was now living in New York and friends with Sissle. Both insisted that Florence was capable of the transformation, and convinced Sissle to let her take her shot. After all, she did have one quintessential attribute that all the chorus girls for the show needed to have: light skin.

The desire to cast light-skinned Black performers was partly a reflection of how Black creators had to bend in different directions to appeal to white theatergoers whose expectations were often logically inconsistent and capricious at best. Those audiences wanted to see light-skinned chorus girls with facial features and hair textures similar to those of their white counterparts in other Broadway productions, even as they expected Black performers—male and female—to appear onstage with their faces painted coal black and lips overpainted with red smiles or frowns to exaggerate their phenotypical differences and emotions. But the preference for light skin was also a reflection of Sissle and Blake's internalized racism, an unsurprising result of centuries of white beauty ideals being forced on Black men and women. Color-based preferences in the Black performance world found analogues in other professional realms, like law and business, and in social life, including the dating pool and marriage market. These forces united to create an internal hierarchy in which lighter-skinned people dominated the ranks of America's Black elite and drove darker-skinned people—especially women—to try products that would bleach their skin. They were encouraged by advertisements and articles in papers like *The Afro-American,* which insisted to readers that "there is no complexion, no matter how bad, dark or spotted that will not improve immediately and become light, soft, smooth and velvety when treated with Dr. Fred Palmer's Skin Whitener Preparations."

This kind of colorism almost kept Josephine Baker from getting her part in *Shuffle Along* (she was part of the national tour's chorus from August 1922 until the fall of 1923). She had to audition multiple times before her talent and charisma blew all concerns about her brown skin out of the water. But other performers would not be so lucky.

Just as Florence was auditioning for the role of a lifetime, one that could change the direction of her future, the Bijou Theatre on West Forty-fifth Street and Broadway hosted an event that served as a powerful reminder of the trauma and upheaval of her past. On June 20, 1921, a play written by a white author named Ernest Howard Culbertson and titled *Goat Alley: A Tragedy of Negro Life* had its stage debut. In the introduction to the published version of the play, which was set in Florence's old D.C. neighborhood, drama critic Ludwig Lewisohn claimed that Culbertson "saw that the Negro cannot yet hope, like the white man, to transcend common standards. He must first reach them." Unsurprisingly, the story leaned heavily on disparagement. It described one character as "an old coal-black Negress" who lived in self-induced squalor alongside other Black residents who drank too much, fought endlessly with romantic rivals, and were always the source of their own troubles.

To Florence it must have felt like a moment of divine irony, if not outright cruelty.

Though the theaters they were staged in were physically separated by just over a mile, *Goat Alley* and *Shuffle Along* could not have been further apart. Written by a white man for white audiences, *Goat Alley* was a vehicle for offering a parodic, hectoring assessment of the so-called Negro problem. The phrase was popular shorthand used by white politicians, intellectuals, and ordinary citizens to blame Black people for their own hardships rather than acknowledge the country's institutionalized racism. *Goat Alley* fit easily within this racist way of thinking, serving as easy and unassailable proof of Black people's pathological tendencies. Lines like "Go 'long, yo' ole black wench! Don' yo' give me

no back talk!" and "Yo' be de meanes' [n****h] in Wash'nin'"
brought those tendencies to life as the mostly amateur cast
yelled them at one another.

In contrast, *Shuffle Along* was the first major musical production written, staged, and performed by African Americans, many of whom had college degrees during a time
when only 10 percent of Americans could say the same.
After more than a century of minstrel shows and vaudeville
performances that hewed to white theatergoers' stereo-
typed expectations of how Black performers should look
and sound onstage by confining them to roles as buffoonish
figures with childlike emotions, conveyed mostly through
plantation-style songs while wearing blackface (which in
those days involved the application of dark makeup to dark
skin as well as white), *Shuffle Along* and its cast broke new
ground. The show celebrated its characters' humanity,
showcased their joy, and—importantly—sought to make
audiences laugh *with* the performers, rather than *at* them. It
would also mark the first time that Black audiences got to
sit in the orchestra, closer to the stage, rather than being
forced into distant balcony seats.

Still, there was one thing that both *Goat Alley* and *Shuffle
Along* did have in common, and that was blackface. While
most of the latter show's cast was able to sidestep the tradition, it remained so steeped in American performance culture that the two lead performers still wore it. The decision
was not without criticism from Black audiences, who
wanted to see *Shuffle Along* represent a wholesale rejection
of blackface and all the racist show business practices it represented. Was that too much to ask?

Perhaps keeping blackface in the show was an attempt, like the casting of the chorus girls, to lure in white audience members by giving them familiar and comfortable tropes. Or maybe it was an act of defiance, a way of signaling an awareness that blackface was not going anywhere anytime soon, and that Black performers might as well reap the benefits of its mainstream popularity while also endowing the practice with something less cartoonish and insulting.

Together, *Goat Alley* and *Shuffle Along* represented the complicated spectrum of employment options available to Black performers in the United States, with *Goat Alley* being the more typical option on offer and *Shuffle Along* being the exception that still played by some of the same rules. Both productions required performers to make sacrifices if they wanted to work at all. They tried their best to instill the parts with some depth, to eke out something onstage that was missing from the page, even if all the audience saw were one-note performances.

Of the two shows, only one got the advantage of prime placement and coverage. While *Shuffle Along* was relegated to the fringes of the theater district uptown, "sandwiched between garages and other establishments representative of the automobile industry, [which] was little known to the average Broadway theatregoer," *Goat Alley* had its premiere in the heart of Broadway with a formal pre-show program that was covered by *The New York Times*. On opening night, according to the paper, "the Medical Review of Reviews [journal] has been at some pains to make the point that here was an important play of negro life, a work of some sociological value that should deal frankly and fearlessly with a vital phase of the negro problem." The production also featured someone the paper described as a "medical speaker," which was most likely some kind of doctor, medical professional, or self-styled expert who was willing to promote the popular eugenics discourses of the era that linked biology to social behavior. The medical speaker's presence reduced the characters to specimens of sorts and gave *Goat Alley*'s claims a veneer of scientific rigor and legitimacy before the very first curtain call. The paper would ultimately criticize Culbertson's lack of artistic and sociological originality, suggesting that "the piece would probably have been just as realistic throughout had it been played by professional [meaning white] actors in blackface." Nonetheless, the *Times* described *Goat Alley* as "a serious play."

What could it have been like for Florence, to see a white man who had never lived in Goat Alley, who had never endured its peculiar hardships or the wrenching heartbreak of being taken from his own family, be elevated—by both the medical and the theater establishments—as an expert on it? And how did it feel to have traveled so far over the years to escape those memories, only to end up just a few short blocks from *Goat Alley*? Maybe anger was the only thing Florence could take from all of this. And maybe that anger crystallized into a new vision of herself, one that was no longer innocently demure but capable of rising above Goat Alley: both the place and the play. Perhaps she put that passion on full display at her last audition for *Shuffle Along*, because finally, Sissle saw it: Florence was "Dresden china, and [then] she turns into a stick of dynamite." When she got the part, the contract included a role for Thompson.

Years later, when a reporter tried asking Florence about
her childhood, she waved off the attempt to dredge up old
memories. "I don't like to think of that part of my life," she
said. "It was too horrible. I like to think I started with *Shuffle
Along*." It certainly made for a happier place to start, since
when she joined the production in August 1921 there was an
immediate cascade of rave reviews. *Vanity Fair* called her
"the most skilful [*sic*] individual player" in the cast. "Merely
to watch her walk out upon the stage, with her long free
string and her superb, shameless swing, is an aesthetic plea-
sure: she is a school and exemplar of carriage and deport-
ment." Within weeks, another opportunity came calling.

Lew Leslie was a white performer of unremarkable talent who turned to writing and producing, eventually making a name for himself by putting on shows with all-Black
casts at the Cotton Club. Everyone in the performance
world, Black or white, dreamed of playing there because a
short set broadcast over the radio could make an entire career. The trade-off for Black performers, however, was that
the club did not allow Black guests. Night after night, Black
performers would work up a sweat onstage, only to have to
leave the building as soon as their work was done, without
so much as a glass of water for their trouble. This was despite the club's location in Harlem, and the burgeoning
Black theater audience that was based or willing to travel
uptown. The success of *Shuffle Along* proved that all-Black
casts could do big numbers at the box office, and that Black
theatergoers were a lucrative market who should not only
be welcomed but actively courted.

Few were more eager to exploit this lesson than Leslie,

BEYOND THE SHORES 29

who set his sights on Harlem's Plantation restaurant as the location for a musical revue of the same name that would boast Florence as its headline star. The two-act show soon outsold its uptown location and opened in July 1922 at the 48th Street Theatre, adding some vaudeville numbers to create what *The New York Times* called "a spontaneous outburst of song, dance, color and buoyant spirits." When the *Plantation Revue*'s run concluded a month later, Florence and Leslie moved on to create *Dover Street to Dixie,* which had a brief, complicated run in London in 1923 (more on that later) before they returned to the United States for *Dixie to Broadway,* another two-act revue that featured numbers like "Jungle Nights in Dixieland" and "Put Your Old Bandana On." It ran at the Broadhurst Theatre from October 1924 until January 1925. Both productions won Florence more adoring coverage, not so much for the material as for how her charm and talents transcended it.

The next year brought another starring role. *Lew Leslie's Blackbirds of 1926* opened with Florence leading a cast of seventy-five in front of a sold-out audience of one thousand at Harlem's Alhambra Theater (where ticket prices ranged from fifty cents to a dollar). *The Afro-American* described how Florence made her entrance "from the center of a large birthday cake, that is supposedly for 'Mammy's Birthday,'" before singing a number called "Silver Rose." It was a scene that could have been in the *Plantation Revue, Dixie to Broadway,* or any number of other vaudeville shows of the 1920s. It seemed that the broader theater world learned few lessons from *Shuffle Along.* Even when they acknowledged the bankability of all-Black casts and the desire of Black audiences to see them, they were not ready for Black writers or production staff. Their voices still did not matter.

Florence had gotten exactly what she'd been dreaming of when she sat across from Noble Sissle to audition for *Shuffle Along:* Broadway stardom. But even that came with its share of indignities and disappointments. After years of grueling work on the road, she found herself at the pinnacle of success for Black performers, yet still being handed the same old vaudeville material with the same bad writing, thin plotlines, and cartoonish characterizations of Black people.

This was the era of Irving Berlin and George and Ira Gershwin, who were breaking new ground in musical theater by offering audiences more dynamic songbooks and storytelling in front of far more lavish sets than were typical of vaudeville productions. From Berlin's *Music Box Revue* (1921) to the Gershwins' *Lady, Be Good* (1924), it was an exciting time for performers and audiences alike—so long as they were white. Florence, meanwhile, continued to toil away in the same kinds of roles that, outside of *Shuffle Along,* had always been her lot, and watched from the sidelines as her white counterparts like Adele Astaire (sister to the famed dancer Fred) got meatier opportunities. (George Gershwin's all-Black *Porgy and Bess* would not have its premiere until 1935, more than a decade after the 1922 premiere of *Blue Monday,* which was similarly influenced by Black culture but featured white actors in blackface.)

Broadway in the 1920s was also a direct route to Hollywood for white performers. Florence was aware of this and knew that the only thing holding her back was her race.

There was no other reason: Marion Davies, who got her start as a chorus girl on Broadway, landed a role in the *Ziegfeld Follies,* which she transformed into a career as one of Hollywood's leading ladies.

Black performers were used to finding their own way beyond Broadway. While *Shuffle Along* might not have changed much downtown, it was a different story uptown. Langston Hughes wrote that the show "gave just the proper push—a pre-Charleston kick—to that Negro vogue of the 20's, that spread to books, African sculpture, music, and dancing." In other words, it helped inform the artistic milieux that became synonymous with the Harlem Renaissance.

In addition to Harlem, another venue started to materialize for Black performers: Paris. The city was undergoing its own postwar rebirth, with audiences who were clamoring to see the Black revues that were all the rage in New York. Josephine Baker and the cast of *Revue nègre* led the way, and just one year after her arrival, Baker managed to secure a nightclub of her very own after the completion of the show's run. Florence's Panama Trio colleague Ada Smith had done the same. Nicknamed "Bricktop" for her fiery mane of red hair, she'd first tried her luck in New York after leaving Chicago but soon moved across the Atlantic to open a namesake nightclub on rue Pigalle in Montmartre.

Paris was a place where bigger, better, and more exciting things seemed to be on offer for the Black members of the vaudeville and cabaret circuits. Josephine Baker's early success in the city suggested that a revue performance could be a springboard to one-woman shows and possibly roles in

French films. If they couldn't take Hollywood, well, then, they could try taking Europe. So, when Lew Leslie signed his *Blackbirds* up for a run in Paris, with a premiere date set for the end of May 1926, Florence, the rest of the cast (which included her husband), and their orchestra were more than ready.

BEFORE THEY COULD CLAIM any of their potential fame and fortune, though, they had to get across the ocean. In the late eighteenth and early nineteenth centuries, ocean liners still served two distinct populations. In one group were the wealthy Americans who traipsed across the Atlantic for honeymoons, vacations, and educational opportunities at some of the world's most famous museums, archaeological sites, and universities. These were the types of travelers immortalized in Edith Wharton's novels, elegant men and women who hopped on and off steamers like catching a city taxi. The other group were the millions of immigrants who left behind homes and families in Italy, Poland, and Russia to cross the ocean in search of new opportunities in the United States.

Although these two groups often traveled on the same vessels, their experiences could not have been more different. For their part, wealthy Americans boarded floating resorts for their journeys at sea, sleeping in spacious, wood-paneled cabins modeled after the finest hotel rooms. They spent their waking hours in elegantly appointed dining rooms, smoking lounges, and recreation areas featuring Turkish baths and swimming pools.

In contrast, immigrants crowded into the ships' lower steerage decks where, as one passenger put it, there was "no attention to comfort or decency." They slept on mattresses filled with wood shavings and took their meals out of tin pans while seated in the same cramped spaces. All the while, they jockeyed for better deck positions among their fellow travelers, in the hopes of making the journey a little more bearable by getting fresher air and more expansive views.

There was a shake-up in the steamship industry in the 1920s. With nativist and anti-Asian sentiment on the rise in the United States, Congress passed strict immigration laws to reduce the number of new arrivals. This meant that the major steamship companies catering to immigrants lost a significant source of revenue. They moved away from transporting immigrants in the lower holds and instead targeted leisure tourists and business travelers in the United States, offering them competitive prices for travel to and from England, Germany, and France.

Part of what made the pivot to the tourist market possible was the strength of the U.S. dollar. Favorable exchange rates meant that Europe was a relatively inexpensive place for tourists to travel. And steamship companies were offering transatlantic prices that were comparable to domestic rail tickets, meaning that it didn't cost much more to go to London from New York than to California. In addition to Cherbourg and Southampton (both reachable from New York in seven days), ships now docked at Liverpool (reachable in eight days), Hamburg (nine days), and Antwerp (eight to nine days).

The steerage compartment was renovated to make room for people who wanted, rather than needed, to travel. The cramped, oppressive quarters were replaced by "tourist third class" cabins, which were intended for middle-income tourists rather than the tired, poor, and huddled masses who were yearning to be free on U.S. soil. The cabins came with access to the same public amenities enjoyed by first- and second-class passengers. The British-owned White Star Line, for example, promoted weekly sailings in their third-class cabins on the *Majestic, Olympic,* and *Homeric* vessels traveling between New York and Cherbourg / Southampton with an advertisement that showed a "dining saloon" where passengers could take their meals on a high floor of the ship, an outdoor volleyball court where they could work up a sweat in the fresh air, and a tourist smoking room where they could entertain themselves into the wee hours. The copy read: "Here you will find contestants worthy of your skill in chess, checkers, dominoes, bridge or other games."

In short, the introduction of third-class cabins made it possible for more Americans to travel overseas. But it also transferred already existing land-based hierarchies in the United States to the high seas by bringing people who rarely interacted with one another in their day-to-day lives on land into the same physical space together. Thanks to publications like *The Chicago Defender* and the *New York Amsterdam News* trumpeting the affordability of traveling by sea, African Americans now came on board in growing numbers. They were free to book whichever class of cabin they (or their sponsors) could afford, whether on the upper decks or in the lower holds, but often found that their fellow Americans wanted to draw the same kinds of color lines that governed their interactions at home.

When a group of performers from New York's Cotton Club were booked in third class on board the *Lafayette* to attend the Exposition Internationale in Paris, white passengers complained to the staff about having to travel in such intimate proximity to African Americans in the public spaces of the ship, which did not have a formal segregation policy in place. In response, the *Lafayette* staff arranged for the performers to sit in a separate corner of the restaurant, out of sight of the white men and women whose tickets cost no more than their own. White Americans wanted to carry Jim Crow as far across international waters as they possibly could.

Sometimes, though, things went smoothly, as they did for a group of Fisk University graduates on board the Italy-bound vessel *Conte Biancamano,* who expected to encounter racism but instead found that "every day was filled with sunshine and pleasurable activities and every night filled with moonlight and dancing. . . . We took a part with the others in every activity on the ship, and had some wonderful times. Our dining room steward and waiter saw to it that our every need was fulfilled."

Florence, Thompson, and the *Blackbirds* crew had to navigate this new world of steamship travel to get to Paris, and on May 15, 1926, they made their way down to West Fifteenth Street to board SS *France* bound for Plymouth and Le Havre. The vessel was operated by the Compagnie Générale Transatlantique, which was better known in the

United States as "the French Line." The *France* had been requisitioned by the French navy during World War I and helped repatriate American troops in 1919 before being refurbished and returned to commercial duty in 1920. Known as "the Versailles of the Atlantic" because of its opulent décor and nearly all first-class cabins (there were 150 third-class berths), it was popular among the wealthy white Americans and Europeans who traversed the ocean for work and leisure. Florence and her company were joined on this sailing by the boldface names of white America, like tennis players Vincent Richards and Howard Kinsey, and Rudolph Ganz, conductor of the St. Louis Symphony Orchestra.

It's not known if Florence and company were in first or third class, but they would not have been spending much time in their cabins anyway. They had a show to rehearse. *Blackbirds* was set to open within days of their arrival at the Café des Ambassadeurs, a three-thousand-seat venue located in the iconic Hôtel de Crillon at Place de la Concorde on the Champs-Élysées.

THE LOCATION WAS IN the heart of the heart of the city, which was the first indication that *Blackbirds* was going to be met with great fanfare. Indeed, it quickly became "the sensation of Paris," with the cast performing night after night to sold-out crowds. Florence was a major draw, with a Parisian paper saying she "would stand out among a half-dozen Rolls Royces." Although both the show and its stars were widely chronicled in France and the United States, it was the Black press that took care to note how different the environments on each side of the Atlantic Ocean were. A *New York Amsterdam News* headline said it all: "Colored Artists Holding Sway and Being Treated Like Human Beings by the French."

This kind of coverage served as a flashing billboard for Paris in the United States, not just for other African American artists but also for the audiences who supported their work and the chroniclers who wanted to capture the emerging zeitgeist. Unlike venues in the United States that allowed Black people as performers but not as patrons, or that restricted them to certain seating areas or nights of the week, the Parisian theaters and nightclubs beckoned to them without restrictions. Gone were the days of performing long sets at the Cotton Club and then being refused a seat or a drink of water.

Soon these new arrivals were sharing dinner tables, drinks, and dances with Parisians of all stripes. In the 1920s, the city was home to nearly three million residents, with a large and growing percentage hailing from other parts of Europe, from Latin America, and from French colonies in Asia, Africa, and the Caribbean. While some of these groups had been in Paris for generations, others were more recent immigrants who came to study, to find domestic, factory, and office work, and to pursue varying artistic, intellectual, and political agendas. Together this diverse bunch created a global city with enclaves, alliances, hierarchies, and frictions emerging around racial, ethnic, linguistic, and citizenship lines.

Black enclaves in Paris took up both sides of the Seine,

including Montmartre to the north and Montparnasse to the south. The latter was home to one of the most popular centers of nightlife in the city: Le Bal Nègre, a dance hall founded by Martinicans that served as a gathering place for people from the Caribbean and West Africa. When J. A. Rogers, a reporter for the *New York Amsterdam News*, visited in 1928, he called it "French Harlem." It was an apt label for the mélange of cultures and traditions it was home to: On a given night, patrons could dance to Martinican *biguines*, which derived from the folk songs of the enslaved, Senegalese orchestra tunes that included elements of Cuban music that traveled to African airways and migrated to France, and even some African American jazz. Rogers noted that "the visitor who speaks only English had better take an interpreter with him."

Black Parisians from Martinique, Guadeloupe, Haiti, Benin, Senegal, and elsewhere founded organizations such as the Ligue Universelle pour la Défense de la Race Noire (LUDRN, or the Universal League for the Defense of the Black Race, which had a companion newspaper called *Les Continents*) and the Ligue de défense de la race nègre (LDRN) in the 1920s to defend and protect the rights of Black people in France, condemn the abuses endemic to French colonial rule, and insist that French colonial subjects should have full citizenship rights. They were among the many organizations that cropped up throughout the African Diaspora around this time, including the Pan-African Association, which was co-founded in Paris in 1921 by the African American intellectual W.E.B. Du Bois, the German branch of the LDRN, and the Jamaican activist Marcus Garvey's Harlem-based Universal Negro Improvement Association.

The very existence of the LUDRN and LDRN was proof that Paris was far from a racial idyll, and that France was not that different from the United States when it came to how it treated its Black population. But the absence of Jim Crow made it seem like a haven to African Americans. Perhaps nowhere best embodied this vision of Paris than Bricktop's. Owner Ada Smith welcomed old friends from home like Florence and the writer and poet Langston Hughes, as well as white American guests, including F. Scott Fitzgerald, Cole Porter, and Gertrude Stein, who helped spread the word that the nightspot on rue Pigalle was the place to be. "Go to her cabaret any night," said J. A. Rogers. "The list of distinguished guests would vie with guests at a reception at King George's court, or sound like a Who's Who in Wall Street. She is the very life of her place. It is simply impossible to have the blues in her company."

These white American guests would likely have balked at the idea of sitting at the same table or in the same section with a Black person in the United States. But when white visitors came to Bricktop's and other hot spots, they understood that the rules in Paris were different. For them, crossing racial lines was part of the local experience, but it did not change white Americans' attitudes about African Americans or race in general.

None of Gertrude Stein's visits to Bricktop's, for example, ever stopped her from deploying racist characterizations in her fiction, or from filling her letters to her friend and fellow writer Carl Van Vechten with anti-Black epithets.

In one letter, she referred to an essay she wrote in *Useful Knowledge* titled "Among Negroes" as "the little [n****r] thing," and in another letter told Van Vechten, "I am looking forward enormously to the [n****r] book" (referring to Van Vechten's *Nigger Heaven*). Stein didn't see any conflict between her racist beliefs and her enjoyment of Bricktop's hospitality. Cole Porter was no better than Stein: Although Bricktop was the conduit through which he made his success in Paris, the friendship proved one-sided when Bricktop eventually returned to New York and Porter refused to see her or take any of her calls.

The nightlife of 1920s Paris was increasingly American-centric thanks to the combined punch of a strong U.S. dollar and the high sales taxes levied on customers in cafés and clubs as a means of boosting the French economy in the post–World War I era, when income taxes proved an insufficient source of revenue for the state. Because incomes were difficult to assess, and attendant taxes were difficult to collect, officials resorted to levying taxes on food and beverages, which made it even harder for Parisians to enjoy their own city's nightlife. A reporter for *The Afro-American* pointed out that few Frenchmen could patronize the cabarets where Black performers were headlining, since they struggled to afford the cost of a beer or whiskey once inside. In contrast, "French women can always find a gallant overseas visitor delighted to take her to one of the exotic cabarets."

Not every white American was content to fraternize across the color line. With more and more establishments serving a primarily American customer base, Paris and its nightclubs started to see a wider mix of white Americans who had no intention of treating African Americans any differently than they did back home. Just because they were thousands of miles away did not mean that the rules of Jim Crow did not apply.

It's no wonder that years later Josephine Baker revealed, "When I heard an American accent in the streets of Paris, I became afraid. I would tremble in my stomach. I was afraid they'd humiliate me." And she had plenty of reasons to be afraid. One incident that was fueled by the racist outrage of white American patrons occurred in June 1926 at the Café des Ambassadeurs, where Florence made her French splash weeks earlier. On a typical night there, the band would play while some folks enjoyed the music from their tables and others spun around on the dance floor. On this night, according to a report in *Variety,* a Black man named Frisco started dancing with a white woman. This was typical, too, for him, for his partner, and for countless others at nightclubs all around town. But some white Americans in the crowd didn't like what they were seeing and took their complaints to management.

Maybe if it had been the year before, when white Americans made up just a small segment of the crowd, management could have ignored them. But now club owners and promoters were worried about alienating the very people who were keeping the lights on, which meant that someone on staff decided to head out to the dance floor, tap Frisco on the shoulder, and ask him and the lady to take their seats. Of course, the move was out of step with what Frisco and others had come to expect: Confused and insulted, he shrugged off the request and kept on spinning around the floor with his partner. After all, they weren't doing anything inappropriate—they were only dancing, just as Black-white pairs had done every other night before this one.

Whether it was because the club's staff knew that the white American customers would not let this go, or out of their own sense of irritation over being rebuffed, management decided that if Frisco wasn't going to stop dancing on his own, they would make sure he didn't have anything to dance to, so the band was instructed to stop playing. But the musicians were Black, too, and like Frisco, they didn't see why there was a problem. It was Paris, after all, not New York. So they kept right on playing, and the couple kept right on dancing—right up until someone called the cops.

When the police arrived, the woman's white husband stepped forward to explain the situation. It was his idea, he told them, for Frisco to pair off with his wife on the dance floor. According to *Variety,* the "nationality of the husband and wife was not mentioned in the cable [as for Frisco, he turned out to be British]. It may be presumed they are French. On the Continent the colored race is not discriminated against as a rule."

The tension over how locals treated Black people—with basic respect for their humanity—and how white Americans wanted them to be treated—like second-class citizens—was something African Americans noticed wherever they went in the world. When Robert S. Abbott, publisher of *The Chicago Defender,* and his wife went on a monthslong tour to South America, they found warm welcome among locals in Brazil, Peru, Argentina, and Chile. But when he attempted to enter American-owned and -operated hotels in Rio de Janeiro, Brazil, and Valparaíso, Chile, he was turned away. In Panama, he saw store signs noting that "gold" lines were for whites, and "silver" lines were for non-whites. The labeling system intentionally mirrored the market hierarchy that made gold a more valuable commodity than silver. Abbott shared insights he had learned abroad: "One of the big lessons he had learned was that South Americans do not feel prejudice, that Americans are its chief distributors, that Race groups in South America are so unaware of it that they have not awakened to fight the American infiltration, and that it must be our duty here in America to keep up the fight for the eradication of prejudice at home as the first step in checking its spread abroad." From Abbott's perspective, it was useless to think of international travel as an escape from U.S. racism if racist white Americans were traveling to and doing business in the same places.

Encounters with racist white Americans were a particular cause for concern in Paris because exorbitant sales taxes continued to have a devastating impact on the city's nightlife. As fewer locals could afford the clubs, audiences became more American. Facing the possibility of performing before the same white American crowds that had sent them sailing for Europe in the first place, the so-called Race Musicians started to try their luck in other parts of Europe. Jim and Jack, "the nifty steppers," had a show in Leipzig, Germany, at the Crystal Palace, and Emma Maitland and Aurelia Wheeldin's show toured in Milan, Rome, Genoa, Turin, and Verona. Even Josephine Baker decided to strike out from Paris, accepting an offer to do motion picture work in Berlin.

The performers' dispersal fueled expanded international coverage in *The Chicago Defender* and other Black newspapers. In one article, a reporter described taking in a performance by Teddy Drayton, of the dance duo Greenlee and Drayton, at the Grand Café Astoria in Zurich, Switzerland, before setting off to cover other performances at the Royal Orpheum in Budapest and at Le Negresco, a hotel in Nice. In addition to writing about Black acts that were taking the stage in Paris, London, and Berlin in the 1920s, Black journalists explored other sites—for example, the beautiful pastoral landscapes of places like Ireland and Scotland—and encouraged their readers to consider doing the same. Reporting like this helped to fuel their readers' interest in these locales as tourist destinations.

The presence of African American performers in Europe was not lost on the white American press, but the coverage was less concerned with acknowledging the circumstances that sent them away from the United States to begin with, or the differences they encountered abroad. When, after twenty-two months in Europe, Emma Maitland and Aurelia Wheeldin returned to the United States and spoke to a *Variety* reporter about their journey, Maitland, unprompted, shared the highlight of their time away: "Miss Maitland declared their treatment throughout was most cordial, and their color at no time brought them any embarrassment." Not only were African Americans learning that the harshest limits they encountered were from white Americans, they wanted white Americans to know that they knew it. It was a clever way to slip in a critique, too, since it made white Americans sound provincial and unsophisticated compared with their European counterparts. White *Variety* readers might not have been ashamed to be outed as racist, but they would certainly be ashamed to be considered gauche.

FOR THEIR PART, FLORENCE and company set out for London in the fall of 1926. *Blackbirds* debuted at the London Pavilion at Piccadilly Circus, one of the grandest, most popular music halls in the city. Just as in Paris, the show was given prime real estate, and critics responded accordingly. They were especially keen to shower the lead star with praise. One crowned Florence the "Sensation of the Season," and another described her as "the greatest coloured entertainer this country has ever seen." The Prince of Wales himself was a huge fan who bragged about having seen the show twenty times.

Like Paris, London had a mix of residents who came from all over the world. In the 1920s, they arrived from various corners of the British Empire, including Hong Kong, India, Jamaica, Kenya, Ghana, and Sri Lanka. But there was a difference between the two cities: In London, these groups were targets of large-scale racist violence. This was true elsewhere in the United Kingdom as well. In January 1919, Glasgow was the epicenter of a riot that started out as a skirmish between Black and white sailors over scarce jobs and quickly descended into chaos when other white Glaswegians joined in, using guns, knives, bricks, and makeshift weapons against the Black sailors before moving on to other Black residents, South Asians, Chinese, and Arabs. Word spread to other port cities in the United Kingdom, and by August, whites in places like Cardiff, Liverpool, and London were emboldened to carry out similar attacks.

The United Kingdom and the United States had this kind of history in common. They also shared more systemic practices like housing and employment discrimination and quotidian ones that made life difficult for Black Londoners and visitors alike. Reporting on his visit to England for *The Chicago Defender,* the paper's publisher, Robert S. Abbott, described the problems faced by Black Britons as well as his own experiences. He noted that local newspapers made it "difficult even for the worst cracker papers in the South to show more anti-Negro venom," and spoke to a Black Liverpool resident who pinpointed the irony of the United Kingdom enlisting Black soldiers from its colonies to fight in World War I while subjecting them to racist violence as soon as their utility ran out. "When the war was on," the Liverpudlian said, "they made the biggest sort of fuss over us, but no sooner was it over than they were mobbing us from one end of the country to the other." Abbott got a glimpse of this hostility himself, having been refused entry to approximately thirty London hotels.

London's theater world was no exception. Back in 1923, when Florence was first in the city for *Dover Street to Dixie*'s run at the London Pavilion, several local artists' guilds came out to protest the idea of an all-Black cast. Just as the rioters in 1919 blamed their violence on job scarcity, the Actors' Association, the Variety Artistes' Federation, the Musicians'

Union, and the National Association of Theatrical Employees all complained to London's city council that the *Dover Street to Dixie* cast was taking jobs from out-of-work white Brits. Their campaign succeeded, and in the first half of the show all the Black performers—Mills included—were replaced with white ones who could hardly match the energy and finesse of the roles' originators. The choice all but doomed the show, and Florence and Leslie soon returned to New York.

Three years later, the London premiere of *Blackbirds* saw Florence and her crew perform every minute of the show from start to finish despite protests from the same guilds that had derailed *Dover Street to Dixie*. This time, the strong early success of *Blackbirds* shielded it from needing to make any concessions—all the better for the audience, which included white Londoners who wanted to see "what the negro has made of jazz," and Black Londoners who wanted to see themselves represented onstage. As one drama critic noted, "There were indeed lots of negroes of all shades in the house, all proud of the triumph of their coloured brethren." Florence herself understood the importance of this return to London: In an interview with London's *Daily Express*, she said that she saw it as "the quickest way of showing white people that we are really very like them."

For all her success in *Blackbirds*, there were signs Florence wanted to stretch her wings. At the peak of her triumph in London, she told a local drama critic that she had her sights set on becoming the first Black actress to play Peter Pan, the boy who would not grow up, from J. M. Barrie's classic children's tale. There was a timely reason for her saying so, since a London production was in the works and yet another white actress—in this case, American-born Dorothy Dickson—had been cast in the role. Mainstream audiences had no trouble buying white women as youthful, guileless innocents yet refused to suspend the same disbelief for Black women. But Florence, who used to be mistaken for a teenager, knew she had the goods to endow the role with similar qualities and make theater history in the process.

Unfortunately, Florence had more pressing concerns. She'd contracted tuberculosis and by the summer of 1927 was headed back to the United States for treatment. Whatever her reasons for choosing not to be treated by doctors in Europe, she was thrust back into the stark racial realities of her home country, where a Black woman—no matter how accomplished or famous—was subjected to below par medical care.

On November 1, 1927, Florence succumbed to a post-op infection at the Hospital for Joint Diseases in New York City. The entertainer Lena Horne, whose own screen and stage debuts in the 1930s were made possible thanks to the influence of performers like Florence and Josephine Baker, vividly remembered that day. Her schoolteacher in her hometown of Macon, Georgia, had stopped mid-lesson to impart a somber message to the class. "We've had a great loss to us," she told them. Reflecting on the memory, Horne said, "I think that was probably the first time I was conscious that we looked upon certain people as *ours,* with this kind of pride." The *New York Amsterdam News* reported on Florence's funeral service, describing it as "the largest, most impressive and tearful in the memory of Harlem," where "every stage celebrity who could possibly attend and persons of both races high in the life of the city and nation were present." *The New York Times* put the crowd at the Mother Zion African Methodist Episcopal Church, on 137th Street, at more than five thousand, with many thousands more flooding the streets of Harlem for the procession. Attendees included Cora Green (from the Panama Trio), Gertrude Saunders (who Mills replaced in *Shuffle Along*), and the actress and singer Ethel Waters, all of whom were designated as honorary pallbearers.

To look back on Florence's early years and career highs and lows is to reckon with a formidable, singular talent. But her legacy would be overshadowed by her untimely death. By comparison, Josephine Baker lived long enough to conquer stages and screens, serve her adopted country by spying on Nazis for the French Resistance during World War II, and become an icon on both sides of the Atlantic. What feats would Florence have accomplished if she had survived the health problems that sent her back into the clutches of the United States, just as she was starting her ascent in Europe? Would she have ridden the wave of her European success to film roles and life as a full-time expatriate? Or would she have parlayed her name recognition into a chance to play Peter Pan back in the United States, breaking one barrier after another? The fact that we can only wonder is also why her story matters so much. For, as tempting as it may be to think in terms of adventure and possibility when we think of African Americans going abroad, we must also take care to remember that tragedy lay at the heart of it, too.

Dusha v
Dushu

IN NINTH GRADE, A FEW of my teachers got together to buy me a book. It was the middle of the school year and I had just received an achievement award from the local chapter of The Links, Incorporated, a Black women's social and community organization founded in 1946. Everyone was proud. The inside cover was inscribed with notes, including one from Mr. Rice. "Thought you might like this book," he wrote. "It serves to connect ninth grade stuff with your life too—*dusha v dushu*."

What he meant by "ninth grade stuff": It was the early 1990s and the Cold War had just ended, so in place of a typical history course Mr. Rice, our in-house Russophile, led us through a yearlong exploration of Russia and the Soviet Union. He filled the hours with stories about his friend Sasha and their youthful exploits in Moscow, lessons in vocabulary and how to write our names in Cyrillic, and case studies about the member republics of the USSR. I loved every minute.

What he meant by "your life": I was one of a small handful of Black students at our private K–9 school. By that point, I had been there for almost three years, on scholarship, commuting to the verdant seven-acre campus in Denver's wealthiest neighborhood from Montbello, my working-class community on the other side of town. It was by turns an intellectually exhilarating and profoundly isolating existence.

What he meant by *"dusha v dushu"*: The book was Yelena Khanga's *Soul to Soul: The Story of a Black Russian American Family, 1865–1992.*[*] *"Dusha v dushu"* was Russian for "soul to soul."

Despite these connections and the initial intrigue that they sparked in me, I did not get around to reading the book until years later. In part it was because I was busy with schoolwork and applying to get into private high schools for the next year. But, in truth, I had also intentionally tucked the book out of sight and mind.

The reason for that came a few weeks later, after Mr. Rice announced that he'd be taking a group of students on a trip to Moscow and St. Petersburg over the summer. The news initially came as a thrill: Whatever grades we needed to earn or application essays we needed to write to get on the list, I was ready. For years I'd sat mute on the sidelines while my classmates casually traded stories about their sleepaway camps in the Adirondacks, lacrosse clinics in New England, and family vacations in Mexico, complete with all the new friendships, crushes, and inside jokes that defined them. I knew without needing to be told that the

---

[*]   First edition. Subsequent editions of the book had a different subtitle: "A Black Russian Jewish Woman's Search for Her Roots."

summer months I spent at my grandparents' house in Colorado Springs, where my mom sent my sister and me while she worked a second job, had no place in these exchanges. Much as I relished spending time with my grandparents, no one wanted to hear about my waking up early to hang laundry on the clothesline, weeding the garden before it got too hot out, shucking peas on the covered porch, or watching *Jeopardy!* after dinner. But meeting the famous Sasha and sneaking vodka past Mr. Rice? They'd die to hear about that.

It turned out, though, that I'd already lost the only contest that mattered: The class trip would include only the students whose families could afford the several-thousand-dollar price tag. Mine, of course, was not among them, so I would be going to my grandparents' house once again.

I hadn't started the school year thinking there would be a trip, but somehow with Mr. Rice's late-breaking announcement came the sense that I'd be able to do more than just study Russia. I'd be able to see the Moscow of his memories with my own eyes, to use the words we'd memorized from his lessons, and to find some reason to sign my own name in another script and language. That sense, in turn, further sharpened my focus in class. So, when I learned that money, not merit, would decide whether any of those things would ultimately happen, suddenly to my fourteen-year-old mind everything we were learning seemed pointless. By then, *Soul to Soul* was no longer attached to the success of my recent award; instead, it became an emblem of my failure to get the same educational opportunities as my rich white classmates. I couldn't handle such a tangible and glaring reminder of this cruel fact, so to the bottom of the basement bookshelf at home the book went.

Years later, on a break from college, my mom tasked me with sorting through some boxes she'd stored in the garage of her new house after a recent move out of my childhood home. In one of them was *Soul to Soul,* its paper cover still as crisp as the day my teachers bestowed it upon me. This time, I was finally able to read past the first page of inscriptions without my eyes welling up in resentment.

I felt an immediate sense of kinship with Yelena Khanga, the author, for reasons that were visible to Mr. Rice all those years ago—and for ones he never knew. "When I was growing up," she wrote of coming of age in Moscow in the 1960s and '70s, "I thought of my color not as a target for discrimination but simply—and not so simply—as a mark of separateness . . . a reminder that I wasn't like everyone, or anyone, else." She described being self-conscious about her short Afro when all her classmates had cascading manes, and spending years convinced that "no man would ever want to touch my nappy black hair." Even with the vast distance and decades between us, Khanga could have been talking about my experience in private school in 1990s Colorado, where being Black was less about being called racist names and more about being asked how I could wash my hair every night with braids in, and about being overlooked by all the boys I had crushes on.

She could also have been talking about my own life when she described the refuge she found at home, where the air was filled with the music of Billie Holiday and Ray

Charles, the bookshelves with the writings of Langston Hughes, and the coffee table with issues of *Essence* magazine. But how was that possible? Why did her Russian family share and revere the same totems of African American life and culture as my own did? As I kept turning the book's pages, I discovered that the answer traced back, in part, to her grandfather: Like mine, hers was born in the Jim Crow South, grew up with its unrelenting violence and indignities, and made his escape the first chance he got.

CHAPTER 2

THE NEGRO COMRADES

Joseph J. Roane *and* Oliver Golden,

YANGIYUL, 1930S

FOR MOST OF HIS LIFE, the only Kremlin Joseph J. Roane knew was in Virginia. Part of Westmoreland County, in the northeastern part of the state, Joseph's hometown was a place most other Virginians did not even know existed. But it was as real as the other, better-known Kremlin, where the twenty-six-year-old and his new wife, Sadie, now found themselves standing on a cold winter's day in November 1931.

Depending on how you counted, it had taken either weeks or years for the young couple to arrive. Weeks if you factor in the crossing on SS *Deutschland* from New York to Southampton, the train to London, the few nights spent there before returning to the ship, the last leg of the journey to Hamburg, the train across Germany to the Baltic Sea, the ferry to Helsinki, and then the train to Moscow, which rolled into the ornate Oktyabrsky rail terminal on

November 7. It took years if you include how long Joseph had pursued a bachelor's degree in agronomy at Virginia State College at Petersburg, and the time he spent attempting to find work in a profession whose experts studied and shared best practices in both field crop production and soil and land management. But the fact that Joseph was Black mattered more than his training, even though said training was exactly what the country needed in the middle of a depression, since it could help feed more people and contribute meaningful solutions to pressing problems. No one would hire him, full stop.

Either way, it had been a considerable journey. And Joseph and Sadie had yet another long train ride to go before reaching their ultimate destination, but that would come later. For now, their hosts—the Soviet government—wanted to welcome them to Moscow.

And what an auspicious day to do so. Their arrival coincided with the fourteenth anniversary of the 1917 Bolshevik Revolution that overthrew the czarist government and brought Vladimir Lenin to power, and the occasion was marked by a ceremonial program in Red Square. The vast, cobblestoned public space, which was flanked by the Kremlin to the west, the State Historical Museum to the north, the State Department Store to the east, and the landmark St. Basil's Cathedral to the south, with its colorful pillars like ice cream cones reaching toward the heavens, stood at the very center of Moscow in a spatial, political, economic, and spiritual sense, making it the perfect setting for a celebration in honor of Russia's revolutionary rebirth.

According to the front page of the English-language *Mos-*

cow News, on that day Red Square was filled with the "thunder of horses' hooves, thunder of tramping feet, clatter of gun carriages, [and] clatter of tanks." The paper's coverage also included a photo of a multiracial group of foreign workers, with "happy, smiling faces," who joined Soviet citizens carrying signs covered with Joseph Stalin's portrait in a march past buildings decorated with red streamers.

Accompanying Joseph and Sadie as they took in the proceedings from the sidelines were their fellow travelers: a group of fourteen African American agronomists and their wives, all of whom had been assembled thanks to the efforts of a man named Oliver Golden.

A Mississippi-born veteran of World War I and a graduate of the Tuskegee Institute who studied under George Washington Carver, Oliver had been in a position similar to Joseph's years earlier, searching fruitlessly for a chance to work in the profession for which he had spent so much time and effort training. Finding only closed doors, he resorted to working as a waiter in a Pullman railway car to make ends meet and support his first wife, Jane.

That was back in the 1920s. Life might have gone on that way were it not for a chance encounter in Chicago with Lovett Fort-Whiteman, an old buddy from Tuskegee. Oliver later told his friend Harry Haywood that even though the pair hadn't seen each other in years, they eased into their old college banter. "I asked Fort-Whiteman what the hell he was wearing. Had he come off the stage and forgotten to change clothes? He informed me that these were Russian clothes and that he had just returned from that country." The two kept up their jokes for a bit, reminiscing

about their younger days, until the conversation took a
sharp turn:

> Out of the blue, he asks me if I want to go to Russia
> as a student. At first, I thought he was kidding, but
> man, I would have done anything to get off those din-
> ing cars! I was finally convinced he was serious. "But
> I'm married," I told him. "What about my wife?"
> "Why, bring her along too!" he replied. He took me
> to his office at the American Negro Labor Congress,
> an impressive setup with a secretary, and I was con-
> vinced. Fort-Whiteman gave me money to get pass-
> ports, and the next thing I knew, a couple of weeks
> later we were on the boat with Otto and the others
> on the way to Russia. And here I am now.

Oliver was invited to Moscow to pursue studies at the
Communist University of the Toilers of the East (KUTV).
The school was run by the Communist International (Comintern), an organization founded by Vladimir Lenin in
1919 with the mission to "struggle by all available means,
including armed force, for the overthrow of the international bourgeoisie and the creation of an international Soviet republic as a transition stage to the complete abolition
of the state." To that end, the KUTV was established to
educate and train a cadre of Communist leaders hailing
from all over the colonized world, who would return to
their countries to promote and assume leadership roles in
Soviet-style Communist regimes. The student body represented more than seventy nationalities and ethnicities (in-

cluding, in the 1920s, Hồ Chí Minh, who eventually became president of North Vietnam, and Deng Xiaoping, future leader of the People's Republic of China). African Americans were included in the school's mission because the Soviets considered them, like their KUTV brethren, a colonized people (in their case, *within* their own country, by their fellow citizens) and sought to train them to lead Communist movements in the United States. Haywood, a Nebraskan born to formerly enslaved parents, was another recruit of Fort-Whiteman's, and met Golden as a fellow KUTV student.

The school's curriculum focused on classic works from Marx, Engels, Lenin, and Stalin. "But unlike schooling we had known in the past," Haywood later noted in his autobiography, *Black Bolshevik,* "this whole body of theory was related to practice. Theory was regarded not as dogma but as a guide to action."

By all accounts, the Goldens' time in Moscow was enjoyable, surrounded as they were by Haywood and other Black people from the United States, Africa, and the West Indies. Although the Black students were a small minority in the city of four and a half million, to their relief Muscovites displayed only friendly curiosity toward them. Even Jane found her place, taking classes at the KUTV as well. As the only Black woman in the group at the time, she became a kind of touchstone for the Americans, reminding many of them of the sisters and mothers they'd left behind.

Then tragedy struck. Jane suddenly fell ill with a kidney infection and died shortly thereafter. The school and its leadership took over the funeral arrangements, and the

couple's friends and classmates assembled at the cemetery
to pay their final respects, later taking Oliver to one of their
apartments where they toasted to Jane's memory with
vodka. Still, despite the support of the community he had
in Moscow, the loss proved too much for Oliver, and not
long after burying Jane he returned to the United States before finishing his program.

Back home, whatever hopes he had for his career
were thwarted by the Great Depression, which hit African
Americans especially hard. Oliver resorted to working as a
dishwasher in a New York City hotel. It was the exact set of
circumstances that made the American Communist Party
a kind of refuge in those days. Its members were heavily
involved in the labor movement and in anti-racist activism,
promoting a vision of racial equality that made Communism an attractive ethos. As an official for the National Association for the Advancement of Colored People (NAACP)
put it at the time, "the greatest pro-Communist influence
among Negroes in the United States is the lyncher, the Ku
Klux Klan member, the Black Shirt, the Caucasian Cru-
sader and others who indulge in lynching, disfranchise-
ment, segregation and denial of economic and industrial
opportunity."

Oliver's attraction to the party was strengthened by his
Moscow experience. Though he had never been politically
involved at the KUTV, instead seeing the experience in
largely intellectual and social terms, he carried warm memories of the Soviets' comradeship during a time in his life
when he needed it most. It felt like a homecoming, in a certain sense, to join the party.

The Communists also saw something in Oliver. As one of the few African Americans who had experienced the Soviet experiment up close, and who was schooled in its underlying theories, he was quickly placed in a leadership position that had him doing community outreach. This put him in the path of a Soviet recruiter, who invited him to lead a team of African American agronomists on a two-year project in the USSR's burgeoning agricultural industry in Uzbekistan. The Soviets were finally offering Oliver the chance to do the kind of work he had gone to school for, and wanted to do, for years.

In exchange, the Soviets would pay Oliver several hundred dollars a month, which amounted to a fortune during the Depression, and certainly more than he could ever make in a year of dishwashing. They would also give him a home to live in, an extended paid vacation each year, and the service of a household maid. It was beyond anything he had dared to imagine for himself, even during the hours he spent on his feet in front of a sink that never seemed to empty of pots and pans.

Of course, accepting the offer meant once again leaving his people and home country behind. It was one thing to have gone to Moscow, a place that came highly recommended by a friend and fellow African American. But it was quite another to decamp to Uzbekistan, a place neither he nor anyone he knew had ever set foot in. Still, did he really have a choice in the matter, considering how little his pedigree and patriotism mattered when it came to finding meaningful work? And did it not mean something that the Soviet Union, which had only ever shown him welcome and kindness, seemed to value his intellectual abilities and wanted to embrace him as a leader in his field, not just despite but perhaps even because of the color of his skin?

Oliver had also recently remarried and had his wife's needs to consider. His party involvement had introduced him to a young woman named Bertha Bialek, the daughter of Jewish immigrants from Poland. The United States had never been hospitable to interracial unions, and by 1931 more than half of the country had anti-miscegenation laws on the books that prohibited interracial marriages. Even in those places where it was legal for Black and white people to marry, including cosmopolitan New York, couples had to carefully consider where they lived and socialized to avoid experiencing unpleasantness or outright hostility. In contrast, the Communist message seemed to be one of welcome and acceptance. And so, having considered the kind of future they could have in their home country, Oliver and Bertha decided to cast their lot with their comrades.

Now Oliver was faced with the task of building a team to take with him. He already knew plenty of agronomy experts from his time at Tuskegee, and thought that George Washington Carver, his former teacher-cum-mentor who had shepherded a generation of scientists through the institution, would be the draw to lure all the rest. Oliver knew it would not be easy to convince Carver to decamp for the Soviet Union, but it did not seem impossible. On April 15, 1931, Oliver wrote a letter to Carver that read, in part: "Tuskegee is nationally and somewhat internationally known, but your going to the U.S.S.R and the success of these men will give Tuskegee an international character." Besides, Oliver added, "you owe it to your race." Because Oliver himself had justified his own willingness to participate in the project in terms of a dual sense of obligation, both to his own people and to the USSR for placing so much faith in him and other African Americans, he thought he could make a similar case to Carver.

Oliver also thought that moving from the United States to the Soviet Union would convey, to both his native and adopted homelands, a message of protest and renunciation. What better indictment of the country's racism and exclusionary hiring practices than not only to go to work for the Soviets but to excel at it? It had long been a truism among African Americans that all they needed was opportunity and any doubts about their abilities would melt away. Oliver had proved this in the military, and he was prepared to do it again and again until the message stuck.

Given his own fervor, Oliver was more than a little surprised that Carver rebuffed the invitation outright. On the surface, the explanation was simple: At seventy years old, Carver said that he was not healthy enough to undertake such a journey. But there was more to it. From Carver's perspective, he had an obligation to stay home and fight for equality in the United States. If all the qualified men and women of their race left the country, he argued, who would lead the battle for inclusion at home? What leaders would the younger generations have to look up to?

Both Oliver and Carver had strong, compelling cases and valid reasons for following their chosen paths. Oliver ceded his mentor's point and began to look elsewhere for his team. In this he did have some help from Carver: In a sign of his respect for his mentee and his bold mission, Carver gave Oliver the name of someone who might be willing to take up his offer. John Sutton, another Tuskegee graduate and mentee of Carver's, was born and raised in Texas as one of fifteen siblings (one brother, Percy Sutton, would go on to become the first African American elected Manhattan borough president, an investor in the *New York Amsterdam News,* and owner of the famed Apollo Theater in Harlem). He and George Tynes, a graduate of Wilberforce University in Ohio, were among the first to get on board. As Oliver expanded his attempts to recruit a wider network of African American agronomists—a small world indeed—he eventually reached out to Joseph Roane.

Joseph had just applied to be a train porter for the Pullman Company when he got a letter from Oliver. As he read the invitation from the man whom he had once heard speak when Oliver came to visit Joseph's college in Virginia to talk about his time in Moscow, the weight of the offer on the page started to sink in. Here was a chance to finally work in his chosen profession, arriving at the exact moment when he had lost hope that such a thing would ever happen. It felt like fate.

That did not mean, of course, that Joseph's decision would be easy. Unlike Oliver, Joseph was not involved in the Communist Party, and had not previously spent time in Moscow, so there was no direct connection to Soviet values to sway him. All he had was the word of a man he admired, but who was mostly a stranger.

It was a lot to ask of the scientists, to leave their friends and families and the only country they knew for this strange land. What if these white people treated them just as badly as the ones at home did? At least at home, Joseph understood the racial etiquette and had developed his own tools of survival and ways of navigating white racism. African Americans in Virginia, and elsewhere in the United States, had their own stores, their own banks, and their own schools and churches. Where would they take their business, educate their children, and worship their God if the Soviets refused to make room? Or, worse yet, if American racism managed to follow them halfway across the world?

On the one hand, the Soviets were promising professional opportunity and advancement. On the other hand, there were recent reports in the Black press about an attack on Robert Robinson, a Black engineer from Detroit who was among a group of three hundred Americans (Black and white) recruited to work at the new Stalingrad Tractor Plant. The plant was the beating heart of Soviet industrialization and its claims to being "the fatherland of all workers, including Negroes." The Americans shared the factory line with workers from twenty-six other countries, and things seemed to be going peaceably enough until, one day in July 1930, as Robinson entered the common mess hall, a group of his co-workers surrounded him and delivered enough punches and kicks to send him to the hospital.

The *Norfolk Journal and Guide,* one of Joseph's local Black newspapers in Virginia, devoted regular coverage to the incident. The paper revealed that the aggressors were not the Soviets themselves, but rather Robinson's white American co-workers who had taken their racial hatred along with them to this new land, as though it were an essential piece of luggage.

The paper also reported that, in the aftermath of the attack, the other tractor workers organized a mass meeting of their union wherein they adopted a resolution to "condemn severely this savage, anti-worker, and barbarous misdeed of a group of backward American workers," and vowed that "we will not allow the ways of bourgeoise America in the U.S.S.R. The Negro worker is our brother. . . . We castigate any who dares to destroy in the Soviet land the equality we have established for all proletarians of all nations." True to their word, the union identified the leader in the attack on Robinson as a man named Lemuel Lewis and tried him for his crime. His sentence was immediate deportation.

Perhaps there was comfort in knowing that even though white Americans continued to find ways to unleash their racial hatred, the Soviets refused to let them get away with it. It was more than Joseph and others could say of their own country, where similar attacks on Black workers and Black communities went uninvestigated, untried, and unpunished.

There was other evidence that the USSR saw Black people as human beings deserving of respect and agency. When Universal Studios released the film version of Harriet Beecher Stowe's *Uncle Tom's Cabin* in the fall of 1927, it was well received among white audiences in the United States, but among the Soviets the intended message of the film was getting major pushback. The Soviets felt sympathy for Tom and ire toward the slaveholder character Simon Legree, who subjected him to countless cruelties. At the same time, the Soviets found it "intolerable that the chief character should die a Christian, forgiving his enemies." After the Soviets initially banned the film as a result, they eventually cut a new ending, in which Tom shoots and kills Legree. In this version, *The Afro-American* happily reported, "Negroes are urged by Uncle Tom not to submit or to pray, but to fight back."

There were also reports in the Black press about folks like Emma Harris, a Southern-born entertainer who traveled throughout Europe with several theater troupes in the 1920s before moving to Russia. After studying at the St. Petersburg Conservatory, she found tremendous professional success there, and ended up married to a Russian.

And then there were the letters Black factory and plant workers in the USSR were sending back home. In one, which *The Afro-American* headlined "Russians Need No Prodding Where Justice and Fair Play to Negroes Are Concerned," the author had the following advice:

> Young Negroes, anxious to shake themselves free from American prejudices and circumscriptions, might well look toward Russia. Dancers and jazz-entertainers may find the sledding a little hard there, but WORKERS, especially those more or less skilled in any vocation, will find a welcome.

Perhaps no one captured the guiding ethos of these sojourners better than Homer Smith, a twenty-two-year-old journalism graduate from Minneapolis who had been recruited to help modernize Moscow's postal service. "I yearned," he later reflected in his autobiography, "to stand taller than I had ever stood, to breathe total freedom in great exhilarating gulps, to avoid all the hurts that were increasingly becoming the lot of men (and women) of color in the United States." For Smith and so many others, their own country had become unlivable, and its open hostility to their very existence made them desperate to escape—even if it meant leaving nearly everything they knew and almost everyone they loved behind. The only way up was out.

Still, as a married man, Joseph had to consider his new wife, Sadie. She had gone to college as well, but to be a teacher. What would she do for work? And if there was no opportunity for her to apply her own skill set, how would she pass the days?

In a follow-up letter, Oliver assured Joseph that Sadie would not be alone. His own wife, Bertha, was going, as was the wife of another agronomist, Frank Faison. If nothing else, they, the workers, and their wives would have their own community to navigate this new world together.

There was one more draw, according to Joseph: "I was young and I wanted to see the world. I thought this might be the only chance I'd ever get." Besides, as newlyweds, he and Sadie saw the trip as a honeymoon of sorts. Thus, on October 15, 1931, Joseph, Sadie, and the others said their goodbyes and packed up to take the journey of their lives. When one of Oliver's friends asked when he'd be back, he replied, in a singsong that hinted at his commitment to seeing the new endeavor through: "I'll be back when the elephants roost in the trees."

——

THE BOAT RIDE FROM New York to Southampton on board
SS *Deutschland* had echoes of the one Florence Mills and her
Blackbirds crew had taken several years earlier. Only, instead
of passing the days at sea rehearsing songs and dances and
comedy bits, this group worked on their Russian with the
help of the Soviet passengers they befriended and got acquainted with the concept of collectivized farming.

Once they docked in England, there were signs that
things were already different. As Joseph later told Oliver
and Bertha's granddaughter:

> The first stop was London, where we ran around
> looking at all of those places from storybooks and
> buying long underwear, because we were told it was
> very cold in Russia and you couldn't get it there. The
> wonderful thing about London was that we could do
> whatever we wanted, go wherever we wanted. There
> was no back of the bus, you could just get on and
> ride. For those of us who'd spent our lives in the
> South, always taking a back seat, this was really
> something. I was already glad I'd come, and I hadn't
> even gotten to Russia. I'd never in my life, you see,
> been able to walk in a restaurant and know I would
> be served food, and treated like any other customer.

After that, the group got back on the train to head to
Moscow. The city had its own surprising new world of freedoms in store. A few days after their arrival, Joseph and one

of the other men in the group found themselves in need of
haircuts after being in transit for so long. When they fretted
over where to go, one of their Soviet hosts suggested, perhaps with a hint of surprise at the need to point out something so obvious, that the men should simply go to the
barbershop in the lobby of their hotel. Such an option
would have been entirely off the table in the United States,
so of course it did not occur to them to consider it.

Even as they crossed the threshold of the shop, the men
braced for rejection. Still, they summoned their best bits of
Russian from the *Deutschland* and combined them with a
pantomime of scissors nipping at their heads. If the barbers
were surprised to see them, they didn't let on. They quickly
led the pair to their chairs, right past where two white
American customers were sitting. The latter two immediately began to experience a kind of culture shock of their
own. "What are you [n*****s] doing here?" they demanded.
They were used to a world of segregated barbershops and
did not see any reason why they could not keep it that way,
no matter how far they were from home.

Now this was the reaction Joseph and his companion
expected. The Russian barbers, however, were taken by
surprise. Even though they did not speak English, they understood yelling and body language and sensed the growing tension in the room. Joseph filled them in on the
specifics, or at least he tried to, as the white Americans insisted to the barbers that Joseph and his colleague be re-
moved from the shop. Joseph braced himself for what was
surely coming next: If they were lucky, they might get an
apology from the barbers along with the request to leave,

perhaps even an invitation to come back at another, quieter hour. To Joseph's surprise, however, it was the white Americans who were thrown out, with shaving cream still on their faces. A new world indeed.

Moscow continued to dazzle Joseph and the rest of the agronomist collective during their stopover. While Oliver gave a few informal lectures to the group—ones that no doubt covered some of his old KUTV material, as well as topics related to the work that lay ahead of them—they were mostly free to explore the city and all that it had to offer.

The 1930s were a peak period for American immigration and tourism to Moscow, which held special appeal to laborers, students, intellectuals, writers, and celebrities hoping to get a glimpse of or play a part in the Soviet experiment. Most of the activities for tourists were focused on showcasing the city's factories, plants, and educational institutions. But as the workday ended, the city's nightlife beckoned, and a lot of it was concentrated in hotels. As it happened, the famed author and poet Langston Hughes had recently arrived in town with a crew of actors to work on a movie.

Financed by the Comintern, the film, called *Black and White,* was to be shot in Moscow but set in Birmingham, Alabama. In his memoir, *I Wonder as I Wander,* Hughes, who was hired to help punch up the script, wrote that "its heroes and heroines were Negro workers. The men were stokers in the steel mills, the women domestics in wealthy homes. . . . Its villains were the reactionary white bosses of the steel mills and the absentee owners, Northern capitalists, who aroused the poor white Southern workers against both the

[incipient] union and the Negroes." In other words, it was a
piece of propaganda meant to bolster the Soviet model of
trade unionism and criticize the United States' divisive racial
politics. At the same time, it was also an opportunity for
Black actors and writers to get work. In that way, Hughes
and his film crew were on a kind of mission similar to that
of Joseph, Oliver, and the other agronomists.

There were some paperwork issues holding up their
production, so Hughes's group had plenty of free time on
their hands in Moscow. They held court from their post at
the city's Grand Hotel, which stood just a block from the
Kremlin and boasted "enormous rooms with huge pre-
tzarist beds, heavy drapes at the windows and deep rugs on
the floors," and "a big dark dining room with plenty to eat
in the way of ground meats and cabbage, caviar, and sometimes fowl." When they tired of that setting, the group
made their way to the Metropol, which Hughes described
as "the only hotel with a jazz band, and pretty women available with whom to dance," and other venues like the lobby
of the Bolshoi Moscow Hotel. Somewhere along this circuit
of watering holes, Hughes crossed paths with the agronomists, who were spending this time taking in Moscow's
pleasures themselves. Oliver and Joseph got on with Hughes
so well that they invited him to call on them in Uzbekistan
sometime, if he happened to be willing to make the trip.

For Oliver, the Moscow interlude must have been
fraught with emotion. It marked his first trip back since
losing Jane, and making his way through the streets that he
last walked with her before her sudden death surely resurfaced old memories. Not all of those memories were sad,

of course, and he still had plenty of friends in town. In fact, it was in the lobby of the Bolshoi Moscow Hotel that Oliver reunited with his KUTV classmate Harry Haywood. As Haywood later told it, the pair "ran into a Russian embrace," a popular Communist greeting that consisted of three deep hugs, alternating between the left and right sides. They caught up on what had transpired since Oliver left in 1928. Haywood had also been back in the United States, traversing the nation on behalf of the Negro Department of the Communist Party. He arrived back in Moscow in late summer as a delegate for the Twelfth Plenum of the Executive Committee of the Communist International, which took place in August, and stayed on through the winter to arrange for his wife Ekaterina (known as "Ina"), whom he'd met during his KUTV days when she was a ballet student and married in 1927, to return with him to the United States.

Oliver's old Tuskegee pal Lovett Fort-Whiteman, the one who'd recruited Oliver and Haywood to study at the KUTV, was also in Moscow. He was involved in several endeavors at the time, including working as a science teacher, helping to pen the *Black and White* script, hosting dinners to promote the Communist cause among visiting and resident African Americans, and making trips back to the United States to do the same.

It was a pleasant time, until into the agronomists' and entertainers' Moscow idyll crashed news from back in the United States involving a group of young teenagers in Alabama who had been falsely accused and convicted of raping two white women on a train. Known as the Scottsboro

Boys, the group was facing the death penalty, and African Americans around the world were working hard to rally international support for their release. Emma Harris, the African American singer who trained at the St. Petersburg conservatory, was doing her part by giving regular speeches in fluent Russian on the subject, as was Ada Wright, whose two sons, Roy and Andy, counted among the jailed teens. Wright traveled around the United States and across Europe to raise awareness about the young men's plight. Her Moscow visit culminated in a procession through the city's streets, with thousands of Soviet workers carrying signs saying "Free the Scottsboro Boys!," which had become a worldwide rallying cry in the case, and others proclaiming, somewhat incongruously, "Down with US Imperialism!" For the Soviets, the Scottsboro case was both a human rights crisis and an opportunity to score political points against the United States, not only with African Americans but with the broader international community as well.

The Russians were consequently on their best behavior. Hughes described them as exceedingly welcoming and polite, offering their seats on buses, their places in line, and, when they had nothing tangible to give, their respect. "*Negrochanski tovarish*" or "Negro comrade," they would say.

AFTER A FEW WEEKS in Moscow, it was time for Joseph, Oliver, and the agronomist collective to board the train for a 1,900-mile, six-day journey to their new home in Uzbekistan. The group had packed light. Apart from cold-weather clothing, their possessions were few, even after the stint in Moscow. As for Oliver's wife, Bertha, she set out with only a Singer sewing machine and a Smith Corona typewriter. She later explained to her granddaughter that the fact that she was headed to such a poor region drove her decision making: "She had no desire to flaunt the kind of material well-being enjoyed by most Americans, even during the Depression, in comparison to most Soviet citizens."

Indeed, poverty in Uzbekistan was at a historic high, and the region was in the throes of a widespread famine. The Soviet government's move to collectivize the means of production (taking control of private farms, equipment, and livestock) had the immediate effect of reducing agricultural output. The unforgiving climate did not help matters, and when the ground was not muddy from rain or slushy from snow, it was frozen solid. These were hardly ideal conditions for coaxing fruits and vegetables from the soil, or much of anything else. But the government was committed to the experiment, and to the idea that it would succeed with the help of trained experts.

That's where Joseph and Oliver's group came in. Their task was to test the soil and determine best practices for developing local agricultural capacities that would sustain the population and generate income. This meant figuring out ways to successfully plant foodstuffs, raise animals for consumption and production, and grow cotton to stimulate the textile industry.

The agronomists knew the task would not be easy. Still, nothing could prepare them for the reality of what they were up against. When their train pulled into Tashkent, their second-to-last stop, there were few signs of the modern, cosmopolitan city they had left behind less than a week before. Gone was the grand railway station out of which passengers spilled into busy streets filled with pedestrians and traffic. In fact, there seemed to be no cars in sight. Instead, local drivers pulled up in *arby*, the traditional Uzbek carts pulled by donkeys, to take the new arrivals to their hotel for a night or two of rest before the last leg of the journey. The only traffic on the street was made up of other *arby* drivers, men on camels, and a handful of streetcars that seemed to provide the only evidence of the city having entered the twentieth century.

The collective had arrived during a moment of transition in the region's history. Tashkent, which means "stone village" in Uzbek, had recently been named the capital and was in the process of transforming from a colonial city with narrow, twisty roads and one-story buildings into an urban center worthy of the designation. The next thirty years would see it grow and expand, with its own Red Square, wide boulevards, and grand buildings. For now, though, in 1931, it was a world away from Moscow.

The sense of distance only heightened over the next few days. One night, while wandering around Tashkent, Joseph got lost in a snowstorm. With a coat of white powder, all the buildings looked the same to him, and all their hand-lettered signs were covered over. All that was left was a maze of medieval streets. There were no cabs, of course, to drive him back to the hotel. When he crossed paths with an Uzbek on camelback, who was wearing a saber at his waist, the man spoke no English or Russian, and Joseph no Uzbek,

so he could not get directions. The moment drove home a
stark reality: They were not in Moscow anymore.

Joseph eventually found his way back to the hotel and
the group soon boarded a regional train for the forty-mile
trip to the village of Yangiyul, their ultimate destination. If
no one had told them they had finally arrived when the
train slowed down to a stop, they never would have known
it. The village did not have a designated train station so
much as an agreed-upon depot for quickly off-loading and
boarding new passengers. The agronomists scrambled to
disembark before the train carried them farther east.

If Tashkent was the gateway to Central Asia, Yangiyul
was its rural epicenter. It was a primary site of the Soviet
struggle, begun in 1917, to Europeanize the largely Muslim
region, and the agronomists moved into a large home on
the outskirts of town that had been divided into private
apartments. Almost immediately, they found themselves
with their feet planted in two completely different worlds.
One was the modern future the Soviets envisioned (to
which they saw the agronomists as a key to realizing), and
the other was a region steeped in centuries of tradition.

The Soviet government had recently adopted a policy of
repressing religious ideas and practices. But even as their
mosques were closed and their imams and mullahs were
arrested, rural Uzbeks retained their generations-long connections to Islam. They continued to pray and fast when
possible, kept shrines, and sought out religious teachers
who had escaped arrest and managed to hide in plain sight
by publicly earning their living on collective farms while
privately dispensing Quranic advice.

The tension between the world of the Soviets and the rural Uzbeks was embodied by the day-to-day lives of the agronomists, on one hand, and their wives, on the other. The agronomists were brought in to use their expertise to breathe life into the barren landscape and impart wisdom to colleagues and subordinates who were eager to hear it. It was by no means an easy task, but when they went off to work, it fell to their wives to interact with local Uzbeks to carry out the work of managing their households. Grocery shopping was a job in and of itself, and the wives fretted over how to put food on the table like everyone else in Uzbekistan living under collectivization. As part of their recruitment package, the Soviets promised the Americans access to special markets that were slightly better provisioned than those frequented by locals. But the women were still strangers in a strange land, as yet unaware of what kinds of foods would be on offer or what their local names were.

Having grown up in Tidewater Virginia, Sadie Roane (formerly Russell) was accustomed to a diet rich in fresh crabs and oysters. She had no idea what to expect in landlocked Uzbekistan, where most people had never seen the ocean, much less eaten from it. But she knew she could make the egg breads, sugar-baked apples, and chicken and dumplings of her youth if she could find the ingredients she needed—or at least come close. She might have spent hours at the table each morning, writing down lists of foods and consulting the Uzbek maid using whatever method of communication they could manage—gestures, drawings, bits of Russian and Uzbek—to determine local equivalents, sometimes writing a phonetic pronunciation next to each item. Then off Sadie went to the market to try to track it all down. Fruits and vegetables would have been one thing; figuring out how to read package labels or ask for help identifying unfamiliar products or spices was another. She could lose time in the store, leaving little to prepare something with the hodgepodge of goods to welcome Joseph home after a long day at work.

For Bertha, who had been an activist alongside her husband back in New York, living in Yangiyul provided an opportunity for continued political engagement—now related to the women who were her new neighbors. Rural Uzbek women continued to wear traditional veil combinations known as *paranji-chachvon*. The *paranji* was an oversized robe that covered the woman from head to toe, and the *chachvon* was a net made of horsehair that was intended to cover her face and the front of her body. Not only was the *paranji-chachvon* a sign of their piety, but it was also a form of resistance during a time when their religious identity was under attack by the Soviets.

The Soviets were launching a movement to unveil Uzbek women when the agronomists arrived. Bertha, searching for her own role to play while Oliver began his work, dove headlong into the effort. For her and other women activists, the goal was not to make veiled women more European, or even more Russian, so much as it was to help them secure the freedom to show their faces and wear what they chose in public. This was part of a broader vision of social egalitarianism in the region, and of equality for women everywhere. But it also, unfortunately, had the same elements of the "we know what's best for you" rhetoric that defined the Soviets' approach, and was therefore met with local resistance.

For her part, despite the language barrier, Sadie likely felt an affinity with the women of Uzbekistan. Another African American visitor to the region around this time was Louise Thompson, one of Hughes's fellow members of the *Black and White* film crew. After a long delay, the project had gone belly-up because of a change in the Soviet Union's status vis-à-vis the United States. The 1917 Bolshevik Revolution had set in motion sixteen years of nonrecognition from the United States that finally came to an end in 1933. In exchange for diplomatic recognition, the Soviet Union committed to dialing down its anti-American propaganda, including strong criticism of U.S. racism. The Comintern-financed *Black and White* film was no longer viable in this new context. While some of the crew went back to the United States, Thompson decided to take some time to travel across the Soviet Union. Of the Uzbeks in Tashkent, she later said: "The people looked like many of us. They were brown; a number of them were very dark brown. The only thing they didn't have that we had was curly hair."

In addition to physical similarities, there were social ones. Anyone from the United States riding trains in the region would have noticed the old, faded signs separating the nicer "European" sections from the more run-down "Non-European" ones and thought back to Jim Crow. So, to Sadie, her new neighbors were a kind of kin. She would not have stood out so much as a Black woman, but rather as a woman who went about unveiled. It's possible she chose to wear something to cover her head, even if it was a simple scarf, out of deference for these cultural norms or simply to avoid standing out more than necessary. But she did not take the same interest as Bertha in Uzbek women's unveiling.

Sadie had other concerns. In addition to making a home for herself and Joseph, she also needed to prepare for life as a new mother. It was hard enough being away from home, and her own mother, during a time like this. But she was also the first of the wives to be pregnant and not yet fluent in the language or local birthing customs.

Little did she know that what was typically a private affair, for both Americans and Uzbeks, was going to be attended to with great fanfare in this instance. The child she was carrying would be the first African American baby born in the Uzbek capital, and the Soviets wanted to mark the occasion. When her delivery date approached, in the summer of 1932, Sadie was ferried to a hospital in Tashkent where doctors graciously welcomed her, and reporters eagerly waited outside for news.

When her son arrived, the doctors proudly proclaimed his name: Yosif Stalin Roane, in honor of the Soviet leader. Shortly after, the infant would be "Octoberized," which was ceremonially similar to a christening, but which anointed each baby a child of the October Revolution of 1917.

Bertha and Oliver were the next among the agronomist collective to welcome a child, a daughter they named Lily. As the single men in the group met and married Uzbek or Russian women (something that was easy enough since the Soviet Union, unlike the United States, had no laws banning interracial marriage), they likewise started to have children of their own, growing their community in ways that made this remote outpost feel more and more like home.

Yangiyul was not a major destination in those days, as the only people who spent time there were those living and working in the agricultural sector, or the occasional intrepid visitors who had the wherewithal to make the trek. Langston Hughes was one of the latter. Like Louise Thompson, Hughes had decided to stick around the Soviet Union for a bit longer after the end of *Black and White,* and spent several months traveling by train, with rides punctuated by card games played with fellow travelers. After making his way to Tashkent, he decided to take the agronomists up on their invitation to pay them a visit in Yangiyul.

On the journey from Tashkent, Hughes realized, just as the agronomists had a year before, that trains did not really stop in Yangiyul. "As a convenience," he noted in *I Wonder as I Wander,* employing the same wry tone that characterized so much of the book, "they did slow down." And so, he jumped off and landed in a mix of slush and mud that covered his ankles. It was not a great start to the visit, but Oliver and Joseph, who had been waiting, pulled him out of the muck, and together they went to Oliver's house for a meal prepared by the agronomists' wives.

By his own admission, Hughes let the weather and humble surroundings, coupled with mounting homesickness, get the best of him. He refused to join his hosts in a game of bid whist, a familiar card game from down south, and sat glumly by the fireplace nursing one cognac after another and wishing he could be anywhere but there. The behavior was not lost on the Americans, and decades later, Bertha recalled to her granddaughter how rude he was. But there was one thing, according to Hughes, that eventually dragged him out of his self-pity:

> Christmas day was wonderful. We even had pumpkin pie for dessert, and the tables were loaded down with all the American-style dishes that those clever Negro wives could concoct away over there in Uzbekistan. That morning I didn't feel homesick at all when I got up and found a stocking full of halva, cashew and pistachio nuts hanging on the head of my bed. They were delightfully amiable hosts, these cotton-collective Negroes from America in the middle of a mud-cake oasis frosted with snow.

The dinner was the result of a profound group effort that unfolded over a relatively short period. In just over a year, Sadie and Frank Faison's wife had managed to get the hang of shopping in Yangiyul and hone their skills to create a taste of home (even though Hughes only mentioned the "Negro" wives, it's almost certain that Bertha was among them in the kitchen since everyone was gathering in her house). By then, their husbands had started to succeed in their work, which resulted in benefits they could reap at home, like ducks to raise, rice to cultivate, and more bountiful provisions. Together, the group's work yielded a Christmas feast of stewed rabbit, hot bread, buttered squash, and pumpkin pie.

AFTER THEIR TWO-YEAR CONTRACTS were up, some members of the agronomist collective returned to the United States while others moved on from Yangiyul for opportunities elsewhere in the Soviet Union. George Tynes ran several duck farms, first in Georgia, then in Crimea, and then in the Volga region, before finally settling in Moscow with his Ukrainian wife, Maria. Joseph and Oliver both received promotions and soon joined Tynes, with their wives and children, in Moscow. There, the families continued to host African American visitors (more made it to Moscow than Yangiyul), asking them to bring records and mementos from home if they could fit any into their luggage. When the singer Paul Robeson went to Moscow in December 1934, at the invitation of the Soviet government, he and his anthropologist wife, Eslanda (whose two brothers, John and Francis Goode, had moved there years before), visited with the agronomists and their families. Years later, Yosif recalled Robeson playfully hoisting him on his shoulders.

If Oliver spent time with his old college friend and KUTV recruiter, Lovett Fort-Whiteman, that reunion would come to a mysterious, foreboding end by 1936. Fort-Whiteman had been growing increasingly frustrated with—and vocal about—what he perceived as the Communist Party's failure to call out racism more aggressively in the United States. His criticism put him on the wrong side of the Soviets, and one day in the spring of 1936, he was arrested by the secret police and never seen in his adopted city again. Homer Smith, the young, yearning Minnesotan who moved to Moscow to work for the mail system, had become good friends with Fort-Whiteman over the years and, after not hearing from him for a while, went looking for him at his house. Fort-Whiteman's wife, Marina, a Russian Jewish chemist, answered the door. She had no idea where her husband was but knew enough to be afraid: "I beg you never to come here looking for him again!"

His wife and friends did not know it at the time, but after his arrest Fort-Whiteman was banished to the distant Soviet region of Semipalatinsk. Despite being so far from Moscow, where he'd built a life and community, Fort-Whiteman found a way to get by for a few months. He found a job as a language teacher and boxing instructor, and even became a bit of a local celebrity in a place that rarely saw Westerners, to say nothing of African Americans. Since his banishment did not prove to be punishment enough, it was not long before Fort-Whiteman was arrested again, tried for anti-Soviet agitation and other crimes, and sent off to a gulag in the tundra after his conviction. He suffered every day until his last. One friend heard that "he died of starvation, or malnutrition, a broken man whose teeth had been knocked out," in 1939, but his death was officially classified as the result of "weakening of cardiac activity."

Even without knowing where Fort-Whiteman had gone in 1936, Oliver, Joseph, and other African Americans in Moscow would have sensed the same shift in the Soviets' tone toward the United States that had provoked the doomed man's criticism. They would not have seen as many protest signs proclaiming "Down with US Imperialism!" or as much anti-American propaganda as in previous years. But since the men and their families were living comfortable lives that were the products of professional opportunity and success, as far as they were concerned the Soviets were still fulfilling their promise.

Another promise the Soviets had made to the recruits back in the United States was that they would have generous vacation time, which could be used to explore other parts of the Soviet Union, spend time in Europe, or visit their home country. In the summer of 1937, six years after the Roanes made their initial life-altering journey, they decided to pack up for a three-month trip back to the United States. To get there, they retraced the steps they had marked across the continent in 1931, and boarded SS *Lafayette* in Southampton.

Seventeen days after leaving Moscow, on August 28, the family debarked in New York City and made their way down to Virginia, where they were to stay with Sadie's family. The shrinking of their world from one side of the ocean, where they could sit and eat wherever they wanted, to the other, where they were confined to "Colored" sections of railcars and restaurants, would have been top of mind when they spoke to a reporter from the *Norfolk Journal and Guide* about the past few years of their Soviet lives. By then, Joseph was working at a scientific research institute in Moscow in the field of experimental agriculture, which involved testing Russia's soil and climate to determine whether the country could grow the kinds of fruits and vegetables found in other parts of the world.

The couple were proud to reflect on how much their

lives had changed since moving to the Soviet Union. When they had first left the United States, they were young newly-weds taking a leap into the unknown. Now, they were a family of three, with a young son who had been born in a hospital in Tashkent. In Moscow, the family communicated entirely in Russian, even with one another, so much so that they were now fluent. Not only that, the reporter noted, but "it has become almost impossible for them [referring to Joseph and Sadie] to speak English without a slight accent." Young Yosif spoke Russian (and Uzbek, according to the paper), but no English.

The reporter asked Joseph what he thought about the Soviet system of government beyond being appreciative of the employment opportunities extended to him. "Well," Joseph began, "because it does provide these opportunities without regard to race, but only on the basis of qualification, I would say unhesitatingly that it comes nearer approaching the ideal form of government." He wanted to make clear, though, that he did not run away from the United States, "but simply saw in the offer to go to the Soviet Republic an opportunity to apply the knowledge I had gained at Virginia State College to the best advantage."

Joseph was clear that he and his family had found exactly what they were looking for in the Soviet Union, and that they were eager to return to the life they had created for themselves there. In fact, with the zeal of a convert, Joseph encouraged other African Americans to consider doing the same. To another visiting reporter, this one from the *New York Amsterdam News,* Roane went as far as to address the paper's readers directly. "If you have dependents," he said, "the Soviet government will be ever so glad to have these people come to Russia where they can be adequately taken care of." Joseph further boasted that his own income allowed him to afford a three-month vacation.

Was this a vacation or a recruitment visit? The line between the two was a bit blurry. It was not surprising that the Black press would take such an interest in the Roanes' story, or that the Roanes would happily seize the moment to share the details of their fulfilling new lives. But Joseph also seemed to be speaking for the Soviet Union, as though he had dispensation to say that the government would "be ever so glad to" welcome and take care of African Americans. It's possible that the Roanes had become diplomats of sorts, engaged in a form of soft propaganda on behalf of their adopted homeland during a time when it would have been unwise from a foreign relations perspective for the Soviet government to engage in more direct criticism of the United States.

In a photograph that accompanies the *New York Amsterdam News* feature, Joseph, Sadie, and Yosif sit on a sofa, holding an earlier edition of the same newspaper, above a caption that begins: "GLAD TO READ FRESH news of their people." In that family photo, smiles are plastered on their faces. But to a modern viewer looking at them as they read English-language headlines about local cultural and political goings-on that were no longer familiar, there seems to be a hint of melancholy on their faces. Even though they claimed to be happy in their new country, they also look homesick. But for where?

The Roanes would not have chosen these circumstances

for themselves if given a real choice. They had adapted very well, and even thrived, in an environment where they were unencumbered by institutionalized racism, but there was also another, slightly less tangible cost. What must it have been like to return to a place they would have preferred not to leave, with an accent that marked them as being foreign? Had their new country truly embraced them, or was their acceptance conditional upon serving as symbols of the Communist cause and cudgels against the United States?

The Roanes' return to Moscow proved to be short-lived. Later that year, they were caught in the crosshairs of political strife in the Soviet Union, when Joseph Stalin sought to rid the Communist Party of any disloyal elements. Lovett Fort-Whiteman, it turned out, was just one of millions who were sent to gulags between 1936 and 1938, including intellectuals, artists, and scientists, during a process known as the Great Purge. There were also daily executions, with citizens rounded up on allegations of treason and foreigners accused of spying on behalf of their home governments. Oliver was on vacation with his family when the secret police came knocking on his door in Moscow to arrest him. When he got back home and learned from his worried neighbors about the visit, he brazenly stormed into the secret police headquarters and said: "Arrest me if you think I'm an enemy of the people." "Comrade Golden," came an officer's reply, "don't get so upset. We've already fulfilled the plan of arrests for your area. Go home and work in peace."

Living in peace, it turned out, would come with conditions. Oliver, Joseph, and the other agronomists who were still residing in the Soviet Union were presented with an impossible choice: renounce their U.S. citizenship and declare enduring fealty to the Soviets or return to the United States. It was an inverse of the choice that had led them to the USSR in the first place, but they had little time to mull things over the way they had done back in 1931.

The Roanes decided to return to the United States. Joseph later claimed that the decision was not made out of fear; he and Sadie simply wanted to spend more time with their families. He was initially hopeful that his Soviet résumé would allow him to land on his feet as an agronomist. As he later told Oliver and Bertha's granddaughter, "In just a few years—you'd be surprised—you could forget what segregation was like." But he struggled to find employment until, at a tremendous pay cut, he became an instructor of vocational agriculture at A. T. Johnson High School, an all-Black school in Westmoreland County where he worked until his retirement. He and Sadie lived in Virginia until their last days. As for Yosif, he quickly learned English and adapted in Virginia, but never forgot the land of his birth. Speaking to a reporter for Sadie's hometown paper in 1943, he said that he "remembers Russia very distinctly, and expresses the hope of yet returning to that country." That return did not ultimately come to pass, but in the years before his death in 2021, Yosif kept the family's Soviet connection alive thanks to a series of interviews with outlets in the United States and Europe. Part of that coverage also revealed a connection between the agronomists' work and one of Uzbekistan's most famous exports. "As far as I know," said one biology professor from Uzbekistan, "Uzbeks still grow the types of cotton created by the Americans."

As for Oliver, well, he did once say that he'd return to the United States when the elephants roosted in the trees. During the Stalinist era, he opted to renounce his American citizenship and become a Russian citizen. While living with Bertha and their daughter, Lily, in Moscow, Oliver remained close to George Tynes, one of his original recruits who also chose to make the city his permanent home.

When Oliver died in Moscow, shortly before World War II, he took a lifetime of stories with him. His daughter, Lily, and her daughter, Yelena, were both devoted to piecing together their family history, with Yelena eventually publishing a memoir, *Soul to Soul: A Black Russian American Family, 1865–1992*. The process of writing the book took her to the United States, where she retraced her grandfather's roots and route from the South to New York and back again to Moscow, his ending and her beginning.

Whites Only

MY GRANDPA, JOHN, WORE HIS war story on his face. It was there the whole time I knew him, from my earliest days, but I never really knew how to read it until long after he passed away.

The story's broad outline lay in the incongruence between the colors of his eyes, one a deep dark brown and the other a grayish blue. He'd lost his second brown eye, and half the sight he was born with, to a piece of shrapnel flying along a Normandy beach on D-Day. He would have faced a lifetime of disfigurement had it not been for the scientific advancements that produced the prosthetic eye he was eventually fitted with, which came complete with a white sclera, a pupil, an iris, and painted-on blood vessels. Still, the timing could not have been worse: He was one of thousands upon thousands of soldiers who lost their eyes to battle or disease during the war, and the United States struggled to meet their demand. By the time it was John's turn to get a new eye, his only option was blue.

Maybe white veterans ended up with mismatched eyes, too. But they certainly got the first and best pick of everything else. Back home in Montgomery, Alabama, John stood by as white veterans took plum manufacturing and defense industry jobs that rewarded their tactical expertise, enrolled at the University of Alabama and Auburn to prepare for career changes, got specialized vocational training to start their own businesses, and received loans to buy homes for their growing families during what would come to be known as the baby boom.

Meanwhile, none of those options were available to John or the other African Americans who fought in the war and helped hold down the home front. The latter group had worked (along with white women, Chinese Americans, and Mexican Americans) in factories and defense plants that were desegregated by presidential order so they could help build tanks, planes, and weapons to support overseas troops, only to get laid off at war's end to make way for white veterans. Those layoffs saw years of economic gains, professional development, and social progress come to a grinding halt. Training for new career paths was almost entirely out of the question since local universities and trade schools refused to admit African American applicants, which resulted in endless waiting lists at historically Black colleges and universities. Added to that was the double bind created by Federal Housing Administration–endorsed racial covenants that prevented African Americans from buying homes in white neighborhoods, and redlining practices that prevented them from getting mortgages to invest in their own.

Even if John could have managed to sidestep just one of those hurdles, there were others still blocking the way in the form of white staffers at government agencies. The

ones at the Veterans Administration found arbitrary reasons to deny African Americans' access to the GI Bill of
Rights, even as they freely signed off on subsidizing white
veterans' educational and wealth-building dreams. And the
ones at the United States Employment Service, which was
supposed to help veterans find jobs in the defense industry,
instead steered African Americans toward janitorial work,
restaurant service, and porter jobs, none of which required
the specialized training or expert skills acquired on the battlefield and factory floor. The local banks were in on it, too,
refusing to underwrite African American vets' home or
business loans, even with government backing.

John wanted to marry his sweetheart, Willie Mae, and
start a family. But what kind of life could they lead in Montgomery? How would he be able to keep a roof over their
heads and food on the table, or provide for any children
they hoped to have? He found himself thinking back on
how skeptical he'd been when he was first drafted, how
afraid he'd been to risk his life for a country that would ask
so much after giving so little. And he began to wonder if
he'd made the right choice.

So little had changed in this world he had sacrificed so
much to keep safe. It was 1945 and he still had to sit in the
back rows of streetcars and buses. He still had to climb the
stairs to the stifling-hot balcony sections of movie theaters.
He still had to trudge to the back of gas stations to relieve
himself in filthy outhouses, and sneak into dark alleyways
when the sign on the only restroom said: "Whites Only."
He still had to endure the rudeness of white cashiers at the

stores where he spent his hard-earned money and listen to white men call him "boy." And he still had to tread lightly in the face of such insults, lest he end up one of the lynching victims he read about in the paper.

Amid this piling on of injustices, the United States was sending billions of dollars in aid to rebuild postwar Europe and promote American-style democracy. John read about it in the *Montgomery Advertiser* and the *Alabama Journal,* the same newspapers that showed indifference to Black people's suffering, even blaming them for their own experiences of racial oppression and violence. Their front pages trumpeted the benefits of the Marshall Plan (named after its chief architect, former U.S. Army chief of staff turned secretary of state George C. Marshall), insisting it was the only way to halt the spread of Communism from the East.

John marveled at the hypocrisy. Like so many African Americans, he wondered how the United States could bang on about democracy without ever truly practicing it. Black newspapers around the state and country, together with the newly founded *Ebony* magazine, a Chicago-based publication that John would read from its first issues until the day he died, amplified these questions and warned of a foreign policy failure if domestic civil rights issues weren't resolved. Their writers knew that the Soviets were using their own propaganda machines to spotlight the United States' hypocrisy and gain support for the Communist cause, particularly among African Americans. And they knew that even the Western Europeans on the receiving end of U.S. largesse were skeptical of the country's claims of moral leadership when it treated its own citizens with such cruelty. They heard it with their own ears when they went to places like London, Paris, and Rome.

They also knew that the American money flowing into Europe had a way of silencing open criticism there, no matter how righteous or necessary. But what they did not yet know, could not yet see, was that the United States had the means to extend its power and influence in ways that would make even the farthest reaches of the world feel, to African Americans at least, like they hadn't left home at all.

CHAPTER 3

THE *HIJO NATIVO*

Richard Wright,

BUENOS AIRES,
1940S

I T'S THE MOMENT THAT WILL change everything for Bigger Thomas. The moment that will propel him from a
wayward kid from the South Side of Chicago to a man on
trial for murder. Thomas always knew he had it in him to do
something rash, something he could not walk back—so palpable was his rage at white people for hoarding every opportunity for themselves and leaving only scraps for Black
people to fight over. He could never get used to it. And now
here he was, in the stately home of his white millionaire
boss, Henry Dalton. He'd just spent hours driving Dalton's
daughter, Mary, and her boyfriend around town while they
sipped from a flask and locked lips in the backseat. Before
retreating to his sleeping quarters in the basement, next to
the furnace he'd wake up early the following morning to
tend to, Thomas helped the drunk woman to her bedroom.

He stared at her dim face, the forehead capped with curly black hair. He eased his hand, the fingers spread wide, up the center of her back and her face came toward him and her lips touched his, like something he had imagined.

The kiss is a crucial plot point. Mary is too incapacitated to fully realize it is happening, yet Thomas attempts to take things even further. He's mounted on top of her when, suddenly, her blind mother enters the room and begins calling out her name. Thomas panics. What if Mary comes out of her drunken haze and alerts her mother to his presence? Seized by guilt and fear, and perhaps even some of that poorly suppressed rage, he puts a pillow over Mary's head, using all his strength to halt her bucking and scratching until, finally, her body goes limp.

The scene and everything that flowed from it made waves when Richard Wright first published his novel *Native Son* in 1940, and again when Orson Welles staged it on Broadway starring Canada Lee a year later. And now, in 1949, on the elaborate set that had been built in a suburb of Buenos Aires for the book's film adaptation, it was about to take place once more.

This time, Richard himself was playing Thomas. Even though no one knew the character better than him, it was not a foregone conclusion that he would take on the lead role. For one, Lee's performance had been a revelation, propelling him to international stardom (so much so that he was becoming a true movie star, filming a role in Europe around the same time that the film adaptation of *Native Son* was coming together). For another, Richard was a writer, not an actor, and most important, he was forty-one years old, married, a father of two, and more than twice Bigger's age. Much as he might have wanted to be the person to bring his most famous character to life onscreen, he didn't see a way to do it convincingly. But a meeting with a compelling duo in Paris, where Richard had recently moved with his family in 1947, helped to change his mind.

Pierre Chenal was a French Jew who made his name in noir films in the 1930s but was forced to flee Nazi-occupied France during World War II. He set up in Buenos Aires, a bustling Argentine city on the banks of the Río de la Plata that since the late nineteenth century had welcomed European immigrants as part of a large-scale attempt in Latin America (including places like Mexico, Cuba, and Brazil) at modernizing through whitening. The goal, as local governments saw it, was to outpopulate Indigenous, Black, and racially mixed people with white ones from Spain, Italy, the United Kingdom, and France, to compete on a global stage with the United States and Western Europe. Argentina also stood as a refuge for Jewish people fleeing pogroms in Russia and Eastern Europe and continued to beckon during the rise of Nazism (at the same time, it would also become a postwar destination for Nazi officers and collaborators fleeing punishment for their crimes), which meant that Chenal was among many Jewish creatives who came to call the country home.

While in Buenos Aires, Chenal crossed paths with Uruguay-born producer and screenwriter Jaime Prades, whose first film was *Volver a vivir* (Return to Life). Released in 1941 by Argentina Sono Film, the country's leading studio, the story centered on a young man struggling to rebuild his life and family after falling into criminal activity. A few years earlier, Chenal and Prades had both seen *Sangre negra*, the Spanish-language stage adaptation of *Native Son* that literally translates to "black blood." The production was put on by the Narciso Ibáñez Menta company at Buenos Aires's El Nacional theater and had a 150-show run, starring a cast of local actors. The story's subject matter appealed to Chenal's interest in noir, to Prades's soft spot for troubled men trying to make good, and to both men's careerism. They decided to pay Richard a visit in Paris with the idea of selling him on a film adaptation, insisting on top of everything that the author was the only man in the entire world who could bring the character of Bigger Thomas to life on the big screen.

Although Richard suspected that Chenal and Prades were leaning a bit heavily on flattery, he was touched by their vision for the film. It was not the first time he had been approached about adapting *Native Son,* but every other proposal had been too insulting to even consider. Never far from his mind in those days was the letter he received from Hollywood's Harold Hecht Company, which proposed that a white screenwriter named Joseph Fields helm the project, and suggested a critical change to the story itself:

> The plans are to change the leading Negro character
> to an oppressed minority white man, but rest assured
> that we have every desire to preserve the integrity of
> the original work. . . . Mr. Fields has a tentative idea

which calls for the picture to start with a Negro, a Jew, and a Pole or Italian, all applying for the same job. The Negro and Jew step aside for the other man. He needs the job more than they because of some personal reason, perhaps because he is married. At the end of the picture we will tie this together by a scene with the Jew and the Negro who realize that it could have happened to them, or to anyone who does not have the opportunity of living in equality with other people; that when one group is disenfranchised the meaning and the basis of what we live for is destroyed. . . . It will have a relationship to life as it is lived in this country and not be a glamorized, fictional Hollywood report.

MGM had made a similar pitch, offering him $25,000 on the condition that the cast be all white. For their part, and to their credit, Chenal and Prades had no such designs on stripping *Native Son* of its core premise and features. In the Buenos Aires stage adaptation both men had seen, all the local actors wore blackface, and they understood how necessary it was for the Black characters to be played by Black actors if the movie was going to have any sort of meaningful impact.

In other words, Chenal and Prades had finally presented Richard with a respectful offer that was worth considering. But there were important details to iron out. The first concerned the rights to the script. The film was going to be based not on Richard's book but on the play adaptation, and because the play was written in a complicated and contentious collaboration with the white dramatist Paul Green, the rights were jointly owned by Richard and an entity called Wellman, Incorporated (which itself was owned by Green, Orson Welles, and the actor and producer John Houseman). To move forward with the film, Richard and Wellman, Incorporated needed to be bought out to the tune of $6,000.

Chenal and Prades agreed to pay the fees. Since Richard lived in Paris, they initially offered to buy him out in French francs. However, at the time the franc was notoriously unstable. While it made Paris attractive and affordable to Americans, the currency had no place in business as far as Richard was concerned. "Oh no," he had told them. "Under no circumstances will I accept that amount of money in a country where the value is in such doubt. If you can't come up with American dollars, then the whole deal is off." The pair promised that they would raise the money, and Richard agreed to sign pre-option papers, with a more detailed contract to follow.

Next came the question of where to film the movie. Richard preferred to do it in Europe, but no country that was part of the Marshall Plan, an economic recovery and anti-Communist program that distributed aid from the United States to Western Europe in the aftermath of World War II and at the dawn of the Cold War, wanted to risk alienating the United States. Hosting a film shoot with content so critical of the country's treatment of African Americans could spell the end of U.S. financial support. Not even Richard's adopted homeland of France, for all the refuge it provided against American racism, was willing to do it. But

Chenal and Prades had a better idea: They should film in Argentina. It was Chenal's adopted homeland, a place where he and Prades had already had success in the film business, and—most important—it was not dependent on Marshall Plan funding. It would welcome the cast and crew to make the film they wanted. They would shoot it at Sono Film studios.

With most of the high-level details sorted out, Richard left his wife Ellen and their young daughters behind in one Paris—the one to which he'd written and would continue to write countless love letters—to set up camp in another. This one, the "Paris of the Americas" (as Buenos Aires was known by locals and in the burgeoning travel industry), bore a resemblance to its namesake, with its grand boulevards, elegant cafés, picturesque parklets, and Haussmann-style buildings. It would loom almost as large in Richard's life as the Paris that is most closely associated with his name. Yet Richard would ultimately say so little about Buenos Aires that his time there remains something of a mystery. Why would a man given to so many words about the places he lived in and traveled to, both within and outside of the United States and Paris, including writing an entire book about Spain, be almost completely silent about his year in Buenos Aires?

Part of the answer is simple: It was one of the darkest times in his life.

THE ROUTE TO BUENOS AIRES involved traveling first from Paris to New York on the *Queen Mary,* and then boarding another steamship for the passage to South America. Before setting sail from New York, however, Richard made a detour to Chicago in September 1949. He'd lived in the city for years after arriving from Mississippi as a teenager but had not been back in the nearly ten years since publishing *Native Son*. The plan was for Richard to get there first and welcome Prades, Chenal, and the head of Sono Film, Atilio Mentasti, when they arrived to film exterior shots for the movie to lend it some regional verisimilitude, and to do some initial casting for it for the same reason.

Richard wanted to set up shop in the downtown Loop. "I desired to stay in the Loop," he wrote in a 1951 article for Johnson Publishing's Black-interest *Ebony* magazine, "because I wanted to be centrally located near the casting agencies, the photographers' and movie unions; I wanted to be in a spot where I could swing out to any section of the city at a moment's notice on my errands to seek locations and backgrounds for filming." He asked his friend Louis Wirth, a white sociology professor at the University of Chicago, to make the reservation on his behalf. Wirth told the staff at the Palmer House hotel that Richard was staying as a guest of the American Council on Race Relations, an organization Wirth worked with from its founding in 1944 to its dissolution in 1950 in researching the root causes of racial problems and programs to address them. Richard had correctly calculated that the reservation would be honored if the staff thought he was there for official business in service to an organization well equipped to ring the alarm of racial discrimination. But while Richard was indeed able to check in himself, he still ran into problems. A visit to the front desk a few days after his arrival, to make a reservation for Jaime Prades, resulted in his being told there were no rooms available for the next two weeks. Richard knew better than to believe it. He asked a Black waiter in the hotel if it was as booked as the front desk claimed. "Hell, man, this damn hotel is a third empty," the waiter told him. "There's plenty of room." Richard understood. "Chicago was still Chicago. The old racial lines and attitudes still ruled."

This time, Richard enlisted another white friend to call and make reservations for Prades, who managed to immediately secure a room with the front desk. "Perhaps the clerk had thought that I had been trying to make reservations for another Negro!" he wrote. When it was time to make reservations for Mentasti and his wife, Richard went directly to the hotel manager and let him know that the Mentastis were, in fact, white. It worked. These complications and their ultimately easy resolutions were at once a sign of how differently Latin Americans could be treated in the United States compared with African Americans, and a reminder to Richard of the world he'd left behind in moving to Paris.

During some location scouting near the University of Chicago, Richard would meet a lovely young psychology student named Gloria Madison. She signed on to play Thomas's girlfriend, Bessie Mears, a character who, like Mary Dalton, also dies at his hands in the story. In the book, Mears works as a maid, but Richard wanted the character to do more in the film before meeting her end and therefore wrote in a new job for her as a vibrant cabaret singer.

Richard also had other business in the Windy City. In an

interview with the *Atlanta Daily World* at the time of his visit, he mentioned that being back in town gave him a chance to sell the home he'd purchased nearly a decade ago for his mother, siblings, and extended family, following the mega success of *Native Son*. He told the paper he no longer had a use for the home since the family had scattered, with some even returning down south, and he was planning to make Paris his forever home. This was all true, but there was more to the story.

Richard ended up using his own money to get the film project off the ground. While he had every intention of holding Chenal and Prades to their promise to buy him out, he was also deeply—even desperately—committed to seeing the project come to life. In an interview with the NAACP's *The Crisis* in 1950, shortly after filming wrapped, he'd said, "To make the screen version of a novel into which I had put so much of myself was a dream which I had long hugged to my heart, and it was quite painful until it happened."

That pain had evolved into a sense of excitement when he reached the agreement with Chenal and Prades, but one that was tinged with worry that Chenal and Prades might take too long to get the money together and that the guys at Wellman, whom Richard had convinced to agree to the buyout, would raise the asking price or simply change their minds. He thus made the decision to buy Wellman out himself, cabling his agent in New York to handle the transaction while keeping it as anonymous as possible. Eager as he was to work with Chenal and Prades, he didn't trust that they would feel a sense of urgency to buy the rights from Richard or Wellman if they knew Richard had already paid Wellman. He worried that the pair might assume that he did not really need the money for his own rights if he could pay Wellman for theirs, or that he was somehow happy to take on this bit of financing. Either way, Richard was concerned that Chenal and Prades would consider the project practically greenlit and not bother to hold up their end of the financial bargain.

The decision to front the money for the film put a dent in Richard's reserves, and his financial anxiety was now at an all-time high. In addition to selling his family home for much-needed extra cash, he stopped by the downtown headquarters of *Ebony* magazine, where he signed a contract to publish a few pieces, one about his stop in Chicago and another about his time in Argentina. Both would end up being published in the January 1951 issue of the publication. A third piece, "I Choose Exile!," was a manifesto about his rejection of life in the United States. That manifesto would prove more complicated to place in the magazine. The publishers worried that its readers, African Americans who had mostly opted to remain in the United States despite its challenges, and its advertisers, mainstream corporations dipping their toes into the African American market, would take offense at the piece, so they opted against publishing it. But that would come later. On this autumn day in 1949, Richard left the offices feeling reassured. Whatever happened with the film, he would always have his writing to fall back on.

Then it was back to New York for the sailing to Buenos Aires (a trip that was also on his own dime, which only added to the financial pinch Richard was feeling). To play the part of young Bigger, Richard adopted a grueling diet and exercise routine from the moment he boarded SS *Argentina* in October 1949. He did not let up until he lost thirty pounds, just in time for shooting to begin the following month. He may not have looked as young as Bigger, but he certainly looked as hungry.

TRAVELING ACROSS THE EQUATOR meant leaving behind the cold temperatures of late fall in the Northern Hemisphere for springtime in South America. Arriving at the busy Port of Buenos Aires on a sunny and warm October day, Richard hailed a taxi and made his way to the nearby Residence Golden Home at 1557 Posadas Street. The eight-story building was on a down-market commercial strip in the upscale neighborhood of Recoleta, nestled among cabarets, dance halls, and nightclubs.

A *New York Times* reporter, in town to cover the shoot, would later describe the Golden Home as "a small, unpretentious, midtown hotel." Indeed, the bachelor-style quarters were a step down from the large, airy family apartment the Wrights lived in back in Paris, which was in the fashionable district of Neuilly-sur-Seine and just steps from the Bois de Boulogne. But Richard was still out of pocket for the rights to the play, in addition to sending money to Paris and fielding requests from his aunt and mother to send money down south for a seemingly endless list of home repairs. Besides, as Richard had once said, "I've never been able to take much pride in having a material advantage over other people," so this humble choice of accommodations was unsurprising. Whether or not he might have ultimately preferred to stay in posher quarters, since he couldn't afford to spend a lot of money it was nice to know that he really did not need much at the end of the day.

Although the hotel was unremarkable, it was nonetheless steeped in history. Rumor had it that it was the preferred place for the city's most powerful men to house their girlfriends and mistresses, to whom they would be close enough to visit before clocking in at their offices downtown, and again before heading home for dinner with their wives and children. Just a few years before Richard's arrival, in 1942, a young actress named Eva Duarte was one of its residents. The accommodations were a step up from the crowded apartments she was sharing around town with various girlfriends while waiting for her big break. She was finally able to afford a room at the Golden Home after having booked an acting gig with the local Radio Belgrano station. Duarte lived there until 1944, when she met a middle-aged widower and former military colonel named Juan Domingo Perón and moved in with him at Posadas 1567, a few doors down.

Perón was waiting for his own big break in those days. When he and Eva first met, he was secretary of labor and social security in the military government's Department of Labor, but he had much loftier ambitions. Together with Eva, whom he married in 1945, Perón began campaigning for the presidency. He could not have done it without her. Through the soap opera radio program *Toward a Better Future,* which the actress starred in thanks to some behind-the-scenes machinations on Perón's part, she promoted her husband's activities, accomplishments, and plans for a populist presidency.

By the time her husband won the 1946 election, Eva was a star in her own right, affectionally known as "Evita." The pair moved to Palacio Unzué, a nineteenth-century mansion in the neighborhood where they would reside until Evita died there in 1952, and where Perón would remain until the end of his second term in 1955.*

Even though they did not live at the Golden Home or on Posadas Street at the same time, Richard felt the presence of the Peróns during his stay. So did everyone in Argentina in 1949, thanks to a recent change to the constitution that granted the president far-reaching powers. On the surface this was done to improve the country's foundering economy, since the United States, frustrated with Perón's professed neutrality in the conflict with the Soviet Union, blocked Marshall Plan countries from buying Argentina's agricultural exports. But it was also a smoke screen that allowed Perón to arrest students on college campuses for speaking out in favor of democratic freedoms, imprison his political opponents, and suppress newspapers and radio stations that were critical of his regime. The result was a climate in which ordinary citizens and visitors were afraid of expressing anything close to dissent.

There was no getting around it: The film crew had set up shop in a dictatorship. Whether or not Richard fully grasped this fact before arriving in Buenos Aires, the reality

---

* Perón would serve a third term starting in 1973 until his death in July 1974.

would soon become inescapable. When he first got to town, he would sit at his desk in his room at the Golden Home to write letters to Ellen, to his agent, as well as to an assortment of professional contacts and friends. Soon, though, he started to notice that his incoming mail arrived opened before he received it. Then, cables to Ellen went undelivered. Richard later told his friend and biographer Constance Webb that locals informed him that there were government spies inside the cable offices, looking through everyone's correspondence for signs of criticism of the government or outright treason. He started personally ferrying his mail across the river to neighboring Montevideo, Uruguay, where a pilot he managed to bribe would fly his correspondence out of the country.

That might have solved one problem, but there were still others. The United States had also stepped in to make Richard's experience in Argentina as difficult as possible. An attaché from the U.S. State Department, recognizing that "[Richard's] personal manners are sufficiently charming to win him a considerable following here in Buenos Aires," suggested that the United States plant stories in the local papers about his political leanings as a way of discouraging the press from taking an interest in him. The plan worked, to a degree. Instead of welcoming him like the world-famous celebrity he was, Argentine officials treated him like a suspicious foreign agent.

Whether or not Richard was aware of the U.S. intervention as it was happening, he would not have been surprised by it. He had been a member of the Communist Party from the early 1930s until around 1944, when his disillusionment

led him to publicly sever ties, and the FBI placed him on
their Security Index for supposedly dangerous subversives
in 1942. During the sailing from New York to Buenos Aires,
in between his rigorous exercises to trim pounds from his
frame, he penned the lines to a now-famous poem, "The
FB Eye Blues." Its third stanza was almost a prediction for
the year to come:

> Everywhere I look, Lord
> I see FB eyes
> . . . .
> I'm getting sick and tired
>   of gover'ment spies.

Added to all this was the fact that when Richard first arrived in Buenos Aires, he still didn't have a contract for the
film, and still had not been paid for his share of the rights.
This wasn't an immediate cause for concern, since he had
gone into the project believing strongly that it was a "communal idea and undertaking." He wanted something more
collaborative and respectful than his earlier work on the
play adaptation with Paul Green, whom he had once considered a friend but who proved to be not only difficult to
work with but also tremendously condescending. Green
took credit for the final product, referring to Richard in interviews as a kind of research assistant who offered occasional colorful insights about the Black experience. This
time, Richard thought, would be different.

Finally, after a couple of weeks, Prades sent a contract
over to the Golden Home. But it was written entirely in

Spanish, which Richard could not read. After taking the paperwork to a lawyer who could translate its terms into English, Richard learned that the contract was filled with ambiguous language and bore no traces of the agreements the group had provisionally reached back in Paris and drawn up in French.

Richard had brought the pre-option contract with him to Buenos Aires—or at least he thought he had. After visiting the lawyer's office, he went back to his room to compare the Spanish-language contract, now that he understood it, to the earlier, French-language one. He looked on his writing desk where he remembered storing it but could not find it among his files.

Richard might have been willing to concede that he forgot to pack the French paperwork before leaving Paris, or accidentally left it behind somewhere in Chicago or New York, but as he looked around his room it also appeared that someone had gone through his luggage. Was something more sinister going on? He stood in the center of his temporary home, alone, emotionally frail, physically exhausted, and increasingly panicked, surveying every inch of the space in search of proof that he had not agreed to come all this way to be taken advantage of by white people who thought they were smarter than him.

The moment marked the beginning of a period during which Richard started to question whether Chenal and Prades were plotting to take advantage of him, or if the Argentinean government was keeping tabs by snooping around his hotel room, either for its own reasons or on behalf of the United States. He was right to be suspicious, even if he did not yet know who had put a target on his back or why.

BACK IN THE REAL PARIS, Ellen confided to the writer Simone de Beauvoir, a friend of the couple with whom Ellen had grown close during Richard's absence, that her husband's letters had become few and far between as the months ticked by. She didn't know that his attempts were, in fact, being intercepted, and that, in the beginning at least, Richard was dialing down his communication as a result of his growing suspicions of the postal service and his feeling of being under constant surveillance.

Richard might have collapsed under the weight of this accretion of stressors if he hadn't found small relief in the world outside the Golden Home. Richard became fast friends with his younger co-star, Jean Wallace, who played Mary Dalton. She was not the first choice for the role, but several white actresses had refused to sign on to a story that required them to kiss a black man, because of either their own racism or their fear of backlash. As for Wallace, she was never one for following the rules: She was divorced, with an ex-husband who retained custody of their two children, and had already lived through her share of backlash because of both. Besides, this was the biggest role of her career. She was not going to let the chance at success pass her by because of her co-star's race. Nor would she refuse to spend time off set with him, especially since filming outside of Hollywood and the United States meant being free from the expectation of segregation among cast members.

Here, she and Richard could dine, shop, and stroll around in the toniest—and whitest—parts of the city, like *Barrio Norte,* without encountering the kind of hostility or rejection from restaurant servers, store clerks, and residents they would have been subjected to in the United States. This is not to say the pair went unnoticed. A Black man and blond woman would have been an unusual pairing in many parts of Buenos Aires, especially its wealthy enclaves, and Richard would have stood out given the poor socio-economic conditions in which Afro-Argentines tended to live (more on that below). Both circumstances might have resulted in the pair getting an initially frosty reception, but Richard and Wallace's status as Americans would likely have warmed things up.

Richard also found a friend in Gonzalo Sánchez de Lozada, a Bolivian who had recently graduated from the University of Chicago and was an assistant director of the film.* He had come to Argentina to find a job in moviemaking and lucked into his high-profile position at his young age because he spoke English. The pair's ability to communicate in English opened the door for Richard and Sánchez de Lozada to build on their shared association with Chicago and interest in the film industry and develop a close friendship. Sánchez de Lozada would drive Richard around town, where he was warmly received in literary and expatriate circles, especially in those opposed to the Peronist regime. Richard became acquainted with Jorge Luis Borges, and sat for a portrait by

---

* He would also twice be elected president of Bolivia in the 1990s and early 2000s.

the German-born Jewish photographer Gisèle Freund, who
was living in exile in Argentina after fleeing from the Nazis.
Later, Richard remarked to Constance Webb that the city's
elites hid themselves away in their mansions, so fearful were
they of running afoul of the dictatorship. As he acknowledged, "to be in trouble with the government of Argentina
is no light matter."

Richard had plenty of time on his hands since the film's
cast and financing were still being pieced together. The
slowness of the production was one reason Richard would
end up spending such a long time in Argentina, but so, too,
would the delay become a convenient excuse to avoid returning home to Ellen and the children. Aside from Gloria
Madison and Jean Wallace, who were playing Bessie Mears
and Mary Dalton, respectively, there were still major parts
to fill. Willa Pearl Curtis, an "Eastside housewife and actress," from Los Angeles, was cast to play the role of Bigger
Thomas's mother, Hannah. She flew down to Buenos Aires
on her first trip abroad. The local Black press covered her
casting and departure with pride, noting that she was "believed to be the first person of her race taken out of the
country for such a part." The same was true of Madison,
who had flown down from Chicago, but the point was
clear: It was a big deal for African American actors to be
involved in a major international production.

Argentina proved a curious place for the movie to film
given its own racial dynamics. The country's history of slavery dated back to the sixteenth century, when Africans and
their descendants began toiling in domestic service, cattle
ranching, and other sectors, until the institution was abol-

ished in 1861. At one point, Afro-Argentines made up one-third of Buenos Aires's population, but by the 1950s, their numbers had dwindled due to race mixing, dispersal into other parts of the country, and through censual sleights of hand that saw them folded into other racial categories like *mestizo* (which referred to people of Indigenous and European ancestry) and vastly outnumbered by European immigrants. The effect was that, officially speaking, Argentina did not have many Black people—not enough to really matter.

In addition to denying the meaningful presence of an Afro-Argentine population, officials in the country denied the existence of racism itself. Evita Perón had even given a speech proclaiming that the country believed in "fundamental human rights" without regard for race, sex, language, or religion. But the reality was that Afro-Argentine women, like their enslaved forebears, were confined to jobs in domestic service, while Afro-Argentine men were limited to manual labor. A few managed to exceed these limits, like the famous tango bandleader Enrique Maciel, whose stylings Richard and others could hear in local nightclubs or by tuning in to Radio Buenos Aires. There was also Raúl Grigera, a ubiquitous nightlife icon who rose to fame in the early twentieth century and made cameos in a few of the country's silent films, but whose life was ultimately reduced, even while he was still alive in the 1940s and '50s, to a sad parable of a buffoon who was depicted in the press and popular memory as a representative of a dying, dispossessed race.

The adaptation of *Native Son* was the first film in Argentina to grapple so explicitly with Blackness. That is, of

course, Blackness in the United States. It was not a coinci-
dence that rather than being literally translated into Spanish
as *Hijo nativo,* which might have allowed viewers to think of
Bigger Thomas as someone who belonged as much to Buenos Aires as to Chicago, the book, play, and film were all
given the name *Sangre negra* when they debuted in Argentina. And while the play doubled down on this kind of Afro-
Argentine erasure by casting only white or white-passing
actors in blackface, the film took a different, somewhat more
complex tack to round out the cast. A multinational reper-
tory was assembled: Lidia Alves, a Brazilian student and
first-time actress, was cast as Bigger's younger sister, Vera;
George Green, who was of unknown origins but had been
making a living dancing in Buenos Aires nightclubs, played
Bigger's friend, Panama; and Leslie Straughn, who had been
working as a mechanic in Uruguay but was originally from
New Guinea, signed on to play Bigger's brother, Buddy. The
casting of nonprofessional actors was in part a reflection of
the small size of the Afro-Argentine and broader Afro–Latin
American acting community in Buenos Aires, which was itself a result of the dearth of parts for such performers. At
the same time, it's not clear why more Afro-Argentine entertainers, like Maciel and Grigera, were not cast, aside from
those who filled out scenes in the background and went un-
named in the credits. That said, it's clear that the production
drew interest from across the Afro–Latin American diaspora.

That *Sangre negra* was a film about the United States,
and U.S. racism, must have been a source of combined excitement and frustration for the actors, whom we know

little about beyond their names. Maybe they were excited to be part of a truly global production, one that allowed them entrée into a world of filmmaking that had typically been closed off to them, particularly when it came to playing important roles. At the same time, they must have felt profound frustration that the production was one that required them to erase their own diasporic identities to participate. That frustration would only mount as they saw the African American actors get the star treatment. Like Richard, Madison was becoming a local celebrity in her own right. The January–March 1950 issue of *El hogar,* a popular lifestyle magazine in Buenos Aires, featured Madison in its party pages, sitting at an elegant dinner. Surprisingly, one of her companions was Dixon Donnelley, the State Department attaché who had been planting unfavorable stories about Richard in the press.

Aside from Alves, none of the Afro–Latin American actors spoke English, and Chenal did not seem to have any trust in their abilities to recite their lines well enough to convince audiences that they were from Chicago. Instead, he planned to dub in English dialogue to replace their Spanish dialogue at the editing phase. For the Afro–Latin American actors, who had already reconciled themselves to the fact that this film was not going to be about them, at least not explicitly, being quite literally silenced must have added insult to injury. Chenal's decision was also among the many signs that the final product was going to be messy.

Richard still didn't have a new contract by the time filming finally started in January 1950. Instead of waiting for Prades to come through with one, he went directly to Sono

Film studio head Atilio Mentasti. Mentasti understood that
the project hinged on Richard's participation, and so he
agreed to a direct, backdoor contract that would guarantee
him one-fifth of the profits. With that settled, Richard told
himself not to hold a grudge against Chenal and Prades (or
think too much about whether they had played a role in the
disappearance of the pre-option papers) and hoped that the
pair would do the same when they found out about the deal
with Mentasti. There was still a movie to shoot and money
to make.

With both his reputation and his financial future on the
line, Richard spent long days on set, honing his new craft as
an actor while also supervising dialogue and working to ensure that the film hewed as close to his vision as possible, all
while trying to adhere to the constraints of getting a movie
dealing with race, racism, labor issues, and the justice system past the notoriously stringent U.S. censors. Richard was
already cutting the book's references to Communism from
the script in anticipation of state motion picture review
boards, and even more cuts would come once filming was
over. Adding to the complications once shooting finally
started was the fact that Chenal was tremendously exacting
in his expectations. In take after take, according to *The New
York Times,* Chenal would chide Richard's line readings by
saying, "Oh, Dick, you made the dumb business." He also
had words for the local cast members who had been hired
to play Richard's sister and friends, constantly telling them,
"No me encantó" (the paper translated it to mean "It did
not enchant me," but a more accurate translation would be
"I didn't love that"). All this was said without apparent

harshness, since the article described Chenal as "an infi-
nitely patient and winning director," but it still made for an
exhausting shoot.

While the cast and crew immersed themselves in the
world of 1930s Chicago, Peronist Argentina was never far
away. One day, a contingent of armed soldiers arrived on set
and asked to speak with Richard alone. Remembering the
words of local friends who warned him that if he ran afoul
of the regime, "they [did not] try you; they just [shot] you
or put you away in some cold jungle to rot," he panicked. In
the end, though, the soldiers were simply curious about the
moviemaking business and wanted to use their position to
get photos with the famous American *negro* who was starring in the film, and a behind-the-scenes tour of it. Richard,
relieved if unsettled by the brazenness of their approach,
obliged.

The busy days on set put strain on the Wrights' marriage. Ellen grew worried about the lack of correspondence, and told Simone de Beauvoir that she offered to visit
Richard, but he refused. Beauvoir grew suspicious. "Dick is
still in South America," she wrote in a letter to her American lover, writer Nelson Algren. "Soon it will be ten months.
Nobody ever takes that long to shoot a movie, but he says it
will be a good one. . . . She [Ellen] begins to want an extra-
man, but she does not dare to get one." It was true: Ellen
was becoming lonely enough that she was considering taking a lover. She had no way of knowing that her husband
had already beaten her to it. Busy as he claimed to be in his
sporadic correspondence with her, Richard had nonetheless
managed to find time to spend with a beguiling young ac-

tress named Madelyn Jackson. A woman of mysterious origins about whom nothing has been written except in Richard's biography by his friend Constance Webb, Jackson was apparently based in Haiti but had somehow managed to get hired for a bit part in the film and noticed by its lead. Ellen discovered their affair after Richard sent a parcel of his journals and papers home. Desperate to find out what was going on with her husband, she read an entry declaring his love for the actress.

By June 1950, filming had wrapped, the Americans had gone home, but Richard was still in Buenos Aires with Jackson. It seemed that even a dictatorship was bearable with the right kind of company. Eventually, though, the pair got restless. *The Chicago Defender* snapped a picture of them boarding SS *Argentina* together on July 7, bound for Trinidad, then Haiti, and then New York, where Richard introduced Jackson to Webb and her husband, writer C.L.R. James. Finally, Richard sailed back to Europe, alone, on August 19, 1950. Ellen told Beauvoir that after nearly a year apart, he came back without a kiss for her or the kids. In the face of his indifference, she confronted him about Jackson, and rather than apologizing Richard claimed that he wanted to go back to Haiti with the actress, and if that didn't happen, he'd bring her to Paris. "It's your life against mine," he insisted. "I choose mine."

Fearful of losing her husband, Ellen agreed to let Jackson come to Paris, but Richard had to wait one year before inviting her. Perhaps Ellen thought that by then her husband's affection for Jackson would cool and he'd lose interest in the idea. In the end, though, it wasn't up to either of the Wrights. By Christmas of 1950, Jackson wrote Richard to say that she'd had an affair with another man, a high-ranking politician in Haiti. She'd moved on from him, though, and was now considering an offer from a wealthy Argentine (possibly one she met while she and Richard were dating?) to stay at his ranch. Ellen read that letter, too.

Richard's slow departure from Argentina was not just about Jackson. It was also an attempt, perhaps even a sub-conscious one, to forestall having to face the negative reception the film ultimately received. *Native Son* was a spectacular failure in the United States, despite concessions made after it was initially banned by the National Board of Review of Motion Pictures, which required six single-spaced pages of changes before the film could be released. Gone was the most "offensive" content—namely, the moment when Mary Dalton stroked Bigger Thomas's hair. It wasn't even the kiss that had been described in the book, but it still violated the Hollywood film code's prohibition of "miscegenation." An additional thirty minutes were also cut, excising Thomas's trial and its condemnation of U.S. racism. Richard had been especially proud of that scene, later telling *The Crisis* that "we stuck pretty close to the novel, but we did make a few changes in the trial scene, which we thought too static. We had to put in some action there." Richard was being prag-matic: Cutting this and other scenes stripped the film of its heart and potency, and it was a necessary step to getting the film screened in U.S. theaters. Besides, Chenal promised that the uncut version would air at its premiere at the Venice Film Festival and in European theaters thereafter.

But the film was criticized in the United States regardless. Most of the reviews were negative, like this one in *Variety:* "With a certain modicum of subtlety, the picture seems to have been made with intent to create anti-U.S. feeling." The review goes on to say, "The anti-U.S. impact likely will be strongest when it is distributed in Latin America, particularly Panama, Brazil, and other countries with a large proportion of colored population. Presumably it is for that public that contrasts between the rich sections of Chicago and those of the Negro slums are shown with crude sensationalism." Even the Black press, which had breathlessly chronicled the casting news and filming schedule, panned it. "I think it stinks," pronounced the critic for the *New York Amsterdam News*. The only saving grace, according to the paper, was Gloria Madison. "She, even though she did not turn in an impressive job, is the only encouraging spot in 'Native Son.' . . . Oh, yes, Gloria can't sing . . . But, for that matter, neither can Lena [Horne]."

Despite Chenal's promises, the same Frankensteinian version of the film was screened in Europe. It was mostly a flop there, too, although it did find some fans in Richard's adopted homeland of France. The only audiences that saw the original version as it was intended to screen were in Buenos Aires, where it opened to rave reviews in March 1951, at the famed Gran Rex theater. By then, Richard's film debut had cost him dearly: He was paid only $3,000 for an initial investment of more than $6,000. And when he tried to get his hands on the uncut version of the film, which he had hoped to distribute in French film houses, he faced constant evasion from Sono Film, until the studio finally told him that there were no original copies left.

According to the media historian Ellen Scott, *Native Son* "could have been the quintessential African-American film noir." Instead, it was plagued by a host of problems that doomed any chance of success. "Over-dark cinematography often obscures visual cues essential to the narrative—literally frustrating our vision. The dubbing of foreign actors is obvious, and many of the American actors give forced and unconvincing performances. The film is visually dark but the stylized, high-contrast noir cinematography is missing. In its place is a blunt, frank darkness." And that's just what made it onscreen. As one of Richard's biographers put it: "So now he had a taste of how big business was conducted on three continents—Europe, North America, and South America. Richard had got the worst of it. Like so many American blacks who leave the States, he had had a blind faith that he would be treated well because he was a 'refugee.' Not even in the deepest recesses of his basically suspicious and distrustful soul had Richard believed he could be so easily duped."

Perhaps it is no wonder, then, that Richard had so little to say about his time in Argentina. In fact, in his 1951 *Ebony* piece about the creative process behind the film, titled "Richard Wright Explains Ideas About Movie Making," he adopts a distant and confusing tone, referring to himself in the third person and refusing to make direct points: "What the writer actually sees happening is a collective, organized creation of images designed to evoke and control currents of feeling. Slowly the writer's hostility ebbs; he senses that this, too, is artistic expression, but self-conscious, technical, and forceful." Richard seems to be meditating on the difference between the writer's solitary creative process when it came to writing books and the necessarily collaborative process when it came to making films, but struggles to find the right words to convey what that process truly meant for him.

His other reference to Argentina comes on the first page of *Pagan Spain*, his 1957 travelogue-cum-ethnography of his journey through Madrid, Barcelona, and other parts of Spain. By way of examining why it had taken him nearly a decade of living in neighboring France before he finally managed to visit, he wrote: "I had been born under an absolutistic racist regime in Mississippi; I had lived and worked for twelve years under the political dictatorship of the Communist party of the United States; and I had spent a year of my life under the police terror of Perón in Buenos Aires. So why avoid the reality of life under Franco? What was I scared of?" He didn't have an answer.

For Richard, the "Paris of the Americas" was no Paris. Not in the ways that mattered. In fact, it was more like the country of his birth in terms of its terrors. But that is still only part of why he never wrote about it. After all, he did write and say quite a lot about the United States—even long after he had moved away. Perhaps the best explanation for his silence about Argentina is the silence itself. Indeed, he spent a year of his life chasing the dream of a film career, along with a woman who ultimately rejected him, all while losing sight of the very thing that had sent him to Buenos Aires in the first place: his writing.

17 Reichenhaller Straße

THEY SET SAIL FROM New York City on June 20, 1952, bound for the port of Livorno, Italy. She was twenty-five years old, her two children just four and three, and they were all alone. Her husband, their father, was already an ocean away, having flown over several months earlier to begin the military posting that made the young trio's journey necessary in the first place.

After its annexation by Nazi Germany in 1938 and surrender to the Allied forces in 1945, Austria was under a quadripartite occupation by the Soviet Union, the United Kingdom, France, and the United States. The U.S. Occupation Headquarters were in Salzburg, a baroque "City of Churches" in the foothills of the Alps where the husband was now stationed, waiting for his family.

The apartment he'd found for them was at 17 Reichenhaller Straße. It occupied one sunny half of the second floor of a three-story building that was built before World War I, on a quiet residential street in a middle-class neighborhood just west of the Salzach River and about a ten-minute walk from Mozart's birthplace. For the next several years, the apartment, the neighborhood, and the city that enveloped both would be the family's home.

The young mother would soon develop a friendly acquaintance with the Austrian housewives in their building, communicating through smiles and gestures as she tried to figure out where to do the shopping and how to work the laundry machine in the basement. The children would learn German under the unyielding hand of a schoolteacher who refused to grant bathroom breaks when requested in English, eventually speaking enough to help their mother at the butcher and to order their own ice cream in one of the many shops lining the way home.

Two more sons would come along, one in 1953 and the other in 1955, joining a family that by then had found a sense of material comfort, dignity, and safety that was almost unheard of for African Americans in the United States. It was the first time, in fact, that they would feel—and be treated—like Americans. That feeling would last right up until the 1955 signing of the Austrian Independence Treaty, which would send all the Americans home and the family back into the grip of U.S. racism. But first, the young woman and her children needed to make the crossing.

They had already made it through one leg of the journey, which was arguably the hardest. The train ride north from Montgomery, Alabama, the only home any of them had ever known, must have been harrowing. I say "arguably" and "must have been" because, even though the young woman was my grandmother, the children were my oldest uncle and aunt, and the man waiting for them over in Europe was my grandfather, I cannot ask them. My grandparents and uncle are all dead, and my aunt was too young to remember the trip.

I grew up hearing bits and pieces about this time in my family's life. I heard about the apartment, the neighbors, and the trips to the butcher and ice cream shops. I also heard about the weekend card games my grandparents hosted and attended, where they played alongside Black and white servicemen and their wives while the children entertained themselves. And I heard about how impossible any of this would have been in the United States. I knew my grandpa had joined the army as a young man in Alabama, lost his right eye on a Normandy beach during World War II, and eventually settled with his wife and kids in Colorado Springs near the military base at Fort Carson. Those were basic facts that explained everyday facets of my life. Like the way my grandparents both spoke with a southern twang, why my grandpa had a glass eye, and how we ended up being among the small handful of Black people to call the mountain state our home. But in my self-absorbed youth, I'd rarely given much thought to his life and career beyond that. I'd always assumed that the knickknacks on every shelf and in every cabinet around the house—beer steins from Austria, chinoiserie vases, porcelain dolls dressed in Korean hanboks, and stacks of old postcards—had come from friends or flea markets. It had never occurred to me that my grandpa had been to other parts of the world beyond the battlefields of France, or that my grandma and the eldest of their nine children had also traveled with him.

There was so much, though, that no one ever spoke of. They never spoke of the beginning of the story, the journey itself, or the early days and months of adjusting to their new world and way of life. No one spoke, either, about the complexities of being Black in what was once part of the Third Reich, of being American in an occupied state, or of being back in the United States after all those years away. And I, living proof that grandparents are wasted on the young, never asked about any of it. It never even occurred to me that there were so many questions to ask, about the beginning and the end and all the points in between, until it was much too late.

I'll never get answers to those questions now. At least not the ones that only my family knew and that, to me, ultimately matter most: *Was Grandma afraid? Was Grandpa worried? Were they happy?* But because my family's history folds into a much broader and well-documented history of African American soldiers and their families leaving the United States to help rebuild Europe and promote democracy after the war, and of returning home to a country that refused to live up to its own ideals, I can at least get somewhere close.

CHAPTER 4

THE MOTHER OF
(RE)INVENTION

Mabel Grammer,
MANNHEIM, 1950S

MABEL GRAMMER WAS SICK. As she later described it in an interview in *Good Housekeeping*, the problem started when she first got to Germany in the spring of 1951. It came on as a general sense of malaise, a feeling that things just weren't quite right, then blossomed into a series of headaches that refused to go away, no matter how many pills she took or hours she slept in her darkened bedroom. Eventually things got serious enough to warrant calling an ambulance to take her to the local hospital.

She was attended to by a young female doctor who carefully examined her new patient. The doctor couldn't find anything physically wrong; Mabel was the picture of health. "You're just feeling sorry for yourself" was the unofficial diagnosis.

What did she have to feel sorry about? She was married to a man she loved and enjoying a comfortable life in

Mannheim, where she was part of a vibrant community of American GIs and their families. But that was also the problem. In this corner of the world, which was almost exclusively the domain of workingmen, stay-at-home mothers, and children, Mabel struggled to adapt. She'd once had a career of her own back in Washington, D.C., writing a long-running column for *The Afro-American*. Her days were busy and exciting then, filled with interesting people who took what she had to say seriously. Still, Mabel had been willing to leave it all behind for love.

The loss of one identity and set of responsibilities might have been more tolerable if it were replaced with another, but as Mabel told her doctor that day in the hospital, a pair of operations (the details of which she kept to herself) had left her unable to bear children. Where did she fit in, then, if not as a mother? How would she spend the days, months, and years that lay ahead?

Mabel kept her early life, the one that set her on the path to Germany, close to her chest. She told *Good Housekeeping* that she was born and raised in Hot Springs, Arkansas, but never pinned down an exact birth date. There may have been a boring reason for that: As was true for tens of millions of Americans, Mabel's birth certificate wasn't officially issued until 1942, when it became the necessary proof of citizenship to get a job, marry, obtain health coverage, and secure other benefits during World War II. It's possible that Mabel did not know when, exactly, she was born (that said, her birth certificate showed a much earlier date than she usually indicated). Or, more intriguingly, perhaps she simply did not want just anyone to know such details. Because

Mabel kept things vague, not only in the *Good Housekeeping* piece but also in other interviews she would eventually give over the course of her life, suffice it to say she was born in the first or second decade of the twentieth century.

Mabel's hometown was nestled in the Central Ouachita Mountains and known for a cache of thermal waters around which a vibrant and segregated resort community sprang up in the 1880s to offer restorative soaks, Turkish baths, steam treatments, and massages, all under the direction of trained physicians and therapists. Like most Black residents of Hot Springs, Mabel's father, Edward Treadwell, formed part of the workforce in the myriad establishments—bathhouses, hotels, restaurants, and gambling halls—that served the tens of thousands of tourists who passed through each year.

According to Mabel's birth certificate, her father supported a wife and three children on his wages as a waiter. It could not have been easy, but one saving grace came in the form of a book that Mabel said got passed down through the generations to her mother, Pearl. Called "Poor Man's Recipes," it had instructions for feeding lots of mouths with just a few ingredients. It included a recipe for a family-sized dinner that involved mixing a pound of ground beef with breadcrumbs, onions, garlic, and eggs, frying it all up, and portioning it out over several slices of toast, followed by a pudding made with a stale loaf soaked in a batter of canned pineapple and coconut cream and baked until golden brown. As Pearl used to tell Mabel and older brothers William (Bill) and Timothy (Big Tim): "It isn't how much you make, but how well you spend it."

For all its hardships, life in Hot Springs did have one ad-

vantage for a family like the Treadwells. While the town's
main artery, Bathhouse Row, catered to white tourists and
strictly enforced Jim Crow in and out of the waters running
through its collection of grand Victorian buildings, Hot
Springs was nonetheless a premier destination for Black tourists from all over the country. They spent most of their time
just east of Bathhouse Row in the city's Black business district, where they stayed at the Pythian Bathhouse and Hotel
(formerly the Crystal, which was damaged in a 1913 fire that
engulfed much of the city) or, if there was no room there, in
the nearby homes of Black residents. The Pythian was owned
and operated by the Knights of Pythias of North America,
South America, Europe, Asia, Africa, and Australia, a frater-
nal organization of Black men that was formed in 1869 after
the Knights of Pythias Supreme Lodge refused to accept
them as members. The organization counted prominent
businessmen, professionals, and community leaders among
its membership and offered them discounted rates at the
bathhouse. With them came their colleagues, friends, and
wider circles, who turned the building into a place to relax,
visit, and make plans for shopping, dinner, and nights out on
the town.

Against this backdrop it's easy to picture Edward coming home at the end of each day with tales of serving Black
doctors from Cleveland and dentists from Chicago and
club owners from New York City. To envision Pearl and the
kids running into some of them during their daily errands
around town, with mother and daughter admiring the
women's dresses, hats, and hairstyles, and the boys standing in awe of the big-city men strolling confidently in their

suits. And to imagine the whole family getting filled with a sense, each in their own way, of just how much bigger the world was than Hot Springs.

BILL WAS THE FIRST of the Treadwell children to leave. He headed for Ohio and was joined in short order by Big Tim and then Mabel. For a time, Mabel worked as a cosmetologist in Cleveland and took classes at The Ohio State University in Columbus. The school had enrolled its first Black student in the 1880s and began slowly accepting handfuls more in the decades that followed. Among them was a promising young sociology student from the town of Wilberforce (home to the historically Black Wilberforce University) named John C. Alston, member of the class of 1937.

With such a small Black student community, it was inevitable that John and Mabel would cross paths. They started dating, fell in love, and married not long after Alston's graduation, which was soon followed by his getting offered a job as a research assistant at Howard University. The school had been training generations of Black professionals in every field since its founding in 1867, but by the 1930s it was enjoying something of a golden age. Leading thinkers like the political scientist Ralph Bunche, the sociologist E. Franklin Frazier, and the philosopher Alain Locke were helming its classrooms, where students like Thurgood Marshall were taking careful notes.

If Howard and the surrounding Shaw neighborhood were the intellectual heart of Washington, D.C.'s Black community, U Street was its soul. The corridor stretching from Seventh to Sixteenth streets N.W. was home to "Black Broadway," where theaters, concert halls, and nightclubs provided jobs and entertainment for a Black population that was excluded from similar possibilities in other parts of the heavily segregated city. Both U Street and neighboring Columbia Heights were also filled with hundreds of Black-owned banks, doctors' offices, schools, grocers, and restaurants where residents could meet all their daily needs.

Together, these institutions and neighborhoods made the city an easy draw for John and his new wife, who was now known as Mabel Alston. The position at Howard also granted the couple a smooth entry into Black Washington's elite. News of their arrival was reported in the society pages of *The Afro-American*, the Baltimore-based weekly that published a Washington edition and others around the country. The October 1938 write-up noted that Mabel was working as a cosmetologist at the Inez Beauty School. It was accompanied by a large photograph of her—hair in a pin-curled bob and coronet braid, body draped demurely over the arm of a sofa, hands crossed at the wrist, chin resting upon them, and eyes cast to the side—under the headline "Beautiful Beautician."

Mabel also had a byline, her first, in that same issue of the paper. It was the debut of a national column initially titled "Your Face Is Your Fortune" but soon changed to "Mabel Alston's Charm School: An Institute of Beauty Advice Conducted for AFRO Readers by an Expert Cosmetologist." The rebrand made sense: Her beauty may have gotten her face in the paper, but it was going to take more than that to keep her name in it.

Mabel quickly staked out a place for herself as a researcher, curator, and guinea pig who was willing to read up on the latest beauty advances and test them out before deciding which to recommend to her readers. She told them how to enhance their bosoms (with tinctures massaged into the skin before bed), how to eliminate blackheads (by applying an astringent before putting on makeup powder), how to ensure the longevity of color highlights (with regular scalp massages), and how to maintain a trim figure (through controlled exercises focused on the abdomen, hips, and thighs). She also engaged in an early version of branded content, writing articles sponsored by the Madam C. J. Walker Manufacturing Company about the best ways to wash one's hair to promote luster and growth.

Through all this, Mabel insisted that a woman's vanity was not a superficial or even a selfish pursuit: "A woman lends to the comfort of the home by her attention to household duties, but she makes the comfort in heart and mind—the home atmosphere—by attention to herself—to mind, heart, and body." It was a fitting philosophy from a woman who had ambitions beyond being a devoted wife. The move to D.C. may have been for her husband's career, but she was going to make it work for her as well.

The column was a hit. This was partly because of Mabel's conversational, big-sisterly writing style, partly because of the breadth and depth of her recommendations, and partly because it dangled before readers the possibility of seeing themselves in its pages. Mabel might answer one of their letters or, if they were lucky, choose to include them in her weekly "Pin Up Girls" photo features. The

"Pin Up Girls" each possessed some quality, such as clear skin, beautiful hair, exceptional style, or an enviable combination thereof, that reflected the best of the "Charm School" column's teachings, while also embodying the kind of lifestyle *The Afro-American* tended to celebrate. Week after week, Mabel's feature profiled a steady stream of college students, teachers, office workers, and government employees—women who, like the column's author herself, had grand ambitions for their lives.

By 1940, Mabel was a full-fledged society editor. She chronicled the lifestyles and life-cycle events of prominent figures, interviewed foreign dignitaries and entertainers when they came to D.C., and represented *The Afro-American* at various cultural events ranging from beauty contests and theater performances to panel discussions about current affairs.

Through it all, Mabel dressed the part of a woman on the town. As the *Cleveland Call and Post* noted years later, she "had a reputation of being one of the fashion plates, sporting exquisite Parisian gowns and coats which ran the gamut from Petinia [Patina, or orange-colored] Fox to Blue Mink. . . . Mabel collected fur coats like other women collected pieces of bric a brac." The clothes weren't just a perk of the job; they were an asset to it. Mabel looked like someone who belonged in the grand lobbies of D.C.'s finest hotels, where she had a penchant for "associating with swarthy diplomats of many nations [who] gave her [open] sesame to circles where her more timid sisters feared to tread."

She also used her position to draw attention to the politics of the era. One column spotlighted Black women's home front activities during World War II, as they took jobs left open by men who went off to fight and saw the white women who were hired after them get promoted to be their bosses. Additionally, Mabel was among a dozen journalists who accompanied the War Department to Camp Lee, Virginia, to spend the day with the Ninth Regiment of the Quartermaster Corps, a combat support unit that was part of the U.S. Army Logistics Branch. And she attended an interracial luncheon at the K Street YMCA on Christmas Day 1943, where the featured speaker was Eleanor Roosevelt. "The eyes of the nations of the world are upon us," Roosevelt said, "looking to us for leadership in living together and being happy together as one family." Although Mabel didn't know it at the time, she would eventually come to play a leading role in a war-related effort of her own. For now, though, she was a woman with a high-profile job composed of equal parts glamour and substance.

In between her forays around town in gowns and heels and furs, Mabel hunkered down at *The Afro-American*'s Washington office at Eleventh and S streets N.W. There, she was one of the in-house "Little Rays of Sunshine," a group of young female employees whom the paper featured in a series of photos above cheeky captions. There was "Miss Margaret Lewis, alias Maggie, alias Salvation Sal, alias the religious editor," "Mrs. Verna Frazier, circulation department clerk, or she with the Veronica Lake coiffeur usually finds herself punch-drunk on Fridays after battling with newsboys on Thursdays," and, of course, "Mrs. Mabel Alston, society editor, a combination of sugar and spice and everything nice, but somebody dropped in a bit of horseradish and red pepper. Makes things particularly hot around the office on Tuesday afternoon and Wednesday morning deadlines."

The office was just a ten-minute walk from Howard University's campus, where John was now an assistant professor. Perhaps husband and wife found time to meet for lunch in the afternoons or walk home together in the evenings, trading details about their busy days. Or maybe they even took each other as dates to work functions like departmental dinners with John's colleagues or society events Mabel was covering for *The Afro-American,* so that each spouse could put faces to the names in the other's stories. Perhaps they did all of this and more to stay connected, as often as their busy schedules allowed. In the end, though, the couple's marriage did not survive these years in D.C.

Unlike the minor fanfare that met the couple's arrival in the city years earlier, there was no public announcement of, or reason given for, the Alstons' divorce. But the end of their marriage seemed to coincide with the end of John's time in the city, as his path led him to Atlanta University (now Clark Atlanta University), where he chaired the Department of Social Research. While there he also co-authored an *Ebony* magazine article with Langston Hughes on the city's social and cultural life titled "Atlanta: Its Negroes Have Most Culture but Some of Worst Ghettoes in World." Then, in 1947, he accepted a position as chair of the combined departments of sociology and social administration at the Central State University College of Education and Industrial Arts in his hometown of Wilberforce, Ohio, where he would eventually meet his second wife, Dolores, and work for the rest of his career.

A 1945 "Charm School" column provides an indirect window into both the end of John and Mabel's union and the silence surrounding it. Writing about the topic of broken engagements, Mabel remarked that an "old proverb and a fairly true one is, 'To wed in haste is to repent at leisure.'" She went on to extol the wisdom of breaking an engagement over choosing a lifetime of unhappiness, before dispensing a bit of advice: "At this time, suggests the writer, it is important for the young woman to conduct herself with the utmost dignity and self-possession. She is not expected to make any announcement nor offer any explanations." Mabel seemed to anticipate the intrigue the divorce would cause (or to recognize what it had already caused), especially for a couple with careers at such storied institutions in D.C.'s Black community, and wanted to shut it down. She published her last regular "Charm School" column in December 1945, a few months after her piece on broken engagements. That last piece read like all the others that came before it and gave no hint of the fact that she would soon leave D.C. herself.

Taking note of her physical absence from the society events she typically covered in the pages of *The Afro-American*, as well as the disappearance of her well-known byline, the *Cleveland Call and Post* referred to this as "an interim of seclusion." The reality was not that simple. Mabel was now almost as famous as the boldface names she'd covered, thanks to her regular attendance at society events over the years and the fact that her column appeared in editions of *The Afro-American* that were published around the country. Gertrude "Toki" Schalk, a society editor for *The Pittsburgh Courier,* reported on one sighting in the new year: "Well, well," she wrote, "Helen Garland is basking in Mexico's sun. Said she saw Mabel Alston in Hot Springs en route to the land of the hot tortillas."

Ultimately, though, Mabel's absence from D.C. was short-lived. In the spring of 1947, she was back to representing *The Afro-American* at beauty contests and society dinners. Writing in *The Pittsburgh Courier* about the International Night festivities at the National Council of Negro Women conference, Toki Schalk took to her column with another report about Mabel. "What we liked best about the party was seeing folks, some of whom we hadn't seen in yahs [years]," she wrote, including "Mabel Alston and her brother, Bill Treadwell (who used to live in Columbus)."

Despite her return to the city, Mabel's byline in *The Afro-American* was certainly less frequent by then, until it all but disappeared from the paper's pages. That did not mean she had given up on her career, however. Her name resurfaced a couple of years later, near the end of 1950, as the byline on a couple of "Advice About Beauty" columns in the *Cleveland Call and Post*. Then she disappeared once again. Whether by choice or circumstance, Mabel seemed to be finding her way toward a different kind of life.

Indeed, by 1951 she had met and married Oscar Grammer, a New Orleans native, World War II veteran, and current warrant officer in the U.S. Army. On the surface, it

seemed that the two had inhabited entirely different orbits—
Mabel the urbane society reporter, Oscar the war-hardened
soldier—but they did share a strange connection that preceded their first meeting and endowed the encounter with a
sense of destiny.

Just as Mabel had enjoyed lunch on Christmas Day with
Eleanor Roosevelt at the YMCA, Oscar had his own meal-
based encounter with the White House. When he was a
young army sergeant during the war, Oscar was stationed
in Honolulu, on the island of Oahu. One day in 1944, according to a report by one of *The Afro-American*'s war cor-
respondents, President Franklin Delano Roosevelt made a
surprise visit to the island. After a tour of its military instal-
lations, he invited a group of 125 enlisted men to dine with
him in the mess hall on base. Oscar was one of them. United
by history and joined together in love, Oscar and Mabel em-
barked on their next new beginning.

THEY SET OUT FOR a country that happened to be getting its
own fresh start. World War II marked the beginning of a
long U.S. military presence in Germany that continues to
the present day. From 1945 to the mid-1950s, Americans
formed part of an occupying force alongside the other Allied powers (France, the United Kingdom, and the Soviet
Union), with each taking control over a portion of the de-
feated nation. The American occupation zone was in southern Germany and encompassed Hesse, Bavaria, and the
northern portions of present-day Baden-Württemberg. Its
headquarters were in Frankfurt (Hesse). From the begin-

ning, the stated goals were to help rebuild, keep Nazism at bay, and promote democratic ideals. Another element of the U.S. mission emerged following the outbreak of the Korean War in 1950, which was to increase the American military presence in Europe amid escalating tensions with the Soviet Union.

It was into this world that the Grammers stepped in 1951. Oscar was assigned to Mannheim, a city in Baden-Württemberg that sat at the confluence of the Rhine and Neckar rivers and was almost destroyed in the war. It was also a common deployment location for African American GIs who, despite their contributions on and off the battlefield during the war, in the European and Pacific theaters as well as on the home front, were relegated to second-class status in the postwar era. While the army sent white GIs to big cities like Frankfurt and Heidelberg, where they were assigned to intelligence and tactical units, African American GIs were posted to rural areas and smaller cities that suffered the most damage during the war. In Mannheim, they lived in segregated barracks and worked in segregated units loading and unloading supplies, repairing military transport vehicles, distributing food to locals, and performing in the 3rd and 427th army bands, all usually under the command of white officers. Here, there were few signs of President Truman's 1948 Executive Order calling for desegregation of the U.S. Armed Forces.

Amid this institutionalized racism and segregation, Oscar was an exception for his time, race, and place. As a chief warrant officer, he was one of the few African Americans to make it to the officer ranks, in his case with a rare combination of both leadership and technical skills. None of this, however, protected him from slights from white GIs of all ranks. Once, as he entered the Mannheim base, a sentry refused to do the most basic act of saluting him.

Afro-American reporter Ollie Stewart, whose "Report from Europe" column covered the African American presence on the Continent in the postwar era, got an earful about how the army treated African American GIs. "It's asking too much of human nature," one GI told him, "to put a man into the Army on a segregated basis and expect him to fight for what the white man calls the Free World. The biggest idiot in the world can see through that kind of farce."

Still, there were bright spots. Oscar and Mabel belonged to a larger community of African Americans in Mannheim, other parts of Germany, and elsewhere around Europe that provided a bulwark against the army's racist abuses. It included not just fellow GIs and their families, but also auxiliary corps members and civilians who had crossed the Atlantic to work, study, and see the sights. They'd visit one another on holidays, driving and taking the train between countries as easily as if they were crossing state lines. In fact, it was demonstrably easier than in the United States. Back home they would have needed to worry about whether the restaurants and hotels along the way would accept Black guests or reject them at their hungriest or most in need of fuel or relief. Here in Europe, however, they shouldered few such concerns. They also fit in stops at local bases and military communities, where they could visit old and new friends before setting out on museum tours and riverboat cruises. Mabel, a lifelong Catholic, added pilgrimage sites to her plans, including Lourdes, France, to see the Grotto of the Apparitions, where a local teenager claimed to have seen the Virgin Mary in the 1850s.

Ollie Stewart's columns regularly tracked these itineraries and meetups, noting in one case that "people coming back to Paris [were] still talking about the holiday party given in Mannheim, Germany, by 1st Sgt. and Mrs. Moody Staten, Los Angeles."

Despite the segregation that remained in the U.S. military, the local German population offered something of a respite from Jim Crow. Mannheimers regularly filled their city's streets to cheer on the 3rd and 427th bands during parades, opened their stores, restaurants, cafés, and bars to African American GIs, and rented homes to them and their families in residential areas like Feudenheim, where Oscar and Mabel lived.

Despite these moments of hospitality, inspired in cities across the country by gratitude to the United States for its commitment to the postwar rebuilding of ravaged cities, Germany had a long and enduring history of anti-Black racism that dated back to its short-lived colonial presence, from the 1880s to 1920, in Togo, Cameroon, German Southwest Africa (now Namibia), and German East Africa (now Tanzania, Rwanda, and Burundi). During this period, some Africans came to the country as personal servants of colonial officials or as members of the German merchant fleet; others arrived to receive formal educations or military training. From early on they faced limits on their movements, aggressive forms of discrimination, and social isolation that persisted even after Africans fought for Germany during World War I. The 1920s and '30s saw Africans and German-born Blacks effectively locked out of the labor market, finding opportunities only in menial sectors and in *Völkerschau,* or human "zoos."

These spectacles fit within a European tradition of putting foreign people on public display that dated back to the medieval period and usually involved captives taken from their homelands. For their part, German *Völkerschau* called upon Africans and Black Germans to embody the worst stereotypes of the "Dark Continent": handling weapons while crouched in a fighting posture, making animal noises, and pretending not to speak or understand German despite many being native speakers. Even human zoos of the late nineteenth and early twentieth centuries involved captives, or at best groups invited under false pretenses. As late as 1958, Belgian officials invited a delegation of more than seven hundred Congolese police officers, tourists, journalists, dancers, students, and soldiers and their families to Brussels under what soon became clear were fraudulent misrepresentations. While the visitors thought they were participating in a cultural exchange with their counterparts around the country, it turned out that their presence was purely intended to populate the Congo Pavilion at the Brussels World's Fair. They were sequestered within the confines of the exhibition hall, where visitors gawked, threw bananas at them, and generally treated them like animals.

The weight of these insults took its toll on Congolese of all ages. In one memorable instance, a young child sat in the middle of a re-created village in the pavilion while reading a book when a white woman approached him and placed a candy bar between his knees. At such a tender age, he could not understand why an act as ordinary as reading was constantly being made into a spectacle, but he'd clearly grown tired of it, not to mention the invasions of his space and comfort that were part of the whole experience. He grabbed the candy bar and chucked it at the woman, startling her and the rest of the crowd of gawkers. Soon thereafter, the Congolese group departed en masse and returned home.

The rise of Hitler only heightened Black people's precarity: The 1935 Nuremberg Laws (made up of the Reich Citizenship Law and the Law for the Protection of German Blood and German Honor), which had notoriously denied citizenship to Jewish people and targeted them for mass murder, would eventually be extended to apply to Black people, Roma, and others with so-called alien blood.

In other words, there was little daylight between Germany and the United States when it came to anti-Black racism. African American GIs noticed this, too. They told stories about being spat on by Germans, being asked if they had tails, and being on the receiving end of harsh, withering stares. There was more to this dynamic than just racism given the fact of the U.S. occupation. All American and Allied soldiers were reminders of Germany's defeat in the war. But African Americans provoked a specific kind of ire. "We were deeply hurt when you Americans sent Negroes to Germany in soldiers' uniforms," complained one politician. "How can America do this to us, a white people?"

That said, the occupation exposed the faults in both countries' racial logic. Many Germans who once feared and resented African American GIs began to see them as fellow human beings, appreciating the food they handed out and the music they played. And they saw the United States' hypocrisy in criticizing Nazi ideology while embracing Jim Crow in its occupying army. The realizations led to increased fraternization with African American soldiers, who for their part were hardly naïve. They knew Germans' history and could recognize a racial slight when they saw it. They understood the looks they got when they walked into certain establishments, or when they socialized with German women. But in being able to go where they pleased and interact with whomever they pleased, they also understood for the first time what it was like to be American. Mabel would soon come to understand the complexity of these dynamics firsthand. In the meantime, though, she needed to deal with some personal struggles.

Since her arrival in Germany, Mabel's health had been weighing on her. Oscar knew about the operations she said prevented her from having children, as Mabel had told him all about them when he proposed, as if to give him an out, but he took the news in stride. "What's wrong with adopting children?" he asked. That response may have made it easy for Mabel to love him, but the reality wasn't easy for her to live with—especially not now, when she no longer had the job that had once filled her days back in D.C. The trips with the other army spouses were enjoyable, but they could not travel every day. There was shopping to do, the work of keeping house, and, for the mothers among them, the business of raising children.

When she was hospitalized in Germany, Mabel told the

doctor about her inability to bear children. The conversation that followed changed the course of her life. The doctor, a German Jewish woman, shared her own story. She had been in medical school when the Nazis sent her to a concentration camp where they subjected her to experiments that left her unable to bear children herself. The doctor also told Mabel about all the orphaned children who were housed in local *Kinderheim* (a combination orphanage and nursery), including those born to German women and Allied soldiers. "By the time I got home," Mabel later told a reporter for *Good Housekeeping,* "I had stopped feeling sorry for myself." Then she got to work.

THERE'S A GERMAN WORD for everything. For the children born out of relationships between German women and soldiers from all four Allied powers, it was *Mischlingskinder.* The term was not necessarily kind, nor was the country's treatment of the approximately ninety-four thousand such children who were born during the occupation years. Even harsher was its treatment of those whose fathers were African American GIs. They numbered around five thousand, a small fraction of the larger population, but their experience loomed large in both German and American discourse.

These children, known in English as Brown Babies, were not the first mixed-race Afro-German children. The colonial period saw its share of children born out of relationships between German officials and African women, and during the French occupation of the Rhineland region after World War I, African soldiers from the French army had fathered children with local German women. They were known by the pejorative label *Rheinlandbastarde* and, during the Third Reich, subjected to forced sterilization.

Brown Babies would experience their own unique hardships that resulted from entrenched anti-Black racism in Germany and the United States on the one hand, and the specific political dynamics of the postwar context on the other. To Germany they were physical reminders both of sexual relationships between German women and Black men, and of the country's subservience to the United States. To the United States they were reminders that African American GIs freely crossed the color line in Germany in ways they dared not back home.

This didn't just happen in Germany. In the World War II era, many African American soldiers in England and throughout the European theater had relationships and children with white women, often despite the best efforts of local officials, ordinary citizens, and even white Americans to prevent fraternization. In England, the Defence of the Realm Act (issued during World War I) promised to prosecute white women for trespassing or loitering if they were found with African American GIs on military premises. The wife of a vicar in the seaside town of Weston-super-Mare even took it upon herself to issue a multipoint code that dictated women's interactions with African American GIs, with the most important one being that "white women, of course, must have no social relationships with coloured troops."

The NAACP's *Crisis* newspaper reported on "a white Southern lieutenant in a Negro anti-aircraft company who just could not stand to see his men enjoying the courtesies extended by the white women of a certain Eastern [English] town." In response, "he posted a notice that *any* type of association with white women is regarded as rape and reminded his men that the penalty for rape during wartime is death." Certainly, these kinds of rules were often drawn up when it was too late. But they were nonetheless successful at creating hostile environments in which to raise mixed-race children.

In England, Brown Babies were regularly placed in their own segregated orphanages. One advantage of the orphanages, if such a thing existed, was that the children at least had one another. In a CNN interview, two of the children, Deborah Prior and Carol Edwards, then in their seventies, recalled their shared upbringing at Holnicote House in Somerset, England. "There was a group of us all about the same age," Prior said, referring to those born around 1944 and 1945, "who were in the cots together; we even shared potties together, we played together, we ate off the same plate. That was our family."

Babs Gibson-Ward didn't even have that. She was born in 1944 to a white British woman whose white navy officer husband believed that the fair-skinned child was biologically his. The older she got, the more difficult the truth was to hide: Her father was an African American engineer with the U.S. Air Force. The revelation upended Gibson-Ward's childhood when her mother, desperate to save her marriage, sent the child away, first to family members, then to a children's home, then to a foster family where she suffered racial insults and sexual abuse, then to another children's home. At age fifteen, she was put out on the streets.

Brown Babies throughout Europe shared a similar spectrum of fates, from being placed in orphanages and foster homes to having to fend for themselves. Some, though, were placed with African American families in the United States. In Germany, that was thanks in large part to the work of Mabel Grammer.

After learning about the local *Kinderheim* from her doctor, Mabel met a young "bright-eyed" girl. She and Oscar fell in love with the girl and decided to call her Mabel. Then they met Peter, then Roswitha, then Wera, and it wasn't long before the couple had adopted eight children. It was a complicated process, made more so by German officials' misgivings: As Mabel later recounted, "They said we wanted to adopt these children so we could sell them to Southern plantations as slave labor!"

The pair created a happy life for the children. Mabel relied on that book of "Poor Man's Recipes" that had sustained her in her own childhood, and impressed Oscar with her frugality—"Mabel can stretch a dollar until the eagle falls off," he marveled. And while Oscar was at work, Mabel took the children on car trips around Europe. They would have adopted even more Brown Babies if they could have, but there were limits to their home and budget.

Instead, Mabel relied on the skills she had developed in navigating the German bureaucracy to help other families, most of whom were African American, do the same, both in Germany and in the United States. Making sure the children could lawfully enter the United States created its own bureaucratic problems. The profile in *Good Housekeeping* details the process: "She has found adoptive parents for them, made necessary legal arrangements, wrangled them space on airplanes, seen them off at airports. This labor of love has often meant tangling with not only airlines, but also with the West German government and even with the United States Army."

She was not the first African American woman to make these attempts. In 1947, Margaret Ethel Butler, a widowed schoolteacher, was living in Chicago when she first learned about the Brown Babies of Germany. She eventually made her way over and adopted two toddlers. And the author Pearl S. Buck was one of the few white Americans to do the same. But Mabel had one advantage when it came to helping spread the word about the plight of Brown Babies and how to adopt them: contacts in the Black press.

In "What to Do About Adopting War Babies," an article for *The Afro-American,* one of her first since leaving the paper in the late 1940s, Mabel laid out a step-by-step guide for prospective parents. She also provided something of a personal mission statement: "As long as I am in Germany I shall work faithfully to try to give a new life to these deserving children." She seemed willing to accommodate people's desires for the children to "resemble some member of the family," and advised potential adoptive families to send along a photograph with their applications. She made no promises, though: That kind of matching was not only time consuming but could run counter to the spirit of the work she was trying to do. "I am interested," she said, "in finding families who are childless and are interested in giving a youngster love and a new start in life regardless of his family resemblance." The point, in other words, was not to shop as if from a catalog but to create a family.

These implied preferences were an indicator of how complicated the task of placing the Brown Babies would be. Another came in the form of a letter Mabel had received from a Mr. and Mrs. Alonzo Walker, who opened with the couple's take on how hard it was for African Americans to adopt: "Don't allow yourself to be kidded, America doesn't want the brown babies either. It is hard for a colored couple to adopt one." It was both a caution against thinking that the United States was any more welcoming of the orphaned children than Germany was and an expression of frustration. In the letter, Mrs. Walker wrote of her and her husband's previous attempts at adopting three Brown Babies through the U.S. Displaced Persons Bureau, in Washington, D.C. According to Mrs. Walker, the pair were told, first, that they were too old to adopt so many children. Second, the one child that they would be permitted to adopt, a five-year-old, "will have to wait to come in on the quota act of DPB and not under the non-quota act." She worried that the child, to whom she and her husband had already sent birthday and Christmas presents, would be ten or fifteen years old by the time she could enter the country.

In her response, which she published in "What to Do About Adopting War Babies," Mabel acknowledged that there were procedural complications. As she put it, it was not possible to legally adopt a child from Germany; what was possible, however, was sponsoring said child—their visa costs, their paperwork processing fees, their ground transfers, their airfare, and all their food and drink from Germany to the United States. That was where she came in.

Mabel closed out her response with a barbed challenge to Mrs. Walker's claims that the United States did not want to allow Brown Babies into the country or for Black families to adopt them: "I can truthfully write that many people expect for these children to be wrapped in cellophane and sent to them by spending only a few dollars." In other words, as she saw it, the problem was with the prospective parents, not the United States or its process. "Some Americans," Mabel wrote, "do more harm than good."

Mabel may indeed have believed this to be true, but she was also threading a fine needle. She needed to make sure that she could continue to do her work without angering the very country where she was hoping to place the children. The United States in the postwar era needed to think of itself as a model of democracy, since that was the basis of and justification for its presence in Germany and other parts of Europe. Despite the poor U.S. track record when it came to matters of race, the postwar era represented an opportunity for the country to show some moral courage by helping to pave the way for these children to enter with minimal red tape. As for how they would be treated once they finally arrived, the answer was implicit: They'd be subjected to the same ill treatment faced by the mostly African American families who sponsored them.

At the same time, Mabel also needed German agencies to remain cooperative. Many of these children had German mothers who would have liked to raise their children if given the chance and support. But Germany was not willing to offer this kind of assistance, instead believing that the children were better off as wards of the state who could be corralled into orphanages. Nor was it willing to easily cede moral ground to the United States. Perhaps the adoption process was intentionally complicated, an indirect way for the German government to stymie efforts to get the children out of the country. Yet so much could go wrong at every stage of the process that it was hard to pinpoint one culprit. For example, Mabel repeatedly complained about families failing to get the proper signature on affidavits of support, or about the fact that when they were signed, the documents were not properly sealed. It happened enough to suggest that some aspects of the process might not have been clearly understood by prospective parents, or simply were overwhelming for them. But it was clear that—for a variety of reasons—families in the United States really wanted to give the Brown Babies a home.

Journalists who have covered Mabel's story, then and now, have tended to attribute her fervor for adopting and placing Brown Babies to her inability to bear children. Their coverage frequently refers to those operations in her youth as a defining trauma in her life, one that was ultimately resolved through adopting her twelve children.

The *Cleveland Call and Post,* a Black newspaper that had previously published some of Mabel's beauty columns, caught up with her in 1955. By that point, she and Oscar had returned to the United States with eight children. The article, titled "Mabel Switched from Minks to Orphans," compared her old life to her new one: "Before she left Washington . . . Mabel Grammer, formerly of Columbus,

Ohio contented herself with the title of one of the best dressed women in the nation's capital. But when she reached Europe and saw at first hand the problem of the Brown Babies created by the war she found a new mission in life."

There is no doubt Mabel was deeply fulfilled by becoming a mother. As she once said, "Oh Lord, if I had more money, I'd have so many more children." Additionally, her work placing hundreds of Brown Babies with families brought deep meaning to her life, earning her recognition and awards.

At the same time, to think of these days, months, and years as being fulfilling to Mabel simply because they were devoted to the work of family, that caring for her own adopted children and finding loving homes for others were the only things that gave her what she needed, is limiting, because that would ignore her return to work as a journalist.

In addition to publishing articles in *The Afro-American* that explained the ins and outs of adopting Brown Babies and partnering with the paper to sponsor the first groups of children, Mabel managed to carve out a role for herself as a kind of foreign correspondent during that same period. Not surprisingly, she proved a keen chronicler of the African American "society set," as she called them, in and around Germany in the mid-1950s. Just as she'd done back in Washington, D.C., she wrote about their charitable activities and social gatherings, and their family expansions. She also wrote about their European holidays and their hopes and dreams for life back in the United States. In one column, she extolled the virtues of Sergeant W. Seals's famous barbecue buffet in Feudenheim, the neighborhood in

Mannheim where Mabel, Oscar, and other African Americans lived. It "was so tasty that most of the ladies forgot their calorie count and went for the delicacy in a big way." Once he returned to his hometown of Leavenworth, Kansas, Mabel noted, Seals planned to open his own joint.

In that same article, Mabel spoke to Edna Butler, a native Washingtonian and member of the Mannheim Women's Club and the German American Women's Club who described life in Germany as a model for the home front: "If we can live side-by-side in Germany, our children attend the same schools, we attend the same civic and social activities, we can do the same thing at home."

The Grammers eventually returned to the United States and spent a few years there before returning to Germany in 1961 for another of Oscar's deployments, this time as a family of ten living in Karlsruhe, forty miles south of Mannheim. Mabel cared for her large brood while finding time to continue her work on behalf of vulnerable children. She became president of an organization called Give Children Worldwide a Future (also known as the Children Worldwide Organization), whose mission was to provide support to children in unstable homes, children in orphanages, "and otherwise underprivileged children who need help and assistance." And, again, she was helping people adopt Brown Babies, but this time in a less formal capacity.

By the time the Grammers left Germany in 1965 to settle in Washington, D.C., Mabel and Oscar had adopted four more children and helped to place more than five hundred in homes around the United States. For the latter feat, the Vatican awarded the couple its two highest honors in 1968:

the Pro Ecclesia et Pontifice medal and the Benemerenti medal, both of which recognized exceptional service to the faith.

Most of the Brown Babies were adopted by African American couples like the Grammers, including Horace and Louise McMillon. Horace was in the air force, so after he and Louise adopted a little girl they named Doris, they moved around a lot. By Doris's count she'd attended fifteen different schools over the course of her education. Reflecting on her childhood in an article she wrote for *Ebony* in 1982, the WABC-TV New York journalist praised her parents for giving her a good life. Still, the older she got the more she felt she needed to know where she came from and to meet her birth parents before it was too late. Armed with her original birth records and the adoption papers dated March 11, 1953 (both of which Louise had carefully guarded throughout Doris's childhood and which Doris obtained after Louise's death from cancer), Doris knew three things: She was born in Munich, her birth name was Doris Elizabeth Reiser, and her birth mother's name was Josephine Reiser. "About my father," she said, "I knew absolutely nothing about him, but wasn't concerned. I believed that if I found my mother, my father would be easy to find."

It turned out that Josephine was still living in Munich and, thanks to the help of a friend, an ABC correspondent in Bonn, traceable via the local phone book. Doris was thirty years old when she got the news. She was also petrified to call Josephine, instead asking a German-speaking friend to do the initial outreach. "My mother, she said, wanted to see me. And, furthermore, she spoke English." It

was late November 1981, and Doris hopped on a plane almost immediately. She was met at the Munich airport by a
film crew ABC hired to document the first few days of the
reunion. In between stops at tourist attractions and sites of
personal significance, like the home Josephine (who never
married or had more children) shared with her aunt and
mother, Josephine's secretarial office at the University of
Munich, and the kindergarten that replaced the family
home where Josephine and Doris lived in their first few
months together, the pair caught up on the nearly three decades they'd spent apart. They knew one visit was not
enough, especially in front of cameras, and made plans for
Josephine to visit the United States.

Before she left Germany, Doris also got her father's
name from Josephine: Ernest Barnett. With that she con-
tacted the U.S. Army, and eventually found that he was living in New Jersey, just a short bus ride away from her own
home in New York City. She met him on Christmas Day
1981, barely a month after meeting Josephine. He'd married
but never had more children, and after retiring from the
military lived a quiet life punctuated by the pleasures of
blueberry farming. "I am fortunate that these two people
happened to be my natural parents," she concluded, "because even if they were not related to me, I would still want
them to be very close friends."

As for the Grammers' children, they would go on to
continue their parents' tradition of service, with nearly all
of them enlisting in the military. When her mother died in
2002, Nadja West (the future U.S. Army surgeon general)
recalled one of the most important lessons Mabel taught

her: "Just be thankful that your parents gave you life. You
don't know what decisions your mothers had to come up
with, so just forgive them and be thankful you had a second
chance." Mabel, who knew from second chances, might
also have been talking about her own parents, even herself.

But her legacy goes beyond her own family, even beyond
the hundreds of children whose futures were remade by
her work, to remind us of how easily innocent men,
women, and children could be mercilessly caught between
two countries' conflicts and ambitions. And how, at the
same time, those men, women, and children could come to
one another's rescue, too.

Adventure to
the Homeland

THE SUMMER I SPENT AT my grandparents' house while the other kids from my school were in Russia and at sleepaway camps was a summer spent feeling stuck in place. Feeling like I should have been anywhere other than the same quiet neighborhood on the outskirts of downtown Colorado Springs that I'd visited for every school break as far back as I could remember, living the same day of chores and outdoor playtime on a loop while it seemed that everyone else was off exploring new cultures, making new friends, improving their sports prowess, or gaining some sort of academic edge. It was a summer of feeling sure that, by the time fall rolled around, they'd all head back to school cooler, smarter, more athletic, and worldlier than before, while I'd changed not one bit.

It became an afternoon ritual for me, once I was done helping my grandma in the kitchen and bored with whatever my little sister and cousins were up to in the yard, to head into the living room and park myself on the couch next to the burgundy recliner. I knew better than to sit *in* the recliner; that seat belonged to my grandma when she watched her daytime soap operas, and to my grandpa when he watched reruns of *Gunsmoke* or *Bonanza* in the evenings after he got off work in the supply office at the police department (a job he'd taken after retiring from the army). I'd lean into the couch's comfortable cushions and divide my attention between the TV, one of the *Reader's Digest* volumes or Time Life book series from the hallway bookshelf, or the stacks of *Ebony* magazines neatly lined up on the bottom shelf of the coffee table.

I started to notice that scattered among the magazine's features devoted to the role models of Black America, the actors and musicians and politicians and ordinary people who'd made good, were glimpses of what I wanted for myself but couldn't figure out how to articulate or access. They were in articles about the "Getaway Places of the Famous and the Powerful," featuring singer Chanté Moore lounging in the sand on the island of Anguilla, and *Ghostbusters* star Ernie Hudson rhapsodizing about Singapore's sensory delights. Destination profiles extolling the pleasures of Jamaica and the Bahamas with vacation-chic women stepping onto manicured golf courses. Pictures of Fashion Fair Cosmetics staff posing outside of their offices in Paris and London. And offers from McDonald's to enter its "Adventure to the Homeland" sweepstakes for a chance to visit Senegal and the Gambia.

What was I drawn to, exactly, in those magazines? On a basic level, it was the invitation to imagine myself somewhere else, somewhere other than Colorado, since I'd never so much as left the state. Still, none of the articles about "Family Adventures" in Disneyland or New York City made me experience the same kind of longing. I'd seen enough of those places in movies and on TV, plus there was something about the pictures of smiling nuclear families following the dad's lead toward Epcot Center or the Empire State Building that alienated me. My immediate family—a trio formed by myself, my sister, and my mom now that her longtime boyfriend had recently moved out—looked nothing like the pictures, and it was hard to imagine us fitting into the scenes.

But I could see myself, by myself, staring out at the horizon from a sandy Caribbean beach. I could see myself exploring Singapore's streets and architecture and hawker stalls. Working on my golf swing while the tropical sun beamed down on my shoulders. Taking a lunch break from work in Paris or London to visit a museum or pop into a boutique. Visiting the Gambian village Alex Haley made famous in *Roots*, perhaps even stumbling upon my own distant kin.

I was good at solitude, even in mixed company. Since I started attending private school across town in seventh grade, I'd gotten used to walking the halls between class periods, sitting at the lunch table, and whiling away recess time, mostly by myself. I'd gotten used to reading a book or studying a class handout to make it all look like a choice. Isolated as I may have been, there was a relief in it, too. I didn't have to explain my family situation to teachers or classmates, which in earlier attempts had involved clarifying that, no, I did not live with my dad and, no, my mom and her boyfriend weren't married so he was not my stepdad, either, but they'd been together for ten years and I was sad when he moved out, even though, no, that wasn't technically a divorce. The experience was akin to stumbling into false cognates in Spanish class, like when I said I was *embarazada*, thinking it meant embarrassed (about my accent), but was in fact announcing that I was pregnant.

Back on my own side of town, there was also comfort in retreating, this time into the house. There, I didn't have to try so hard to sound and act less like the "White Girl" the kids on my block liked to call me. They had their reasons for the nickname and were within their rights to wonder why I suddenly seemed to think our local public school was good enough for them but not for me, but they were too young to find the words and I was too young to hear anything but judgment. It was as though I had been exiled from one country and granted entry to another, but only on the condition that I not get too comfortable or start to think of myself as a citizen.

Flipping through those issues of *Ebony* gave me hope that there was some place out there where things weren't so black and white, where I could stop trying to contort myself to fit such small boxes. But they also provoked a sense of having been done yet another injustice. I still had no hope of going anywhere myself. Meanwhile, the kids at my school, who already got to feel comfortable and welcome on and off campus, were the ones who got to travel. Would they even appreciate the experience? I also started to wonder why I bothered getting top grades in Spanish—never once complaining when Mr. Norricks taped over the English subtitles for the movies we watched—when it was the biggest whiners with the worst accents who were going to Spain and Mexico with their families, anyway. I deserved these things as much as they did, if not more. I wanted more. And now, even though the travelers I was seeing in the pages of this magazine were Black like me, even though they were proof that international travel wasn't just for the white kids I went to school with, these Black travelers in *Ebony* were still either rich, famous, or somehow lucky enough to win a contest.

Into this mounting, petulant rage crept a counterpoint, one that was plain as day once I'd bothered to acknowledge its importance. It was there in the fact of my uncles' overseas military posts: My uncle Taylor lived in Germany with his wife and two kids, and my uncle John lived in South Korea, also with his wife and two kids. Another uncle, Gabriel, would soon leave Colorado Springs to take his own post in Seoul. Proof that my own family had traveled and lived abroad was on display in the same living room where I'd spent nearly more afternoons than I could count. It was in the set of beer steins on the shelf by the TV, in the pair of large black lacquer vases with painted-on flowers, and in the little porcelain doll wearing what looked like a kimono perched in a corner of the glass-paneled china cabinet. For such a small space, my grandparents' house held evidence of much bigger lives, more expansive paths.

During the commercial breaks between my grandma's soap operas and my grandpa's westerns, I started to point to each of these objects and ask where they came from. I expected to hear that they were gifts from my uncles or family friends. But I was surprised to learn that the steins were from when my grandparents and their four oldest kids lived in Salzburg, Austria, after the war, and that the vases and doll were from when my grandpa was stationed in South Korea. By then, my grandparents had had five children, and my mom was on the way, so it made more sense for my grandma to stay at the army base they'd been posted to in Kansas while my grandpa went on tour. I pictured my grandpa, missing his wife, picking out the vases as a gift, and selecting the doll for the infant daughter he'd be meeting upon his return.

Up until that point my understanding of my grandpa's military service was mostly local and specific to him. My grandparents lived a few miles from Fort Carson, where they did their weekly shopping at the commissary, sometimes taking us grandkids along to help load groceries into the car. I'd assumed that Fort Carson was where he'd been stationed when he came back from World War II, and that this outpost in this mountain state was the only military town my grandma and their children ever knew. It turned out I didn't know the half of it.

As these summers wore on and high school approached, I became convinced that I belonged to a long line of people who lived interesting, even mysterious, lives, and for whom Colorado was just one of many stops along the way. I had no intention of joining the military, but I did start to conceive of myself as destined to enter a kind of family business, one loosely defined since it offered no product or distinct services but that nonetheless entailed what I considered a romantic kind of itinerancy. If I was going to step into it, I told myself, I would need to seize whatever chance came my way.

During the fall of my sophomore year, at a new private

K–12 school, the brochure for our version of "alternative spring break" started circulating, where each teacher led a program focused on deepening our knowledge of the subjects they taught. I knew without even looking that I wanted to go on the two-week trip Mrs. Salisbury, my Spanish teacher, led to Mexico. I also knew without looking that, as was the case with the Russia trip at my previous school, my mom could not afford it.

I had worked so hard to keep up with and then surpass students who'd been enrolled at the school since kindergarten and been given every opportunity to excel, and here I was facing yet another reminder that I would never really have the chance to compete. But this time, instead of swallowing my frustration, I made an appointment with our headmaster.

Sitting in the oversized leather chair, across from the man who commanded every school assembly and classroom he walked into, I should have been intimidated. But my desperation gave me confidence. I wanted a different life, needed a real chance to create it, and I was ready to remove any obstacle in my way. My people had done harder things, I told myself. I had no excuse not to try.

I looked him directly in the eye and began a nervous recitation of the words I'd been practicing in my head all morning. I made the case that it wasn't fair for the school to dangle educational opportunities in front of scholarship students that were ultimately out of our reach. If study abroad trips were part of our education, I said, growing more confident, then everyone—no matter their economic status—should have access to them. Otherwise, they were just vacations, and if they were, in fact, vacations, they should not be held during the school year.

After I finished my speech, we sat in silence for what felt like forever. My heart thudded in my chest. I became more and more certain as the seconds ticked by that he would tell me I was asking too much, and that I should be grateful for the opportunity to attend school there in the first place. I had grown so used to being told by teachers, kids from my neighborhood, and even my own family how lucky I was to be at the school, that a small part of me did wonder if I was being greedy to want this.

To my surprise, the headmaster agreed with all my points. He said he would see what my mom could reasonably afford to send me on the trip and promised to find the money to cover the difference. It wasn't a complete victory, since I knew that another tough conversation, this one with my overworked and underpaid mom, was now ahead of me. How was I going to convince her that I deserved to go to Mexico as an unemployed and increasingly entitled teenager when she was the one holding down two jobs and hadn't managed to take even an out-of-state vacation?

In the end, I didn't even need to make a case. With the same mix of devotion and miracle working that got her through the long drives to and from her daughters' separate campuses, the snubs from the wealthy parents on back-to-school nights, and the extra work she took on to cover the costs of our books, extracurriculars, and sports equipment, she said yes to this opportunity, too. And I, blissfully—also conveniently, if I'm honest—unaware of the true burden she shouldered, started packing my bags for Mexico.

CHAPTER 5

THE BEAUTIFUL
AMERICAN

Philippa Schuyler,

ĐÀ NẴNG, 1960s

A S THE HELICOPTER BEGAN ITS southwestern descent over Đà Nẵng Bay on the morning of May 9, 1967, Philippa Schuyler could see the ground below taking clearer shape. She could see where the bay's dark blue currents turned into frothy waves that crested onto shore, where the white sandy beaches inched toward higher, tree-covered ground, and where the five peaks of the iconic Marble Mountains sprang from the verdant jungle that seemed to swallow up the rest of the landscape until, in the middle of a vast clearing, emerged the military base where the helicopter was set to land in just a few minutes.

Philippa was in the helicopter with its pilot, crew, and nine children from Huế, a city whose location and history made it tremendously vulnerable during the Vietnam War. If Vietnam is shaped like the dragons that are so ubiquitous within the country's mythology and culture, and the west-

ern Annamite Mountains form its prickly, winding spine,
then Huế comprises its eastern-facing navel. This central
position made the city an ideal site for an ancient imperial
center modeled after China's Forbidden City, and the capital of Vietnam from 1802 to 1945, which together made Huế
both a cradle and a powerful symbol of Vietnamese civilization. In 1954, when the First Indochina War drew a line
across the country (which at the time was a French colony;
the war was between France and Vietnam), Huế became
part of the northernmost region of South Vietnam. Because it was right near the Demilitarized Zone (DMZ) that
separated the anti-Communist South from the Communist
North, the threat of an attack on Huế loomed constantly,
and in the spring of 1967 the possibility seemed ever closer.

At thirty-five years old, Philippa had not intended to get
involved in the war. When she arrived in South Vietnam
around Easter, it was to give a series of piano concerts for
American troops. As she went from Saigon to Huế to Đà
Nẵng, she had also been reporting on her experiences and
observations for the *Manchester (N.H.) Union-Leader,* just as
she'd done for other publications over the past two decades
that she'd spent traveling the world as a professional musician.* But this time, her arrival in Huế made it impossible to
simply bear journalistic witness, thanks to an encounter
with some local Catholic schoolchildren. Someone asked
Philippa, or perhaps she decided herself, to help get them
onto the aircraft, out of Huế, and south to Đà Nẵng, where
Philippa hoped that they would be able to enroll in one of

---

* The paper was owned by conservative William Loeb.

the local Catholic schools to continue their education. When or how they would be reunited with their families, however, remained unclear.

Having grown up Catholic herself, Philippa felt a sense of kinship with the children. But her faith and early education had also instilled a missionary spirit that framed the way she saw the world. Just a few years prior she'd published, in Italy, a book titled *Jungle Saints,* which was based on her travels across the African continent and dedicated to "the thousands of Catholic missionary nuns and priests who, with their lives, blood and dedication shaped modern Africa." The book paid homage to the Irish Sisters of Charity, who worked with homeless populations near Nairobi, a Franciscan nun who ran a leprosarium in Zimbabwe, and others whom locals often criticized for collaborating with colonial governments and corporations to promote Eurocentric beliefs, but who were no doubt top of mind when Philippa encountered the children in Huế.

One child who spent the helicopter ride perched on Philippa's lap was around two and a half years old, the same age as Philippa when she made her public debut in the pages of the *New York Herald Tribune,* a newspaper in her hometown of New York City. Philippa's father, George S. Schuyler, had asked her in front of the visiting reporter to name her favorite authors. "Nietzsche, Dostoievsky and Flaubert," she confidently responded. Her father clarified that Philippa had not actually read any of the authors' work, but he wanted the reporter to note her ability to pronounce their last names. After that, George asked her to spell "rhinoceros" and recite verses from the *Rubáiyát of Omar Khayyám.*

A longtime newspaperman, George knew how to sell a story. He got his start around 1912 when he was in the army, working as a reporter for the military publication *Stars and Stripes*. His service and early reporting career came to a dramatic end in 1917, when he tried to get his army boots shined in a Philadelphia train station and the Greek immigrant manning the booth refused, calling him a "n****r." George was a first lieutenant at that point, facing the possibility of being shipped off to World War I, and the incident seemed to crystallize the futility of donning a uniform if his money still wasn't good enough to pay for a basic service. He went AWOL for three months before surrendering and serving a nine-month term in military prison. After his release, he joined the Socialist Party of America and got hired as a writer and assistant editor for *The Messenger,* a magazine co-founded by socialist writer Chandler Owen and the labor organizer A. Philip Randolph (leader of the Brotherhood of Sleeping Car Porters) that originally billed itself as the "Only Radical Negro Magazine in America" but had gradually expanded its focus beyond union politics to include coverage of the arts, culture, business, and sports to attract a larger audience.

George edited pieces sent in from contributors around the country, including white leftists and socialists who saw it as a friendlier outlet for their views. Among them was Josephine Cogdell, a cattle-ranching and banking heiress from Texas who at the time was living in San Francisco while, as she later put it, "studying Chinese philosophy under Kiang Kang Hu, attending the lectures of John Cowper Powys, taking dancing lessons with Ruth St. Denis and Elmira Mori-

sini and posing for artists in ballet skirts *à la* Degas." Pulled
toward iconoclastic intellectual and artistic spaces, Josephine
found in *The Messenger* "a mixture of socialism and sophisti-
cation hard to find elsewhere in America."

The editorial correspondence between George and Josephine blossomed into a personal one, leading the latter to
travel to New York for a three-hour lunch with the former
that spilled over into dinner and dancing at the famed Savoy
Ballroom and a courtship that took them to venues across
the city. "We enjoyed with equal gusto," Josephine recalled,
"an evening of ballet or of jazz, a Harlem theater, a labor
meeting, or a night at the opera." Six months later, George
and Josephine were engaged. By the time Josephine gave
birth to Philippa two years after the wedding, there was no
going back to Texas, at least not with a Black husband and
biracial child. When Josephine did visit her family, she went
by herself.

By the time the *New York Herald Tribune* reporter visited
their two-bedroom family apartment at 321 Edgecombe Avenue in Harlem on a February day in 1934, George and Josephine had come to see their daughter's talents as part of a
larger, familial story about love and perseverance in the face
of long odds. The pair had endured their share of hard
times as an interracial couple, mostly involving the rejection from Josephine's family, and knew that their daughter
would face her own struggles. But they were insistent on
one thing: "Philippa is not a child prodigy." Instead, they
said, "We have just taken the trouble to train her. Any parent could do the same. It's just a matter of patience and
trouble on the part of the parents."

George and Josephine's parenting ethos seemed to be
the impetus for the article, which George likely used his
newspaper contacts to get published. In the years that followed, the pair remained devoted to nurturing their daughter's precocity with a formula of "patience and trouble."
This was particularly evident when it came to the piano
playing that they guided her toward at a young age, which
led to Philippa giving recitals at the Harlem YWCA, winning prizes from the New York Philharmonic, making ap-
pearances on NBC Radio's *Children's Hour,* and sitting for an
interview on CBS Radio. For all this and more, Philippa was
one of the eighteen people (twelve Black, six white) elected
to the "Honor Roll of Race Relations" in 1940. The distinction was based on a nationwide poll conducted by the
Schomburg Collection of Negro Literature of the New
York Public Library (today the Schomburg Center for Research in Black Culture). At just eight years old, the girl
stood as proof "that genius knows no boundaries of color."

That same year, the New York World's Fair declared
June 19 "Philippa Schuyler Day," making her "the first
Negro girl to be honored" with a day named after her (during which she played a series of her own compositions), and
Look magazine published a profile that nicknamed Philippa
"the Shirley Temple of America's Negroes." Josephine took
credit for setting the foundation for the young girl's success,
pointing out to the reporter that she "dieted for three years
before Philippa was born" and raised the family on raw
foods. To a *New Yorker* reporter who stopped by the family's
new apartment at 270 Convent Avenue in 1940, Josephine
proudly elaborated: "When we're travelling, Philippa and I

amaze waiters. You have to argue with most waiters before they'll bring you raw meat. Then they stare at you while you eat." She went on to note that Philippa consumed a glass of milk and twelve teaspoons of cod-liver oil for extra nutrients each day, liked to snack on a raw ear of corn at the movies, and stuffed green peas in her pockets when she went off to school.

Even Philippa's birthday cakes were raw, featuring a mix of ground nuts, dried fruits, butter, and honey that was carefully molded into the shape of the various instruments she had learned to play each year and regions of the world she had studied or visited. Philippa told the *New Yorker* reporter that for her most recent birthday, Josephine made a cake shaped like the map of South America, using fruit and vegetable juices to color in each different country. "It was a swell cake," Philippa enthused.

George's influence on Philippa was equally strong. By this point, he was a columnist and editorial writer based in New York for *The Pittsburgh Courier,* one of the country's leading Black newspapers, and publishing his own novels and nonfiction books dealing in matters of history, religion, and his increasingly right-leaning politics, in the United States and abroad. The bookshelves of the family home reflected his varied interests, which in turn sparked Philippa's own imagination and creativity. She first read from George's eight-volume *Arabian Nights* set when she was just three years old, rereading it several times until, a few years later, she based a piano composition on it called *Arabian Night Suite*.

Despite boasting an adulthood's worth of accomplishments, Philippa possessed a youthful cheekiness. She called her parents "George and Jody" and liked to make them laugh at jokes or challenge them with riddles. "What has four wheels and flies?" she'd ask, before quickly interjecting: "Give up, please, so I can tell you. . . . A garbage wagon." When her father groaned in response, she shot back: "Was it that bad, George?"

PHILIPPA'S SUCCESS WAS AT once a testament to her preternatural abilities, a case study in parental commitment to coaxing them out, and an indictment of the educational system for Black children in 1930s New York. Because, for all their confidence in their daughter, George and Josephine also knew that she would not thrive with formal schooling alone.

Although New York State law prohibited the formalization of school segregation, racist housing policies had created de facto segregation in the school system. The Schuylers' Harlem neighborhood was mostly Black, populated with migrants from the South and immigrants from the Caribbean, which meant that children attended mostly Black schools where the conditions were dismal.

Students sat in dark, overcrowded classrooms with old blackboards and dilapidated furniture. Their textbooks were either recycled from previous grades or discarded from neighboring white schools, castoffs with ripped pages and lessons that erased African Americans' contributions to U.S. history, society, and culture. One widely assigned textbook opened with the words "The Story of the White

Man," and throughout its pages treated being American as synonymous with and exclusive to being white. Adding to this message was the fact that at the front of the classrooms were "a disproportionate number of older white teachers" who, according to one damning report from the era, were "naturally impatient and unsympathetic towards the children."

Just as horrifying as the teachers' harsh treatment of the students, though, was their focus on vocational training rather than a traditional academic curriculum or schooling in the arts. Black parents, teachers, and church leaders, propelled by the combined punch of their children's stories about white teachers threatening to flog them for minor infractions and reports in the Black press about classes focused on service industry etiquette and domestic work, were increasingly raising concerns in the 1930s about the unacceptable quality of their children's education.

George and Josephine were no different. They bemoaned the fact that Philippa was spending her school days learning that Africans were "savages, uncultured and wild," and that enslaved people in the Americas were "docile and happy." Fortunately, they had the time, education, and resources to provide their daughter with careful, more comprehensive tutelage that included Black history. Philippa could go home, Josephine once wrote, "to read in her father's library that there had been 500 slave revolts, that a quarter of a million Negroes served in the Northern Army and Lincoln himself had said the war would not have been won without them."

In the process, George and Josephine instilled in their

daughter a sense of pride, possibility, and deep self-confidence. The parents rounded out Philippa's curriculum with regular exposure to the Harlem luminaries who formed part of their inner circle, including the African American dancer Katherine Dunham and the white chronicler of Harlem Carl Van Vechten, who also happened to be the girl's godfather. Still, one thing that was missing was a peer group. Between school, her rigorous at-home lessons, and the breakneck pace of her accomplishments, not to mention her parents' rarefied circles and unique philosophies, Philippa had few opportunities to cultivate friendships with children her own age.

For her ninth birthday, she posed for a photograph that ran in the *New York Amsterdam Star-News*. In it, she stands in the living room of her family's apartment, behind a table laden with a birthday cake. This year, Josephine shaped it into a harpsichord, with keys made of coconuts and figs, and a filling with the usual mix of ground nuts, fruits, and spices. The whole confection was accompanied by scoops of banana ice cream and cups of fresh fruit juice. Surrounding Philippa and her birthday display are a group of young girls, above a caption that reads: "In the picture, (left to right) are Joan Bates, Frances Sanders, Frances Graham, Margaret Cox, Philippa Schuyler, talented pianist-composer and daughter of Mr. and Mrs. George S. Schuyler, Iris Kirton, Dorothy Davidson and Lucile Davidson. With the exception of Joan Bates and Philippa, the children in the picture are from the Riverdale Colored Orphanage."

George and Josephine always relished the chance to promote their daughter's success; they were proud of her, of course, but also of themselves. They viewed their parenting style as a kind of bulwark against racism, and their daughter as a shining example of its effectiveness. For its part, the Black press was eager to share with its readers examples of racial uplift. (Philippa's parents would collect these clippings over the years, storing them in a keepsake box that they eventually shared with her when she was a teenager.)

Thus, when the time came to celebrate Philippa's ninth birthday, it seemed like a wonderful opportunity for both parents and the press to make the day mean something for the race. With that in mind, George and Josephine invited the orphaned children to have a day out for a celebration, where Schuyler could share her nutritious cake and good example. The photographers and reporters all seemed to believe they could present a story of racial inspiration, as captured by the image of a group of young girls who, no matter the circumstances they were born into, would somehow leave believing they could achieve whatever they set their minds to. The raw cake and banana ice cream, then, were no accident. According to George and Josephine's parenting formula, the healthy treats were crucial ingredients that led to a healthy body, mind, and spirit.

Though she stands in the middle of a group of girls all her same age, Philippa projects an unsmiling sense of loneliness. These children were perhaps the first to be invited into her home, at her parents' urging, and for a photo op no less. She had no real friends to celebrate with on her birthday, and now the whole world would know it. The day, like so many others in her life, had been turned into a media performance. As for the other girls, some are smiling, while others look serious, even solemn. What must they all have been thinking? What became of them afterward? All we really know is that this was far from the kind of child's birthday party any of them had ever attended. And there wasn't even real cake.

THE DISTANCE BETWEEN PHILIPPA and other girls her age only grew as she became more famous. At thirteen, she was invited to perform a piano recital in Mexico, which her mother chaperoned. The trip was an opportunity to showcase her talents to a more global, and hopefully more accepting, audience, while also providing an opportunity to follow in her parents' writerly footsteps. In March 1945, she published a two-page piece about the trip in the magazine *Calling All Girls* (a title targeting young women from the publishers of *Parents* magazine), becoming one of the first Black authors to be featured in its pages.

In an issue filled with images and stories of white American girlhood, covering everything from model-approved diet and beauty tips to what to do "When Sisters Get Under Your Skin," Philippa's smiling picture appeared in the middle of a piece titled "Friends Across the Border: Girls in Gay Mexico Welcome a Chance to Compare Notes with this Young American." A reader unfamiliar with Schuyler might not have noticed anything different about the light-skinned, wavy-haired author wearing a patterned, peasant-style dress with a matching bolero and holding a rattan shopping basket. She looked a lot like all the other "young American" girls in the magazine. It helped that the title and caption did not refer to her race.

In the article, Philippa talked about Carmen, the teenage girl she met on the train ride from Texas to Mexico City who invited her to her house. A few days later, when Philippa arrived at Carmen's "beautiful Spanish villa," her new friend introduced her to her sister Juanita and girlfriends Enrietta and Rosita. Using a combination of English and Spanish (the study of which had been part of Philippa's homeschool curriculum, along with reading *Don Quixote* in its original language), the group quickly got down to the business of talking about life as a teenage girl in their respective countries.

The Mexican quartet "all began to tell me what they would do if they were American girls. They would have dates, wear nylons, and learn to jive." When one of her new friends asked, "What do you like best about Mexico?" Philippa responded that she appreciated the country's rich history, which dated all the way back to pre-Columbian civilizations. "And what," she asked them, "do you like most about Americans?" They did not hesitate with their responses: "Your present good-neighbor policy."

The Good-Neighbor Policy was a cornerstone of then President Franklin Delano Roosevelt's administration and got its name from his first inaugural address. "In the field of world policy," he intoned, "I would dedicate this Nation to the policy of the good neighbor—the neighbor who resolutely respects himself and, because he does so, respects the rights of others—the neighbor who respects his obligations and respects the sanctity of his agreements in and with a world of neighbors. . . . We now realize as we have never realized before our interdependence on each other; that we

cannot merely take, but must give as well." More specifi-
cally, the approach was to improve relationships between
the United States and Latin America by moving away from
a tradition of intervention and toward supporting a key
declaration made at the Montevideo Convention at the International Conference of American States in 1933, which
was that "no state has the right to intervene in the internal
or external affairs of another." Perhaps the editors of *Calling All Girls* steered Philippa to ask the questions she did,
since it would have been appealing to the magazine's readers to see a cosmopolitan image of American girlhood out
in the world, especially in a place that was welcoming to
and appreciative of the United States. But the Mexican girls
needed no prodding when it came to voicing how much
their country's self-determination mattered to them.

Was this everything that Philippa and the other girls
talked about? Dates, dancing, history, and foreign policy? To
be sure, it was a wide-ranging and sophisticated buffet of
topics, especially for a group in their early teens. But other
sources indicate that Schuyler had talked quite a lot about
U.S. racism during her time in Mexico as well.

When speaking about that same trip to the Black press,
she commented on how the locals "constantly said that
they did not like the racial bias of the United States." She
also reported on her encounters with "many Mexicans of
African ancestry." This was particularly true in Veracruz,
where she and her mother saw a dance troupe rehearse an
African-inspired performance.

Yet none of Philippa's references to Mexicans' criticism
of U.S. racism, or her own observations about the African

presence in Mexico, made their way into *Calling All Girls*. If she, Carmen, Juanita, Enrietta, and Rosita had discussed racism or Afro-Mexican culture in their afternoon visit, there was no mention of the subjects in the published piece. Perhaps Philippa knew, even at thirteen, that trying to address such matters in this publication would have put her whole story at risk of being killed. And if she didn't already know, an editor probably made sure to tell her.

Ultimately, *Calling All Girls* readers caught just a small glimpse of Philippa's time in Mexico. This kind of bifurcation of her experience, with some aspects revealed for a white audience and others for a Black audience, was a theme throughout her life. When she was introduced on the stages of churches, concert halls, and stadiums during her tours, her identity as a "Negro" was front and center. But for a biracial girl growing up in the United States, where both law and custom insisted that "one drop" of Black blood made her a "Negro," this designation might have felt incomplete. Philippa shared George's and Josephine's features, and was immeasurably close with both parents, yet there was no label at the time that easily accounted for the complete picture. Still, on this visit to Carmen's house, she might have found some wiggle room. What if, even for an afternoon, she could simply be an American girl?

In *Calling All Girls*, Philippa wrote that one of the first things Carmen said to her, almost as soon as she flung open the doors to her house, was "It must be fun to be an American girl!" Philippa added, "The others nodded enthusiastically." Whatever her response was in the moment, she did not include it in the article.

In the end, Philippa's approach to the piece, whether it was entirely her choice or not, paid off. She got her byline and photo in the magazine, where she got to speak with expertise about being American. And, the following year, she was named an advisory editor of the magazine, the first Black person to assume the role.

After Mexico came trips to South America, Asia, and Europe. By the time Philippa was sixteen, she had a career and lifestyle most adults of any race would have envied. It was therefore no surprise that Carl Van Vechten considered her a worthy subject for his photo sessions, and not just because he was her godfather.

By this point, Van Vechten had moved on from writing. His book *Nigger Heaven,* set in the early years of the Harlem Renaissance, had attracted both controversy and acclaim, making his reputation as a white writer unsteady when there were so many talented Black authors, like Claude McKay, to cover the same ground but with more regard for his subjects. His second act as a visual chronicler of notable figures in New York and beyond, though, was an unqualified success. Among his subjects were Katherine Dunham, W.E.B. Du Bois, Langston Hughes, and the Schuyler family, whom he first photographed together in 1946.

IN 1949, WHEN PHILIPPA was eighteen, she did her first solo shoot with Van Vechten. In it, she models a couple of different looks. One set of photos shows her in an off-the-shoulder dress with a pearled headband. She looks like she's about to grace the stage of a concert hall or perform an original composition in front of a television audience. In another, Philippa wears a Spanish folk costume accessorized with a black lace veil and a paper fan depicting a bullfighting scene. Together, the photos signaled a kind of debut, marking her transition from a precocious youngster whose parents ushered her onto the world stage into a glamorous and independent young woman with a sense of worldly self-assurance.

Soon after, Philippa became a full-time touring musician, logging tens of thousands of miles a year. Although George and Josephine no longer needed to chaperone her travels, Philippa remained close with her parents. Sometimes they would keep her company on her tours; other times she would send them letters so they could feel like they were right there with her.

There was a lot to keep up with: All over the world, in concert halls filled with government officials and adoring fans, she was in high demand, performing original compositions that competed with the classical works of musicians like Mozart and Chopin that she had mastered at an early age. Wherever she went outside of the United States, she was celebrated as a once-in-a-lifetime talent.

On a 1950 visit to Haiti, where she performed in front of an audience of fifteen hundred at Paul Eugène Magloire's presidential inauguration, Philippa—stepping in for her father, who had been invited in his capacity as a journalist but was unable to make it—not only filed several stories about the ceremonial proceedings but also was awarded a diploma and medal as Chevalier of Honor and Merit. And the Black press continued to take obvious pride in and offer fawning coverage about her. Upon her trip to Panama in 1952, *The Chicago Defender* reported that she shined as "an intelligent ambassador of her country and her race among Latin Americans." She also played at Carnegie Hall, in a concert sponsored by the United Nations for the benefit of a Harlem youth center.

In 1954 alone, Philippa traveled more than thirty thousand miles. Her exposure to different cultures and customs made her an expert in more than just the piano. *Ebony* magazine held Philippa up as a go-to source for understanding the ins and outs of different protocols. In a piece on the practice of hand-kissing, which was common in various parts of the world, she dismissed the custom as "out of keeping with democratic ideals as a relic of feudal Europe," but conceded that for women "the handkiss is more graceful than a handshake."

It didn't take long before Philippa had a book's worth of stories, and she published *Adventures in Black and White* in 1960, just short of her twenty-ninth birthday. The book's chapters cover Philippa's multiple visits to Mexico, Cuba, Haiti, Venezuela, England, Sweden, Turkey, the Congo, Malaysia, and beyond, spanning the period from 1945, when she first began touring internationally, until the late 1950s. In the preface, she writes: "This is how I have lived for over a decade, in sixty countries, in black and white moods, among black and white people, and with only my permanent companion, a black and white keyboard."

The book's first chapter focuses on Mexico, with most of the space taken up by Philippa's original visit in 1945. She doesn't mention the afternoon with Carmen and her sister and friends that she wrote about in *Calling All Girls,* or the conversations she had with locals about U.S. racism that she mentioned in the Black press. Instead, she describes visits to museums, bullfights, public parks, and markets with stalls stacked with grilled meats, and her experience attending "a ceremony given by a group of Mexicans descended from African slaves, who had preserved traditions of a strange religion of their own, of Guinea African mixed with diabolic European."

The chapter is reflective of the book's overall focus. Philippa is more interested in giving her readers a sampling of the sights and sounds and smells of the places she visited, and a view of their regional peculiarities through her encounters with locals, than she is in sharing much of her interior life. For example, when Philippa writes about her return to Mexico nearly a decade after her first visit, in what seems like an ideal moment to reflect on how much she has grown and changed, she shares none of that with her reader in the lone paragraph that closes out the chapter. In it, she simply writes: "In 1954, I returned to Mexico, playing in the quaint border town of Juarez; and then in Mexico City. Curiosity led me to look for the chapel of the Black Mass again. The district had changed. A modern movie theatre advertising a film by Mapy Cortes [the stage name of a Puerto Rican performer named Maria del Pilar Cordero, who was a screen star during the Golden Age of Mexican film] was there instead."

Still, glimpses of Philippa's dynamic personality shine through her seeming discomfort with deep self-reflection. Sometimes she comes off as bold and brazen, as in the chap-

ter "Strip-Tease in Saint Thomas," where she writes of having taken the opportunity while touring the home of the
musical director of a local radio station to ask if she could
take a bath in his house. She'd grown tired of hotel show-
ers, she told him, acknowledging his surprise.

She was no pushover, either. Upon landing at Port-au-
Prince for Haiti's presidential inauguration, she notes that
Alphonse Drouet, "supposedly Haiti's most eligible bachelor" and her chaperone from the airport, was a bit of a let-
down. Despite the "languorous perfection of his ebony
skin, finely drawn face, [and] high, arched forehead," he offered only monosyllabic and evasive responses to her questions about the passing landscape, the country's vast class
differences, what kind of work he did, and his hobbies. So,
when he told her, "You know, I'd be all over you in ten minutes if I were alone with you," Philippa quickly and confidently retorted, "You won't be."

Of course, as the title of the book suggests, Philippa was
also a keen observer of the shifting workings of race. When
she returned to Haiti for another inauguration performance,
this time in honor of François Duvalier, she took a short
flight over to the Dominican Republic, on the east side of
the shared island of Hispaniola. To her host, a local journalist, she remarked, "I didn't think the West Indies could be
like this. The symphony orchestra's wonderful—I noticed it
is completely integrated." During this same visit, she also
received an award on behalf of her parents, at a banquet in
their honor, recognizing "the sociological achievement they
had made by their mixed marriage." Similarly, writing about

Jamaica, she notes to the reader how many "mixed couples" she met.

Philippa's racial commentary extends to showcasing her understanding of her privilege as an American. About London, she writes that she never suffered from British racism herself, but spoke to West Indian, Asian, and African friends—all of whom had emigrated from current and former British colonies to London—who attested otherwise. Unlike Philippa, who was not an immigrant, their presence represented competition for jobs and a threat to old ways of life. Still, for all that set her and her friends apart, the specifics of their condition—being denied housing and jobs regardless of qualifications, being resented for wanting to exercise the rights of citizenship, and being targeted by white mob violence (Philippa had arrived in the aftermath of the Notting Hill race riots)—were deeply familiar.

Indeed, for many African Americans who left the United States in the pre–civil rights era, like Josephine Baker and James Baldwin and Richard Wright, their published writings and speeches walked a similar line. Beyond reflecting on how differently they were treated in other parts of the world than in the United States, they were also deeply aware of how differently they were treated in those other parts of the world compared with other "others." This recognition is what fueled their sense of connection to marginalized peoples around the world, and their sense that the struggle for civil rights in the United States was part of a global effort.

At the same time, in Philippa's case, her light skin allowed her different privileges when she traveled. In Asia,

Europe, and Latin America, Philippa stood out onstage, of course, but she also frequently got mistaken for a local (or was told she looked just like one). Upon her visit to Malaysia, she described the reaction to the new red cheongsam she wore to a party given in her honor on her last night. "All eyes were on me," she writes. "The Ministers gathered around me, photographers rushed up. 'How wonderful that you are wearing our Chinese dress!' they exclaimed. 'You look just like one of us! Just like a Chinese Malayan girl!'" These experiences set her apart from darker-skinned African Americans, who were not able to blend in so easily.

Maybe that was the beauty of travel, as Philippa saw it. A chance to step outside of the United States' racial binary and into places where she did not have to be one thing, since, from one place to the next, she could be anyone, from anywhere.

But that could also be a problem. One night, while she was walking alone through the streets of Willemstad, Curaçao, "a sharp voice called to me in bad Spanish from a car." Before she could react, two men grabbed her from behind, stuffed her into the car, and sped off. After a horrifying drive, during which she tried to scream but had her mouth covered by one of the men's hands, the car eventually stopped in a residential area and they pushed her out.

When she was first snatched into the car, Philippa thought the men were police officers. Over the course of the ride and hearing their familiar chatter, she came to understand that they were not. She quickly gathered her composure to explain, in English, that she was on the island per official invitation. With that, the energy shifted, and the men quickly proffered their own explanations. It turned out that they were American, too. Jake, the "blue eyed and dumb-looking one," as she described him, confessed to what was going on: "My buddies had heard about the plane-load of girls they send here from Venezuela every month. Called the 'meat-plane.' The girls take care of the men here for a few weeks. Then they're shipped back to South America. My buddies thought you were one of them."

What stands out in this chapter, aside from Philippa's palpable fear and frustration, is her characterization of the white Americans. They speak bad Spanish, they look plain dumb, and they have no idea who they're talking to and trying to abduct. It must have been a constant source of absurdity to Philippa, who was fluent in Spanish, French, Arabic, and Portuguese, among other languages, exceedingly well traveled, and schooled in the ways of different parts of the world, that white Americans could nonetheless hold themselves up as a superior race.

What also would have struck her was the way the United States was positioning itself on the world stage. "I have found," she writes, "that foreigners throughout the world distrust the sincerity of the United States as a democratic power largely because of the racial situation in the South. We cannot uphold liberty and equality abroad, while permitting racial segregation and discrimination here. We cannot demand free elections elsewhere when those in the states where the Negro is most concentrated, are rigged in a one-party system."

Philippa's invitations to travel abroad often came from U.S. ambassadors, who hosted her concerts at their embassies, official residences, and consulates. She was no doubt aware that it was in the United States' interest, particularly in what was becoming increasingly known during the Cold War as the Third World, to signal that the country recognized the humanity and talents of its Black citizens. It was crucial to its standing abroad and to any legitimacy that it hoped to project on the world stage. But Philippa had also lived her entire life being elevated as an example to her race, by Black and white people alike, and hailed as an ambassador to both her country and her people. And besides, she was used to carving out something for herself even as she served other people's agendas—her own experiences, her own adventures, and her own connections.

It's no surprise, then, that Philippa accepted Ambassador Henry Cabot Lodge, Jr.'s invitation to visit South Vietnam in the fall of 1966, where she gave a concert at the ambassadorial residence in Saigon and another in Huế.* Because Philippa had arrived in South Vietnam during a time when its tourist industry, active until the mid-1960s, was crumbling under the weight of the war, she was in a unique position as an American visitor to take in the country's landscape and culture. Perhaps, during her time in Huế, she was able to travel up and down the gentle currents of the Perfume River, the meandering artery that bisects the lush city, traveling on flat-bottomed wooden sampans while the smell of flowers from nearby orchards filled the air.

She might not have been alone. On the flight from Sai-

---

* The invitation came near the end of Lodge's posting as an appointee of President Lyndon B. Johnson, as the ambassador showed vocal support for the escalation of U.S. military involvement in the war.

gon to Huế, Philippa met a major in the U.S. Army who was heading to the DMZ. The pair struck up an immediate intimacy; she told him she would soon be in Taipei, Taiwan, for another performance, and it turned out he was headed there himself for a vacation. Her mother, Josephine, shared some details about the Taiwan trip in a 1968 novel in verse (one that was no doubt informed by the many letters she and Philippa exchanged during the latter's travels):

> And on that trip to play
>> She played for him alone,
> That love and art were one;
>> And they stood and greeted all
> With this recital done;
>> It was such a happy day
> Then all too soon was gone
>> For he received a call
> And both flew back to Huế.

Nearly everywhere in the world Philippa traveled, there were men who pursued her. Most were unsuccessful, and she seemed to delight in relaying to Josephine the details of their ardent attempts, but some did manage to capture her attention and even her heart. Before the major there was a divorced Frenchman, a Togolese politician, and others. But none of those romances seemed to have developed as quickly as the one with the major. Josephine speculated that the specter of war must have made the pair decide not to waste any time. The next day was not guaranteed.

When Philippa returned to the United States, it was not

for long. She was back in South Vietnam the following spring, not just to give additional concerts but also to see the major again. According to Josephine:

> [L]ove came to Philippa
>   By the Perfumed River's side
>
> For the major had come back
>   And that moment they were free!
> Though the guns went ack-ack-ack,
>   And the distant flares you'd see
> The morrow he might not be—
>   She had to face that fact . . .

Love and art were one indeed.

Perhaps the same seize-the-moment mentality that drove the relationship with the major also emboldened her other decisions. At some point during the visit, and it's not clear how, Philippa came across a group of Catholic schoolchildren. Here is what we do know, from the May 10, 1967, edition of *The New York Times:* "Miss Schuyler had been at Hue in northern South Vietnam and had asked the helicopter pilot if he would evacuate her and a group of elementary school children to Danang. The pilot agreed."

They set out for Đà Nẵng International Airport, the principal base for the South Vietnamese and U.S. air forces. It was one of the busiest airfields in the world, where helicopters with passengers from in and around Huế were increasingly common in the months leading up to the January 1968 Siege of Huế, which was part of North Vietnam's Tết

Offensive and one of the longest, deadliest battles during the war.

But the helicopter crashed in the bay before it could land. By all accounts, everyone survived the initial plunge into the water. But safety was still a long swim away. For all the many hours spent honing her talents as a young girl, one thing Philippa did not learn was how to swim. Harlem's only public pool, the Colonial Park Pool, opened in 1936, but it was not among the spheres she moved through during her childhood. Philippa and the toddler who spent the ride on her lap, who was the same age as she was when the world first got a glimpse of her precocious talents, never made it to shore.

For the funeral program, Philippa's mother, Josephine, wrote a book-length poem about Philippa's childhood, career, and travels called "The Beautiful American: The Traveled History of a Troubadour." It began:

She was Diana—but fairer
    A muse with a passionate soul
Though she lived amid violence and terror
    Music and lore were her goal
She read and believed the old sages
    And collected ancient folk song
To play on all the world's stages
    From the Hague to teeming Hong Kong.

As the two-year anniversary of Philippa's death approached, Josephine put the finishing touches on the Philippa Schuyler Memorial Foundation, which she and

George had established to assist with the growing humanitarian crisis in Vietnam. She also got her own affairs in order, arranging for George to receive all her worldly belongings except her typewriter, which she wanted to go to a friend. Then she sat down at her desk and took out a notepad and pen for the last time. "I am killing myself," she wrote, "rather than go to a New York hospital which today are crowded, dirty, with incompetent nurses, indifferent mercenary doctors and attendants looking like cutthroats from a Georgia chain gang."

George was bereft. Without the wife he'd shared his life with and the remarkable child they'd raised together, writing was one of his few constants—if not the only one. He had long ago renounced the Socialist Party in favor of anti-Communist, right-wing politics that isolated him from other Black writers and publications and tarnished his legacy. When he died in New York in 1977, at the age of eighty-two, *Jet* magazine (a Black-interest weekly) referred to his 1966 attendance at a meeting of the far-right John Birch Society, where he "spoke of Blacks in America being better educated, healthier and wealthier than their African counterparts—and that they should be grateful." He no doubt thought of his own daughter as a gleaming example of what a Black person in America could become, all without acknowledging the truth he knew better than most: Everything Philippa became was in spite, not because, of being born in the United States.

My Grandfather's
Granddaughter

MY HIGH SCHOOL TRIP TO Mexico unfolded over two very different weeks in the spring of 1994. We were led by our Spanish teacher, Mrs. Salisbury, and spent the first week taking classes at a language institute in Cuernavaca, capital of the state of Morelos and about a ninety-minute drive south of Mexico City. I was assigned, along with a girl from my school named Ashley,* to a host family in a middle-class neighborhood. The dad worked in an office while the mom stayed home to raise their two young children and manage the household. Ashley and I shared a room with Priya,† an Indian American student from the Midwest who was spending her junior year of college abroad.

She'd been there for more than six months and was already fluent in Spanish thanks to our host family's insistence on eating lunch and dinner together every day and speaking the language no matter what, even though the fa-

---

*   Not her real name.

†   Not her real name.

ther spoke some English and the kids were learning it in school. If we didn't know a word in Spanish, we had to describe it using the words we did know. Priya also took her upper-level humanities classes in Spanish at the local university. All of this meant that she had no discernible American accent and knew all kinds of slang. The day she invited Ashley and me to tag along to meet some of her friends, we had to practically jog to keep up with her as she confidently zipped across the street, around the corner, and steered us toward the *zócalo*, or town square, all without needing to so much as glance at a map or street sign. Her friends greeted us with cheek kisses and cigarettes before launching into rapid-fire conversation. *This girl*, I thought, *is living my dream*.

The second week of the trip Mrs. Salisbury steered us four hours northwest to rural Querétaro, where we stayed at a co-ed boarding school for orphaned teenagers. The staff was used to having international visitors drop in for a few days to see a side of Mexico that was far from its beach towns, big cities, and tourist attractions. In exchange, we paid a nominal fee and did chores around the property. But the teenagers who lived there, who were the same age as us, bore the real burden of our presence. I wondered, but never asked, why my classmates and I had large dorm rooms of our own—one for the boys, one for the girls, with plenty of space and extra beds in each—in a school filled with so many students. I still don't know the answer. Did the teenagers have to crowd into other rooms to leave the two dorm rooms available, year-round, for visiting guests? Or did some of them live in those dorm rooms, only to be forced to vacate and bunk elsewhere each time new people showed up? Realizing that the other kids had to give up their own comfort so that we Americans had ample space and privacy as a group made me wonder what else our visit was costing them. What did it mean for them to see and possibly get attached to new faces that came and went from week to week, especially when they had already been separated from their families?

This was my first introduction to "alternative spring break," a term coined in the 1980s to appeal to service-minded high school and college students looking for ways to spend school holidays volunteering rather than lounging on beaches. Despite the noble premise of the concept, even as a teenager in Mexico I knew that the afternoons we spent peeling onions and plucking chickens for dinner were not enough of a service to justify our fleeting presence—especially when we made such an adolescent spectacle of how gross we found the preparation for dinner. When we said goodbye at the end of the week, I imagined the other kids stripping the sheets, remaking their own beds, and getting into position to welcome the next round of guests while we headed to Querétaro City for lunch at an upscale restaurant overlooking the town square. I felt like we'd stolen something and used it to pay for the meal.

Was that what it meant to be American? I never felt particularly American before the trip, or even during the first week of it. Back in Cuernavaca most of my outings were with Ashley, who was Black like me, or with Priya, and we never got called *gringos* like my white classmates did when they made their way around town. It would take years before I had studied and traveled enough to know that people probably assumed that Ashley and I were Afro-Mexicans or, more likely, tourists from Barbados or Jamaica or somewhere else in the Caribbean, and that Priya was an Indigenous Mexican. It was obvious, though, that African American and Indian American high school and college students were a rare enough sight to not be anybody's first or even second guess.

We didn't get repeatedly approached by street vendors selling gum or batteries or ice cream like my white classmates complained about, but nor did we get warm welcomes or friendly smiles when we walked into restaurants or stores like they did, either. In that way, strangely, I felt right at home.

Things were somewhat different at the boarding school in Querétaro. I was now part of a package that came with the label "American." We were all *gringos* here, all using the privilege of our passports to swoop in for an educational experience that was by definition rooted in other people's struggles and sacrifices. I had gone into the second week thinking that it would be easy for Ashley and me to bond with the kids there. But the kids didn't see us as being anything like them, or even as special at all. Just like back home, it was our white classmates—and the blondes among them especially—who got all the attention. They were the ones the other kids wanted to hang out with and talk to about American music and movies, not Ashley and me.

For all my fantasizing about leaving the United States, I wasn't prepared for the reality of it to be so complicated. I wasn't prepared to ricochet so quickly between feelings of

elation and frustration, marginalization and privilege, confusion and clarity, indictment and guilt. These were feelings
that would take me by surprise again years later, when I
spent the spring semester of my junior year as a student at
the University of Pennsylvania in Argentina.

I had gone there to re-create Priya's Mexico, or at least
my own version of it. In some ways, I did just that: I had a
kind and loving host mother who asked me my favorite
foods the day I moved in and put variations of them on the
table every night at dinner, where she insisted on our speaking Spanish despite being the daughter of British immigrants herself; a large circle of friends from my program
and the classes I took at the University of Buenos Aires; and
an exciting city to explore.

But I also got stared at incessantly ("It's because you're
so pretty," my host mother told me when I complained
about it), mistaken for a Brazilian prostitute on multiple
scary occasions ("Most *negras* here are from Brazil," she
said, despite Argentina's own history of African slavery,
"and they come to sell sex"), and had a group of doormen
in my neighborhood impersonate screeching monkeys
when I walked past them late one night ("Now that, I cannot explain," she replied).

When the monkey screeching happened, I was on my
way to a *locutorio,* which was a place to make international
calls from private phone booths since Argentines didn't have
international calling on their own home phone lines back in
1999. I would go there once or twice a week to call my soon-
to-be-ex-boyfriend back in Philadelphia, my mom and little
sister in Denver, and my grandparents in Colorado Springs.

I usually went in that order, based on their time zones and evening schedules, and focused on the highlights of my day, like my morning classes at the university and my afternoons spent in museums and cafés, instead of the lowlights, like the stares and innuendo. I wanted everyone to know I was having a great time, that the months away were well worth it, and to convince myself of the same.

This time, however, was different. For some reason, the first call I made was to my grandparents. Something in me knew that theirs was the number I most needed to dial, and that whichever one of them picked up the phone would be the exact person I needed to talk to and be honest with. And I was sure, deep in my bones, that one or the other of them would have something meaningfully comforting to say in response. I was full-on sobbing by the time my grandpa picked up and said hello in his soothingly raspy voice. When I got through the main plot points, stopping short of repeating the exact noises the men had made that were still ringing in my ears, he said, with what I now think was a touch of mirth in his voice, "This reminds me of when I was stationed in Austria. They used to ask us if it was true that Black people had tails."

As a kid, I'd only ever heard about the fun sides of my family's life in Salzburg in the early 1950s, like the stories my grandma told me about befriending their building's hausfraus, the ones my aunts and uncles recounted about ordering ice cream in German, and the ones my grandpa shared about the integrated parties he and my grandma hosted and attended, where they played familiar card games from down south like spades and bid whist. These stories were so familiar that they had fused with my own memories. Hence this new detail was hard to compute. What did the rest of the stories amount to now, if not an idyllic escape from the racism of the United States? Did that mean there was really no such thing?

At the same time, my grandpa's revelation gave the two of us a new language to speak together. We had always been close, but I had never known him to be especially talkative. He'd usually sign off our phone calls before my grandma did, leaving the two of us to talk about the foods I was eating there and the ones I missed from her kitchen, and about the telenovelas I was watching with my host mother and how they compared to the ones she and I watched together back at home. But things changed with that phone call. I felt like he trusted me with something that had clearly caused him pain. Now we both had our war stories, our hardships that ordinary civilians just couldn't understand. Now we really got each other.

My experiences in Argentina made me curious about something. At the time, I wanted to be a teacher and follow the example of Mrs. Salisbury (who led my high school Mexico trip), Mr. Rice (who taught my ninth-grade Russian history class), and other teachers who got to travel for their jobs and inspire young people to think of the world outside of the United States. I became interested in what young people in Argentina were learning in school about racism and anti-Semitism (both had long histories in Argentina that recently culminated in attacks on Korean Argentines and the bombing of a synagogue) and started working on an independent research project on the subject with the help of a local professor. I was surprised to learn that instead of tackling these issues head-on, school textbooks and handouts spoke of slavery and racism as only American problems and of anti-Semitism as something Jewish people fled to Argentina from Europe to escape. Argentina itself stood in these materials as a beacon of universal welcome, despite everything I was going through and reading about in the papers.

My research made me want to dig deeper into the country's history and modern racial politics. I knew that becoming a high school teacher wouldn't allow me to undertake the kind of investigative work that was a fit for my solitary inclinations and had become such a source of intellectual stimulation. So instead of applying for Teach for America when I got back to campus in the fall of senior year, I began applying to PhD programs in history. By the spring semester I had my pick of schools, each offering free tuition and a living stipend.

It wasn't lost on me how different my life was from that of everyone else in my family, even though I was no smarter or more ambitious than they were. I just happened to luck into some fancy schools and, with my family's encouragement and support, made eager attempts, like a hungry bear in a salmon stream, to grab onto as many opportunities flowing past me as possible. The year I started graduate school, I was the same age as my grandpa when he was drafted into the army, and the same age as my grandma and mom when they gave birth to their oldest children.

Then the news that I would step into an even more rarefied position came via email, on a cold afternoon in the spring of 2003 when I was a graduate student at the University of Michigan. It was from my school's international programs office, writing on behalf of the U.S. State Department to tell me that I'd been awarded a Fulbright-Hays Fellowship for my dissertation research in Peru. The program didn't (and still does not) publish statistics on the race and ethnicity of its award recipients, but a couple of years prior to my acceptance it had issued a press release counting several prominent Black figures among its alumni: the composer George Walker (France, 1957–58), the historian John Hope Franklin (Australia, 1960), the playwright Dolores Kendrick (Northern Ireland, 1963–64), the poet Rita Dove (Germany, 1974–75), memoirist and poet Maya Angelou (Liberia, 1986), and the filmmaker Julie Dash (United Kingdom, 1991–92).

When I got my acceptance letter, I marveled both at the idea that my name would be added to a list with so many of my role models and at the strange familial symmetry that my acceptance produced. The program owed its name and existence to J. William Fulbright, who as a freshman senator (and former Rhodes Scholar) from Arkansas in 1945 suggested that the United States direct proceeds from surplus war property sales to the State Department. His idea was to "promote international cooperation for educational and cultural advancement . . . to assist in the development of friendly, sympathetic, and peaceful relations between the United States and the other countries of the world." Like the Marshall Plan, this was part of the same spirit of promoting the country's democratic ideals around the world, only in this case instead of sending money the United States would send its own citizens, who would emblematize its commitment to free and open exchanges.

The start of the program aligned with my grandpa's return from the war. After risking his life and losing an eye, not just for his country but for all the African Americans whose lives he'd hoped his sacrifice would improve, he was treated to one indignity after another. He was confronted with "Whites Only" signs at every turn, even when it came to reaping the benefits of the GI Bill of Rights, including the kind of education I was now getting. The Fulbright felt a little like a debt the country was finally starting to pay off to my family, sixty years later.

With excitement came the realization that I was running out of time to tell my grandpa the good news. He'd had a bad fall a few weeks earlier and was in the hospital, suffering from an infection and a low white blood cell count. By the time I got through to him in his hospital room, not long after opening my acceptance email, he was too tired and his voice too weak to say much. Soon, the weeks turned into months and his long hospital stay turned into a move into hospice. After the school year ended, I spent the summer in Colorado Springs, having consulted with my graduate advisers and made the difficult decision to delay the start of my Fulbright by a couple of months. I figured that it was better to see my grandpa through to the end and leave after the funeral than to miss saying goodbye or risk running afoul of my visa and program requirements if anything happened while I was in Peru. Then I started thinking about not going at all.

You know he'd tell you to go if he could, my grandma insisted.

And so, I went. Within weeks of my January 2004 arrival in Lima, my grandpa took his last breath surrounded by his wife of nearly sixty years, most of their nine children, and several grandkids. I felt guilty that I was not there to support him and the rest of my family when he died, and robbed of a chance to say my own final goodbye. And then I felt stupid for having convinced myself that anything I'd ever experience as a Fulbrighter could possibly make up for what my grandpa went through as a soldier and veteran, and for having felt proud to represent my country when it never owned up to what it had done to him and millions of others. I thought about all the illustrious names on that list I was once so proud to join. I felt like we were all caught up in some kind of international reputation-laundering scheme for a country that, as usual, demanded more from us than it ever gave back.

CHAPTER 6

THE VOLUNTEER

Herman De Bose,

KABONDO AND KISUMU,
1970S

HERMAN DE BOSE HAD TO go all the way to Kenya for someone to call him "Mister." It was January 1970 and he was about forty miles outside of Kisumu, a large port city on Lake Victoria, where he had been assigned by the Peace Corps to teach at Wanga'Pala Secondary School in the village of Kabondo. "Mister Herman," his students and fellow teachers would say, using his first name rather than his last in a way that endowed the moniker with a mix of formality and familiarity that would come to define so many of his encounters during his initial two-year assignment.

Herman was only twenty-three when he arrived in Kabondo, which was a relatively young age at which to be called by anything other than his first name. Black men in the United States were rarely ever given the consideration of "Mister" in those days, at least not by white people. Even when they were the age of Herman's father and grandfather, even when the ones addressing them were young enough to be their children and grandchildren, they were called by either their first names or, more simply, "boy." So, the first time someone addressed him as "Mister"—not just the fact of it but its naturalness, too—was striking enough that he'd remember it more than fifty years later.

Herman would not have been able to find the village, or even Kisumu, on a map just a year earlier. In fact, he knew little about Kenya beyond it being the home country of track-and-field athlete Kipchoge Keino, who had made a star showing at the 1968 Summer Olympics in Mexico City when he won the gold medal in the men's 1,500-meter race. It was no small feat that Keino stood out given that all anyone seemed to talk about during the games were the African American runners Tommie Smith and John Carlos. After taking to the podium to accept their respective gold and bronze medals for the men's 200-meter race, the pair each raised a gloved fist in a Black Power salute during "The Star-Spangled Banner" to protest racism in the very country they were representing.

It was an iconic display during a tumultuous decade in the United States, defined by a steady rhythm of civil rights protests and anti-war activism. Federal desegregation orders and African Americans' demands for equality, combined with the increased U.S. military presence in Vietnam (where Herman's brother, Theodore, Jr., served from 1967 to 1968), led to violence in cities and on college campuses around the country. In the spring of 1969, the era's troubles would come bearing down on the historically Black North

Carolina A&T State University, in Greensboro, where Herman was in his senior year and majoring in sociology.

In the fall of 1968, Herman was looking forward to enjoying his senior year on a campus surrounded by a wide
circle of friends. He was not giving too much thought to
what would come after graduation until, one day, "I'm sitting on the library steps of Bluford," he later told me, referring to the university library. He and his friend William
"Smitty" Smith were enjoying a nice afternoon of people
watching when, suddenly, "this gorgeous young lady walked
by." As Herman remembered it, they called out to her to
see if she'd come over and talk to them. Sure enough, she
stopped, flashed a smile, and approached them on the steps.
Herman and Smitty did not need to think of what to say,
since she took quick control of the conversation with an
unexpected question: "Would you guys be interested in the
Peace Corps?"

Herman had first heard about the organization back at
Williston Senior High School in his hometown of Wilmington, North Carolina, when an alumna named Barbara Ferguson came to talk to students about her service in the Peace
Corps in Liberia from 1963 to 1965, where she taught math,
coached a girls' track team, and helped local adults with
their English lessons. But he had not given much thought to
getting involved in the organization. That day, however,
Herman was in the mood to negotiate. "I said, 'Hey, we're
having a party tonight. If you come to this party, I'll fill out
this application.' She said, 'I tell you what, you fill out the
application and I'll meet you at the party.' And I, like an idiot,

filled out the application. . . . To this day, I have no idea who
that woman was."

Herman did not know it, but both Ferguson and the
young woman were part of a concerted nationwide effort
to recruit Black volunteers for the Peace Corps. The organization's founding premise first took shape during a short
campaign speech given by then–Democratic presidential
candidate John F. Kennedy at the University of Michigan, at
two in the morning on October 14, 1960.

As Kennedy stood before a sea of ten thousand students
who had been gathering since ten the night before, he
opened with a bit of humor. "I want to express my thanks
to you as a graduate of the Michigan of the East, Harvard
University," he deadpanned, making the crowd erupt with
laughter and applause. Then he moved on to a more serious
topic that spoke to the heart of his vision for the country.

He was in the last three weeks of his campaign against
the Republican vice president, Richard Nixon, who like Kennedy was running to succeed President Dwight Eisenhower.
The Cold War was raging, and as Kennedy saw it, the United
States was losing to the Soviet Union and its Communist allies in the battle for global influence. With the 1957 launch of
the Sputnik satellite, the Soviets had bested the United States
in the arenas of science and technology. They were also developing an arsenal of intercontinental ballistic missiles and
other types of weaponry, making them a nuclear and military threat. The United States needed to grow its own roster
of allies, not just in Europe but in Latin America, Africa, and
Asia as well.

For Kennedy, young Americans were the country's best
bet in this effort. And so, from his perch on the steps of the
University of Michigan Union in the hours before the sun
rose that October morning, he asked two questions that
would ultimately come to define his legacy: "How many of
you who are going to be doctors are willing to spend your
days in Ghana? . . . How many of you are willing to work
in the Foreign Service and spend your lives traveling around
the world?" His point was to get the students thinking about
the connections between their personal ambitions and their
country's place in a global community. "On your willingness to do that," Kennedy concluded, "not merely to serve
one year or two years in the service, but on your willingness
to contribute part of your life to this country, I think will
depend the answer whether a free society can compete."

It was on the strength of these kinds of stump speeches,
which cast the United States and its citizenry as moral leaders of the future, that Kennedy won the election on November 8. It was, to date, one of the closest national margins
in the popular vote in American history, and Kennedy became the first U.S. president who had been born in the
twentieth century. He was also the best prepared to meet
the challenges of the era. He was charismatic but substan-
tive, trafficking not in vague promises but in the expectation that the members of the crowds around the country
who gathered to hear him speak—students, labor union
members, suburbanites, and civil rights activists—could
and would join him in making America, and the wider
world, a better place.

The speech at the University of Michigan became the unofficial mission statement for the Peace Corps, which would be formally established on March 1, 1961, with Executive Order 10924. Its purpose was to "be responsible for the training and service abroad of men and women of the United States in new programs of assistance to nations and areas of the world, and in conjunction with or in support of existing economic assistance programs of the United States and of the United Nations and other international organizations."

The Peace Corps' first director was R. Sargent Shriver, Jr., Kennedy's brother-in-law. From the beginning, Shriver understood that the message of the organization would be lost if it sent only white people to deliver it. He also knew that to recruit Black volunteers, he would need help from Black leaders. He appointed several high-profile members to his Advisory Council, including the actor Harry Belafonte and then-president of Morehouse College Benjamin Mays, and organized a network of recruiters that included Whitney Young, the president of the National Urban League, and Barbara Ferguson, the alumna of Herman's high school, who served as a recruiter at Historically Black Colleges and Universities (HBCUs). The visit to her old high school was not a formal recruiting visit, for the students were too young; rather, it formed part of her larger mission to inspire other African Americans to serve in the organization.

There was also outreach to, and through, the Black press. An article in the November 1961 issue of *Ebony* magazine served as both a profile of current Black volunteers and a recruiting tool to entice others to sign up for programs in Tanganyika (part of present-day Tanzania), Colombia, Chile, Ghana, Nigeria, St. Lucia, and the Philippines.

The article described a range of volunteer projects, from working with local farmers to teaching science and engineering classes. As Shriver saw it, it was also a meaningful opportunity for African Americans to serve their country since, no matter where the projects, no matter their specific features, the goal was always the same: "winning friends for the U.S. in places where friends are needed the most." But that was not enough motivation for African Americans. The Peace Corps thus promoted these projects as opportunities to deploy skills learned in college during a period when there was no guarantee that Black degree holders would find work in their chosen fields.

Ebony readers would have been struck while reading the article to come across the photo on the bottom right of page 40, about twenty-two-year-old Brenda A. Brown, a recent graduate of Baltimore's historically Black Morgan State College. Captioned "Philippines-bound," the image shows Brown seated at a cafeteria table and surrounded by white people. It presented a kind of funhouse-mirror version of the pictures of lunch counter sit-ins that were so common during that decade: Instead of immortalizing the contorted faces of white people yelling at Black patrons for simply trying to order food, it captured the smiling faces of white Peace Corps volunteers chatting with Brown over coffee and dessert. The message of the photo was clear: The Peace Corps was different, and so were its white volunteers. Everyone who signed up would be treated, and treat one another, like equals.

Why did recruiting Black volunteers matter so much to the Peace Corps? No one ever spelled it out in official documentation or outreach, but the politics of the Cold War era made it obvious. The United States was engaged in a battle with the Soviet Union for global influence, and it needed to make a strong showing of being a beacon of democracy. African Americans were essential to the message.

The United States had clearly failed to learn its lesson from the 1930s, when the Soviet Union successfully enticed men like Oliver Golden and Joseph Roane to leave their own homeland to work in their chosen professions on farms and in factories and receive dignified treatment from morning to night. But the rise of fascism in Europe gave the United States an opening to try again to credibly promote democratic ideals without reckoning with the second-class status foisted upon African Americans. This time around, it wasn't just the Soviet Union that was watching. The entire world was, too.

To gain influence and build friendships in Africa, Latin America, and other parts of the Global South, the United States needed to present a unified front. But rather than dismantle Jim Crow or make other meaningful inroads into the realm of civil rights for African Americans, which would have changed countless lives in the United States for generations and, in the process, gone a long way toward burnishing its reputation and enhancing its credibility on the world stage, the United States placed the burden on African Americans to convey a message of democratic inclusion.

This, too, was old news. During World War II, the United States asked African Americans to sacrifice their lives on the battlefield, dangling the vague promise that their bravery would be rewarded with equal opportunity back home. That generation left home with the understanding that, in the words of one soldier from the era, "we had two wars to win." Even though the country had failed to deliver on its end of the bargain, African Americans remained hopeful that with their hard work and determination, change would eventually come.

The implicit message to *Ebony* readers in 1961 was the same. But by then it was clear that the sacrifices made by African Americans during World War II had not been rewarded with any sort of victory at home. In fact, German POWs were treated with more dignity in the United States than Black veterans were upon returning from the war, and the ensuing decades saw only minor improvements to their social and material conditions.

By 1968, only about 5 percent of active and returned Peace Corps volunteers were Black. The dismal figure became the subject of that year's July–August *Peace Corps Volunteer* newsletter, the cover of which asked: "Should black Americans join the Peace Corps today? A study shows why many don't."

The study was conducted by the Louis Harris polling firm, which spoke to more than one thousand Black college seniors at fifty schools around the country. They revealed "two major conditions of being black in a white-dominated society" that kept them from applying. The first was career pressure. The respondents wanted to leave college and secure well-paying jobs (mostly in the fields of teaching, social work, and government, where they could directly serve their communities and make an impact on the policies that shaped their lives); for them, the low pay for volunteers and the delayed start in the professional world amounted to "a costly interlude." Race was the second condition. As one respondent put it: "There are enough serious problems facing Negroes in the U.S. and someone who is really concerned about helping others should be working against these problems here rather than going abroad with the Peace Corps." Embedded in this response was an implicit critique of the Peace Corps mission: If it cared so much about helping others, why was it allowing such devastating human rights catastrophes within its own borders?

Still, the respondents viewed the Peace Corps positively, saying it was doing more than foreign aid to improve the United States' global reputation. It was somewhat faint praise since the respondents also said that the "Peace Corps has become more interested in improving the U.S. image than in really helping other countries," but the pollsters saw good reason for the organization to be optimistic.

"If the Negro senior is to become interested in the Peace Corps," they said, "he must see it as a meaningful step into his future, not as a pause or a testing of his mettle before the inevitable confrontation with society. The Peace Corps can offer them (Negro seniors) new options and new opportunities that a discriminatory society is reluctant to provide. But the Peace Corps has not been successful in communicating this to black campuses."

To do that the organization hosted an eight-week training program for an interracial group of newly selected volunteers at Howard University in 1962. Out of the ninety-two trainees, twenty-five were headed to Cyprus while the rest were destined for Niger, Senegal, Sierra Leone, and Togo. *Ebony* sent a reporter to capture a few days in the life of the trainees. According to the article, "Howard was found a 'natural' for preparing volunteers for Africa because of its extensive African study program, its enrollment of some 20 African students and because of the fact that the majority of its regular students are Americans of African descent." In other words, the organization saw it as both an ideal training ground—a little Africa in the middle of D.C.—and a recruitment pool.

The magazine itself was another means of recruiting African American volunteers. It made room for Peace Corps advertisements featuring women like Janet Sledge, who, the organization said, "went to Jamaica to become a better school teacher in Chicago." She helped students build up their confidence in class, trained teachers to develop dynamic lesson plans, started a parent-teacher association, and more. The message was not subtle: Black volunteers didn't have to choose between making a difference at home or abroad, as doing the latter would, by extension, manage to facilitate the former.

Ebony also published profiles of Black volunteers like Brooklyn-born Georgetown graduate St. Clair Bourne, who worked at a newspaper in Peru that "has led [the] poor of Peru to protest slum conditions." In other words, they did not need to think about the work they did abroad as burnishing the United States' reputation but rather as serving the needs of other dispossessed groups.

The Peace Corps also disseminated messages via Black newspapers stretching from California and Cleveland to the

Carolinas inviting anyone who was interested to fill out applications and take assessment tests at their nearest post office location. They dispatched representatives—including officials from the Kennedy administration, members of Congress, and returned Black volunteers—to recruit students at the nation's HBCUs.

One such student recalled how a Black recruiter told her that she could "'help' Black and Brown people throughout the world." Before that, she had simply thought of the organization as being "for whites only," but hearing about the chance to support "Brothers and Sisters in developing countries," she decided that she owed it to herself to sign up to go to India. Another young man, following similar logic, applied to go to Tanzania. When other African Americans asked him, "Don't you think we ought to do something here first?" he reminded them that only good things could come from witnessing models of Black self-sufficiency up close.

AS FOR HERMAN, AFTER completing his application to the Peace Corps, his college life went on as usual. But then a month later a friend at North Carolina A&T whom he'd put down as a reference informed Herman that he got a letter with some kind of questionnaire inside. The pair worked together to come up with answers, and the friend sent the package back to D.C. Herman again filed it all away in the back of his mind as the school year unspooled. And soon enough, there were much more pressing issues.

On May 22, 1969, a student named Claude Barnes, a pop-

ular Black athlete at Greensboro's nearby Dudley High
School, had just lost a student election. It was an unsurprising outcome given that the school had taken Barnes's name
off the ballot because of his suspected ties to the local chapter of the Black Panther Party. But he ended up being the
favored candidate anyway, with six hundred of his classmates writing in his name. The student who ultimately
won received only two hundred votes. Almost immediately
after the results were announced, Barnes and some friends
headed over to the A&T campus. They did not quite have a
plan, but knew that Nelson Johnson, the university's newly
elected student body president, had recently started the
Greensboro Association of Poor People. He seemed like as
good a person as any to ask for help.

Johnson listened to Barnes and sprang into action. He
thought he could appeal to Dudley's administration on the
young man's behalf. When that did not work, he and Barnes
led the Dudley students on a walkout. The day ended with
Johnson being arrested for interfering with the operations
of a public school. This, in turn, got more A&T students
involved. Now the dispute cut across two campuses and involved the denial of rights to two popular young men who
were involved with causes that mattered to them all. Why
were they being punished instead of listened to? Together
with the Dudley students, the A&T students engaged in a
standoff at the high school. And then the police showed up.

The coming days engulfed the community in violence,
with police deploying tear gas and pepper spray, clubbing
students, and locking down dorms on the A&T campus.
The mayor asked the governor to order in the National

Guard. Then a sophomore at A&T, named Willie E. Grimes, was shot and killed. No police or National Guardsmen were arrested because, according to one official, none of their service weapons had been found to have fired the shot. They conveniently ignored the reports from terrified locals who saw police officers brandishing rifles and shotguns from their own personal stashes.

The students were sent home and the city imposed a curfew that worked as a dragnet for students who struggled to pack up their campus lives and leave on short notice. By the end of this three-day stretch, Grimes was dead and eight others, including students, police officers, and National Guardsmen, were wounded.

Back home in Wilmington, North Carolina, with his parents Lauretta and Theodore, Sr., Herman did not know what the future held. It was around that time that his aunt in Philadelphia called him. "The FBI just left here. What have you done?" It turned out that his friend's responses to the questionnaire were solid, and now the government was doing background checks. "So, then I knew it was serious."

At the same time, however, Herman wasn't even sure whether he would get to graduate. After all, the school had sent everyone home before they could take their final exams. He kept calling the A&T administration's hotline, but the phone was busy every time. On the morning of graduation day, June 1, he took his chances. "I drove up to Greensboro with my parents and I said, 'Am I going to graduate?' And they said, 'Yep.'"

That afternoon, Herman assembled with around five hundred other graduates. Elreta Alexander gave the com-

mencement address. She had attended Dudley High before
going on to become the first Black woman to graduate
from Columbia Law School, the first Black woman to be
licensed to practice law in the state of North Carolina, and,
in 1968, the first Black woman elected as a district court
judge. She knew exactly what the graduates were feeling
and was keenly aware of the forces they were up against.
"Youth sees our civilization, our society, and rightly so, as a
colossal flop," the judge intoned.

It was a resonant message for the graduation ceremony.
On a day when Herman, his classmates, and their families—
like their white counterparts on their own campuses in that
same month of that same year—should have been filled
only with a sense of pride in their accomplishments and a
sense of future possibilities, they were instead surrounded
by the wreckage of a campus that still showed signs of the
unrest from earlier in the month. One of the dormitories,
Scott Hall, was riddled with more than fifty bullet holes, put
there by police and National Guardsmen who'd conducted
a siege on the dorm while students were still in residence,
claiming they were looking for snipers and weapons. The
bullet holes would scar the building's exterior for decades,
until it was demolished in 2004.

After graduation, Herman moved north. "I had to get
out of Wilmington," he said, referring to his hometown,
and maybe even to the South more generally. He had an
aunt in Philadelphia, the one who'd earlier been visited by
the FBI, and the city seemed to be a good place to meet his
first post-graduation goal: to get a job that paid at least
$10,000 a year (more than $80,000 today). The closest he

could get, though, was a position in the city's Probation Department, making $6,000 a year. It was not the offer he wanted, but it was one he had to seriously consider.

And then he got a phone call.

It was his mom, back home in Wilmington. "Baby, I got this letter from the government." He asked her to open it and read it over the phone. "Congratulations. You've been accepted for the Peace Corps. Meet in Raleigh, North Carolina, on September 29, 1969, no later than five P.M."

Herman immediately made his way from Philadelphia back to North Carolina, where he got a job in a textile factory in Greensboro, his old college town, working on the midnight shift. He remained there until September 20, 1969, when he returned to his hometown of Wilmington to spend a few days with his family and friends before boarding a bus to Raleigh with more than 120 other young people for the Peace Corps orientation. The gathering was hosted by Shaw University at the Sir Walter Raleigh Hotel and lasted for one week. After that, the group traveled to Fort Caswell, a retreat center on North Carolina's Oak Island.

Fort Caswell was where the group, made up of recent college graduates and young professionals, were transformed into Peace Corps volunteers. They were all bound for various parts of Africa, and Herman was one of approximately twenty African Americans. Seventeen of them hailed from thirteen different HBCUs: Arkansas Agricultural, Mechanical and Normal College (Johnny W. Benton and Johnny E. Washington), Edward Waters University (Reginald E. Baety), Fisk University (Harry Eugene Baker and Mary L. Lewis), Howard University (Stanley M. Browne),

Jackson State University (Dollye R. Walker), Norfolk State University (Luther T. Rountree), North Carolina Agricultural and Technical State University (Herman De Bose), North Carolina Central University (Willie A. Barnes), Shaw University (Janie M. Shack), Southern University (Mattie Miles), Tennessee State University (Richmond Woodall), Texas Southern University (Harold Boyd and Delores Lewis), and Tuskegee University (Jonny E. Anderson and Cozetta M. Butts). The three others had attended Dakota Wesleyan University (Gilbert Witherspoon), Northern Illinois University (Marsha Witherspoon), and William Jewell College (Albert J. Byrd). Together, they represented the fruits of the recruitment campaign targeting African Americans.

Their presence as part of an integrated group of young people attracted local attention. Late one night, they were visited by the Ku Klux Klan, who distributed racist leaflets. It was a scary moment, to be sure, but it did nothing to steer the group from their course. They had work to do. "We did language training," Herman told me. "We learned to speak Swahili. Then we did teacher training because we were going over as teachers." After about a month or so, the recruits were placed in public schools around the state to gain hands-on experience. Herman went to Goldsboro, a town of around thirty thousand in the middle of the state where he taught a middle school history class. After the practice teacher training, the trainees returned to Fort Caswell for approximately one more month of language and cross-cultural training.

Finally, they had become Peace Corps volunteers, ready to be sent out into the field. First, they would spend the holidays with their families and say their goodbyes for the next two years, then meet up in New York City on December 31, 1969, to board their flights. On Herman's flight there were three groups: one going to Liberia, another to Uganda, and still another to Kenya. Following a series of bus-style stops, with the volunteers filing off in turns toward their respective destinies, Herman and his group finally landed in Nairobi.

The Peace Corps volunteers had arrived in Nairobi on the heels of two momentous occasions. The first was the assassination of Tom Mboya on July 5, 1969. Only thirty-nine years old, the handsome, charismatic Mboya was a trade unionist, Kenya's minister of economic planning and development, and poised for greater prominence on both national and global stages. He was emerging as a potential successor to Jomo Kenyatta, the country's first president and a member of the Kikuyu ethnic group that had been responsible for the anti-colonial Mau Mau rebellion that lasted from 1952 to 1960, which was marked by untold violence and spelled the beginning of the end of British rule (and for which Kenyatta had been arrested and falsely imprisoned on charges of leading the Mau Mau, in 1953). As a Luo, Mboya was an oddity in Kenyatta's Kikuyu-dominated administration and further set himself apart through his attempts to put country above ethnic affiliation.[*] He also embraced a capitalist vision for Kenya's economic future, which prompted rivalries with more socialist-minded members of government.

---

[*]   Former U.S. President Barack Obama's father was a Luo, and Mboya was a mentor of his.

Mboya met his end on a quiet Saturday afternoon in Nairobi after stepping out of a pharmacy. An assassin opened fire, striking Mboya in the chest, and escaped in the ensuing confusion. The married father of five died in an ambulance on the way to the hospital.

His death sent shockwaves throughout Kenya and exacerbated ethnic tensions in ways that threatened to tear the country apart. Supporters gathered at the hospital in such mounting numbers that baton-wielding police were called in to keep them at bay. As the days wore on with no arrests made in his murder, the belief spread among the Luo that the Kikuyu were responsible (the implication was that Kenyatta himself was somehow involved or had at least turned a blind eye). Then, on the day of his funeral, a riot broke out. It lit a match that stoked similar disturbances across the country for the next several months.

Not coincidentally, the country only began to see signs of calm in the lead-up to the second event that preceded the Peace Corps volunteers' arrival in Nairobi: the December 12, 1969, celebration of six years of Kenyan independence from British colonial rule. Kenya was the thirty-fifth nation in Africa to gain its independence, and the celebrations in Nairobi attracted global attendees and attention. There were representatives from more than eighty countries present, including England's Prince Philip and a mixed-race delegation from the United States. Among them was *Ebony* publisher John H. Johnson, the historian Lerone Bennett, who was reporting for the magazine, and the diplomat Ralph Bunche, whose long career included distinguished work with the United Nations, winning a Nobel Peace

Prize, and playing an active role in facilitating independence in Kenya and throughout Africa by drawing on transnational connections forged during his studies at the London School of Economics. One of his good friends and classmates was Kenyatta himself, who taught Bunche Swahili in between classes. Bunche was able to put his skills to use upon his first visit with Kenyatta to the latter's homeland in 1938. During that trip, Bunche was made an honorary member of the local Kikuyu tribe and given the nickname "one who has returned." Later, a Nairobi street would bear Bunche's name.

Also in attendance was Supreme Court justice Thurgood Marshall. He'd served as constitutional adviser to Kenya beginning in 1960, for the Kenya Constitutional Conference that had laid the groundwork for independence three years later. Marshall crafted a bill of rights whose familiar-sounding preamble stated that "all persons are equal before the law and are entitled without any discrimination or distinction of any kind, such as race, colour, sex, language, religion, political or other opinion, national or social origin, property, birth or other status, to equal protection of the law." This included not just the native Africans who made up the country's majority but European, Asian, and Arab populations as well.

Bennett described three days of official events that "unreeled against the backdrop of the ultra-modern city of Nairobi, one of the showplaces of contemporary Africa." Indeed, post-independence Kenya was in a growth phase. It was expanding its economy beyond agricultural exports to include tourism, which meant investing in infrastructure by building roads and hotels, upgrading its airport to accommodate jumbo jets and the passengers that filed out of them, and developing attractions that would appeal to visitors from around the world. As the capital, Nairobi was both the center of and the gateway to all these changes.

It also embodied contradictions. After landing at the city's gleaming new international airport (which, incidentally, was built using forced Mau Mau labor and would later be named in honor of Jomo Kenyatta), Herman and the other Peace Corps officers did what most visitors did back then, and still do, which was to make their way via the Uhuru (Freedom) Highway about seven miles north to the central business district for a couple of days.

The area was paved with wide streets lined with palm trees and buildings from a mix of architectural traditions and eras, from colonnaded government buildings and Gothic churches to Art Deco hotels and modern glass skyscrapers. At the center of it all was Delamere Avenue (originally named after an early and notorious white settler but since renamed Kenyatta Avenue), a commercial strip that was home to the InterContinental hotel, which had its grand opening in 1969 and boasted a ballroom, an outdoor pool, a rooftop supper club called Le Chateau, a hunting-lodge-themed cocktail lounge, and views of the neighboring Uhuru Park, which was a lush thirty-acre green space that featured recreational areas, a lily pond, and a man-made lake.

One center of gravity was the iconic Stanley Hotel, whose history and evolution reflected broader national trends. Named after Sir Henry Morton Stanley, the Welsh explorer who was famously claimed to have uttered "Dr.

Livingstone, I presume" when he found the elusive physician on the banks of Tanzania's Lake Tanganyika in 1871, the hotel first opened in 1902. For decades it stood among the many hotels and clubs in Nairobi where white settlers and bureaucrats held court beyond the exterior signs reading "No Africans or Dogs Allowed," confident in their place atop the social order they imposed as a racial minority in the Black colony. These were the kinds of places where, as one reporter for *The New York Times* put it, "gimlets were chilled and the only intrusions of Africa were the sounds of black waiters whose bare feet whisked across polished wood floors."

The hotel also served as a regular rest and recovery site for Ernest Hemingway. The first time was after he contracted amoebic dysentery while hunting in Tanzania in 1933, and again following back-to-back plane crashes on another hunting trip in 1954. (Today, a picture of Hemingway and his wife Mary cuddling a lion cub hangs on the wall of the hotel, which also has a conference suite named after him.)

In the years following independence, the New Stanley (the name given to it after a 1958 remodeling and expansion), like the rest of Nairobi, started to shed some of its colonial features. The hotel welcomed a wider constellation of guests, who included royals, celebrities, writers, students, and journalists from around the world. When Craig Claiborne, the white American restaurant critic for *The New York Times,* made his way to the hotel's Thorn Tree Cafe, he noted, "One pundit remarked that the Thorn Tree is not only the major diversion in Nairobi, it is *the* diversion." During the lunch rush one afternoon, he sat next to a student from Tanzania and was within earshot of a few nuns in habits and American tourists in safari jackets. The restaurant, he wrote, was now where "beggars and bankers, the wretched and the rich, all [formed] part of the scene of one of the world's most fascinating gathering places."

Diners at the Thorn Tree could select from a menu that was typical of post-independence Nairobi and reflected the city's colonial history, diverse population, and cosmopolitan aspirations. It included shish kebabs, curries, fried chicken, shrimp cocktails, French fries, and a local pilsner called Allsop's. Absent from the menu, however, was any sign of traditional Kenyan food. The elision was a subtle hint that the New Stanley, like the new Nairobi, hadn't managed to root out every trace of the old.

Another hint that the old ways would not be easily displaced lay in how white locals and visitors continued to treat Kenyans. A writer for the *New York Amsterdam News* visiting Nairobi in 1971 described seeing "safari-clad Englishmen out of 1930 movies dashing off on cross-country road races and brushing Kenyans aside as though the country was still the property of the Crown. All in all the white settler looked alive and well, pursuing his colonial pleasures with all of the verve of pre-independence days."

For all the vestiges of colonialism that were still visible in Nairobi, it nevertheless represented exciting possibilities. To African Americans, especially, it was an epicenter of African self-determination after throwing off the yoke of generations of Eurocentric colonial rule. Speaking with a visiting reporter from *The Afro-American,* one African

American expat, a doctor "who asked that his name not be revealed because he might some day return to the States and he does not want to be penalized for his views," shared why he was content to call Nairobi home. "You can make more money in the States, but what difference does it all make if someone can come up and call you a n . . . r."

How could both things be true? How could Kenyans seem, at least to outsiders, to be living out scenes from *Out of Africa* (the bestselling memoir written by Isak Dinesen, a Danish settler in colonial Kenya), while African Americans felt like they had found an escape from the racism that had so defined their lives and worldviews? This was the tension that lay at the heart of being an African American abroad, then as now: The only place it was possible to truly feel like an American, and to experience all the privileges that came along with it, was in other countries.

That privilege came with a side of complications, however. According to the reporter from the *New York Amsterdam News*, "Even in the African-managed hotels . . . it is not permitted that African employees fraternize with Black American guests. The West still holds on."

AFTER A FEW DAYS in Nairobi, most visitors would head either west to the wildlife reserves for safaris, east to the beach towns along the Indian Ocean coast for sun and sand, or north to Mount Kenya (the second tallest on the continent after Tanzania's Kilimanjaro) for tests of their physical limits. But the Peace Corps volunteers charted their own course.

In Herman's case, his destination was two hundred miles

northwest in the village of Kabondo. He was driven there by a Peace Corps staffer. As the car wound out of the capital early that January morning, the paved streets lined with bustling institutions of urban life gave way to dirt-packed roads cutting through arid savannas and then lush forests, before the car eventually pulled into a small village after nightfall.

The first sign that Herman was no longer in Nairobi was the utter, enveloping darkness. Gone was the bright cityscape with buildings lit from inside and out. In its place was a poorly marked bus stop without so much as a streetlight. Luckily, the Peace Corps had arranged for local guides to meet him. He was met by Philemon O'Koth, headmaster of Wanga'Pala Primary School. O'Koth invited Herman to his home for a welcome meal of ugali (a dough-like cornmeal ball that was served as a kind of bread), sukuma wiki (collard greens), and fish (tilapia). Herman recalled it as one of the best meals he had eaten. After the meal, O'Koth and other village members walked Herman to his new residence.

Stepping outside, Herman's eyes struggled to adjust to the pitch black. He could barely make out his hosts' shapes as they beckoned for him to follow. Since they knew the route and terrain by heart, they moved quickly. As for Herman, he stumbled every few feet, trying to keep from dropping his luggage and having two years' worth of possessions spill out and get swallowed up by the night.

Finally, they made it to a small wood-frame house, which he would have as a home all to himself. The guides helped him inside and then retreated into the darkness. The first thing Herman wanted to do once he got settled in was use the bathroom. But it was in an outbuilding several yards away, and he no longer had the trained eyes of others to lead him. Plus, he was nervous. He decided to hold on until morning and tried to get some sleep.

When the sun finally rose, he set down a short path to the outhouse, but instead of finding a toilet inside, there was just a hole in the ground. After all that training at Fort Caswell, he was not prepared for this. Anything more than peeing in the daytime was going to be a test of both his lower body strength and his mettle.

Nothing about his Nairobi detour prepared Herman for Kabondo. In that way, it was kind of the perfect introduction not just to Kenya in particular but to Africa in general, where no two places were alike. He had traveled only two hundred miles from the capital city—the same distance separating his hometown of Wilmington from his college town of Greensboro—but was now living an entirely different life.

In addition to navigating new, mostly rural terrain, he was interacting with a different population. Where Nairobi was a city of more than half a million that drew people from all over Kenya and the world, Kabondo was a tiny fraction of its size and dominated by the Luo ethnic group. The region never had much contact with the British government in colonial times, nor did it receive many foreign settlers or tourists. The food was also different. Gone were the hamburgers, fries, shish kebabs, and curries that were on offer in Nairobi's hotel restaurants and tourist establishments. In their place was ugali, a bread that, depending on what was available each day, he ate with fish and grilled meats and dipped into sauces or stews.

THE PEACE CORPS HAD assigned Herman to teach geogra-phy and history at Wanga'Pala Secondary School. To get there, he took a bus down the road from his house. But because it could only get him within two miles of the school, he had to walk the rest of the way (and back to get home). When he walked onto campus his first day, a concerned-looking Philomon O'Koth met him at the en-trance and immediately got down to business. It turned out that the secondary school students had even greater needs than the Peace Corps had previously understood. There were too many subjects and not enough teachers, so Her-man would need to add a few more courses to his reper-toire. He would teach the English classes because, O'Koth told him, "English is your mother tongue." And he would help the students tackle math and science because, well, "you've gone to university, therefore . . ."

On top of that, Herman had arrived during a time when O'Koth and the community were negotiating with the Min-istry of Education to grant Wanga'Pala Secondary School status as a government school so that it could receive fund-ing. A representative for the Ministry of Education had in-sisted that, for the school to be accepted as a government school, a government teacher needed to be at the school. O'Koth pointed to Herman's recent arrival as a Peace Corps volunteer: He was a teacher provided by the government, meaning they had a government teacher. O'Koth further mounted his case by enlisting Herman's help. "Mr. Herman," he said, "will you give us the honor of being head-master so we can get funds for our school?"

The plan worked. The school received its funding and Herman served as the school's first American headmaster for the next fourteen months. He often marveled in those days at how far he had traveled in the past year, from a college student in North Carolina to a headmaster running a secondary school in rural Kenya. He didn't feel like a different person from the guy who sat with Smitty for study breaks on the steps of Bluford Library. Even though he was shouldering some serious responsibilities and demands, he was still young and could always summon the energy to have a good time.

Weekends would often find him in Kisumu, which was one of Kenya's largest cities. When he went by himself, people took him for a Kenyan, if not necessarily a local. "People would say to me, 'What tribe are you from?' because I didn't have the physical characteristics of the locals. And then once I opened my mouth with my broken Swahili, they knew and they would say, 'Oh, where are you from?' And I would say, 'I'm from America.' And they would say, 'But you're not white.'"

Once, at a party, Herman was chatting in English with a young Kenyan woman. A Kenyan man approached and, jealous of their interaction, tried to help the young woman see what was going on. "He's pretending that he's from America," he told her. "He just went and studied there."

This was a big part of why the Peace Corps wanted people like Herman to join the organization—to address a fundamental image problem. As one recruiter put it: "Right now there is the male, White, middle-class stereotype of the Peace Corps. I'm not knocking this. . . . But America is more than just male, White, middle-class people." Yet even as Herman and others received a warm welcome from the organization for their role in better showcasing the United States' diversity, and in better connecting with the populations the Peace Corps served, the volunteers found that how they identified themselves was at odds with how locals identified them.

In Nigeria, locals alternately called African American Peace Corps volunteers "white black" and "native foreigners," while Cameroonians referred to one volunteer as a "Black white woman." The volunteers were in a category alone, distinct both from their white American counterparts and from the Africans with whom they shared ancestry. For David Closson, who taught at a school in Uganda, his relief at escaping U.S. racism and feeling welcomed among the locals was outweighed by the sexism he encountered on a daily basis. His male students argued that "education makes women cheeky," and that husbands should beat their wives. On more than one occasion, he watched as his female colleagues were harassed on the street for showing too much skin.

Herman also got reacquainted with some white Peace Corps volunteers in Kisumu (who he'd previously met back at Fort Caswell) when he was eventually reassigned to teach at Kisumu Technical School, where he taught English, geography, and science for the last several months of his assignment. One of the volunteers was named Maureen

O'Malley, a graduate of the University of Michigan. When he would meet Maureen and other white volunteers at a restaurant, the staff "made the assumption that I was 'an American.' And once that was established, when I'd go to those restaurants . . . I was treated different." Different did not always mean better.

HERMAN LIKED BEING THOUGHT of as Kenyan, liked being understood as American, and simply liked his Peace Corps volunteer life so much that when his two-year contract was up, he stayed on at the Kisumu Technical School for another six months. It helped that Maureen was still there. After that, the pair went back to the United States, where they got married. Herman soon joined the ranks of returned volunteers who helped recruit new classes, not just at HBCUs but at universities all over the country. He was based in the Chicago office and enjoyed the jet-set life. "I got an expense account, I got a credit card, I go out to the airport, I leave on Sunday, and I come back on Friday. I'm staying at the Holiday Inn; I'm staying at these fancy hotels, and I put down a credit card. Now I walk in a classroom primarily of whites and I say, 'I was in the Peace Corps in East Africa.' I mean, people gravitated to talk to me."

After a little over a year, he and Maureen moved from Chicago to Los Angeles, where Herman attended graduate school at the University of Southern California to obtain a master's degree in social work, which he earned in June 1975 all while serving as a campus recruiter for the Peace Corps for the Los Angeles recruitment office. Upon completing his degree, he got a job with Los Angeles County in the departments of health and mental health and worked as an adjunct professor at California State University, Fullerton, and California State University, Los Angeles. His Peace Corps days were never far from his mind, and he started connecting with a handful of other former Peace Corps volunteers. The more the former volunteers talked, the more they cohered around a mission, which was to create a communal identity as Returned Peace Corps Volunteers (RPCVs) and to fulfill one of the goals articulated by President Kennedy when he created the Peace Corps, which was for volunteers to come home and teach their neighbors about the communities where they served. In 1978, they met up with RPCVs in New York, Washington, D.C., and elsewhere to create the National Council of Returned Peace Corps Volunteers (now known as the National Peace Corps Association).

There came a point, though, when talking about Kenya became a poor substitute for actually being there. When a Peace Corps country director position opened up in Kenya, Herman put his name in for it. It took three tries, as he was passed over during his first two attempts, but finally, in 1985, he was selected. By then, he and Maureen had three daughters, and Herman had finished coursework for his PhD in social welfare at UCLA. Accepting the position meant that the entire family had to get on board. Maureen now held an administrative position with Los Angeles's Cedars-Sinai Medical Center. She would need to leave her job. While she certainly had her own connection to Kenya, there still was a question: What would she do there? As for daughters Genevieve, Monique, and Renee, who were seven, nine, and thirteen, respectively, they'd not only have to change schools and make new friends but do so in a place that—unlike their parents—none of them had ever known. How would they adjust after living in Southern California their whole lives? At the same time, the children were among the primary reasons Herman and Maureen were willing to cross over to Kenya. They wanted their girls to have the opportunity, just as they had decades earlier, to live and learn in an African country.

Indeed, when they first arrived in Kenya the youngest two children attended primary school in Kisumu, where Herman and Maureen had lived and worked during the last part of his Peace Corps assignment fifteen years earlier (the oldest daughter attended a religious boarding school). Eventually the whole family settled in Nairobi, where Maureen found an administrative position with the U.S. Agency for International Development and the pair's daughters enrolled in the International School of Kenya. There, they developed friendships that have carried them well into adulthood. (Herman and Maureen's fourth child, son Armand, was born when the family returned to the United States.) They also cultivated the same sense of ease in the world that their father first developed as a young volunteer and that carried him through his post–Peace Corps career in social welfare, a field in which he earned a PhD and taught for twenty-five years at California State University, Northridge, before retiring in 2019.

More than sixty years after the Peace Corps was founded, African Americans still make up a small fraction (less than 10 percent) of volunteers. Now, as then, people like Her-

man De Bose have taken up the charge to recruit them. Perhaps no message of service to one's country will be more
resonant than the one De Bose embodies, and that Barbara
Ferguson (the returned volunteer and alumna of Herman's
high school back in Wilmington, North Carolina) shared in
her 2021 remarks as part of the organization's "Strategies
for Increasing African American Inclusion in the Peace
Corps and International Careers" campaign: "Peace Corps
gave me the courage to do almost anything."

Away to Canada

MY MOVE TO CANADA IN the summer of 2017 was not about the U.S. presidential election, but no one really believed me when I said so. At least no one outside of academia. People in my profession understood that we rarely get to choose where we teach, and that we instead must apply where the openings are. It turned out that one of the best, most exciting jobs in Latin American history, one that I was lucky enough to get in an intensely competitive market, happened to be in Toronto.

I could hardly complain about the chance to move to a diverse city with a thriving arts and food scene. In the best of times, my friends and colleagues who took academic jobs in smaller towns or in red states faced a dearth of all those things. The election brought the added challenge of racist abuses from newly emboldened supporters of the winning candidate, not just off campus but within the walls of their colleges and universities. There was a time when I was being considered for a job at the University of Virginia, in Charlottesville, where I'd held a short-term fellowship, and had things gone a different way I would have been moving there just as tiki-torch-bearing white men marched through campus the night before the disastrous Unite the Right rally. As I sat in my Toronto high-rise near campus and watched the coverage of a car plowing through a multiracial crowd of counterprotesters on the day of the rally, killing Heather Danielle Heyer, I understood what I'd avoided by moving north rather than south.

But still, my answer was the same every time a Torontonian or a fellow expatriate asked me if everything that was happening back home was the reason for my arrival: *No, a thousand times, no.* I understood the reasons for their assumption, of course. The same news outlets that were covering the rise of the far right, the new president's rapturous rallies, and the hate crimes spewing forth from both were also profiling left-leaning Americans who'd made the move to Canada. They extolled the country's progressive legislation on matters of marriage equality, immigration, and health care—all things under attack in the United States—and were happy to report that they never once regretted their decisions to leave. There were even websites cropping up to help prospective movers manage transborder logistics and make the adjustment to a place that was so close and familiar to the United States in so many ways, and yet so different in matters of law and custom.

Well before I got the job offer or even saw the advertisement to apply for it, I had come to think of those self-styled exiles and refugees as engaging in the latest iteration of the old and familiar trend of white flight. Instead of leaving a neighborhood or school, they were now skipping out on the entire country. Sure, their reasons were different this time, and to their minds less racist, but I saw it as using an escape hatch when things got uncomfortable. And I wanted no part of that comparison.

Often in these conversations, there was a follow-up, issued as a declarative sentence rather than a question: *You must be so happy to be here, though.* That one proved a little harder to answer. The truth was that I was at a comparatively safe remove from the descent into far-right, white nationalist madness. And I was indeed very happy to make my home in a city and campus community where I got to live and work with Black and brown people with roots in the very countries being reviled by the White House and its supporters. At the same time, however, I felt like I'd managed to snag a standby seat on a different flight than the one I'd originally booked, only to learn that the latter ended up being hijacked.

Further complicating things was the fact that I wasn't blind to Canada's own horrors, past or present. From its residential schools that indoctrinated and abused Indigenous children to its own far-right renaissance that was indistinguishable in its rhetoric from that of MAGA adherents, the country had not entirely earned its reputation as a bastion of progressivism. It was simply easy to look good in relation to the United States.

A couple of years after I'd moved, I had a moment that encapsulates how meaningful it was to Canadians, that feeling of being better than their neighbors to the south. I was seated in the audience during a Toronto International Film Festival screening of *Harriet*, Kasi Lemmons's biopic about Harriet Tubman. There's a moment in the film when Tubman arrives in St. Catharines, Ontario, an important terminus on the Underground Railroad, after an arduous journey. As soon as the city's name appeared at the bottom of the screen via a chyron, the audience burst into a self-satisfied, sustained round of applause.

With my hands defiantly clasped in my lap, I thought of the lines of a poem my librarian friend David had shown to me as part of the preparations for an exhibit he was helping to mount on Black Canadian history. Titled "Away to Canada," it was written by a man named Joshua McCarter Simpson sometime after his arrival via the Underground Railroad in the 1850s, to honor the wife and family he left behind down south:

> Grieve not, my wife—grieve not for me,
> O! do not break my heart
> For nought but cruel slavery
> Would cause me to depart.
> . . . .
>
> O, Susannah!
> Don't grieve after me—
> For ever at a throne of grace
> I will remember thee.

I thought of how, for Tubman and Simpson and so many others, the joy of that arrival was also paired with a profound sense of pain. An awareness of their American families and communities who were not so lucky. And I thought of how they never stopped looking back.

A strange sensation started to descend upon me in that darkened theater, one that I couldn't, or wouldn't, yet name or consider acting upon. Although I was by no means defensive of the United States, there was no part of me that wanted to celebrate someone being forcibly severed from the land of their birth, the place they had helped make, the people who made it with them. That country belonged to them, too. There was also no part of me that wanted to join the next round of applause that came when the lights turned back on for the Q&A and an audience member declared—rather than asked—how pleased, even appreciative, the director must have been to show her film in Canada considering everything the country had done for its namesake. It all made me feel rather homesick.

It was comforting to know that I was not alone in my mix of emotions, even if it felt like it in that auditorium. When the singer and entertainer Paul Robeson (who'd traveled to the Soviet Union in the 1930s, where he experienced a taste of what he called "full human dignity" and spent time with the agronomists Oliver Golden and Joseph Roane) went on tour in Australia in 1960, he sat for an interview for the Australian Broadcasting Corporation's *Spotlight* program. At one point, he was asked if he felt any pull toward Africa during its era of decolonization. The implication was that unlike the United States, which had shown him and his people such hostility, the continent might offer a more hospitable home and future. In response, Robeson said, with his eyes locked onto his interlocutor's: "I would say that unquestionably I am an American, born there, my father slaved there, upon the backs of my people was developed the primary

wealth of America . . . so there's a lot of America that be-
longs to me yet." His assertion invoked the words that were
first spoken at a convention of free Blacks in New York City
in 1831, who'd come together to protest the American Colonization Society's efforts to promote sending formerly enslaved African Americans to Liberia: "This is our home, and
this is our country. Beneath its sod lie bones of our fathers;
for it some of them fought, bled, and died. Here we were
born and here we will stay." Like Robeson and our nineteenth-
century forebears whose words he conjured up, I wasn't done
with the United States.

CHAPTER 7

THE
FAVORITE SON

Kim Bass,
TOKYO, 1980S

IN THE EARLY 1980S, KIM BASS was an unusual fixture on Japanese television. He stood out from his co-stars not just because he was American but also because he was Black and could speak Japanese. This combination of traits made him a perfect fit for his characters, beginning with his debut in a made-for-TV movie inspired by World War II–era events in which he played the son of a Japanese woman and an African American soldier who was raised in a Tokyo orphanage. Then he scored a role on *Chotto Kamisama*, a popular nighttime soap opera, as a young father forced to rely on and build bridges with his dead wife's estranged Japanese family. Then came a guest-star role on the long-running detective series *Taiyo ni Hoero*, in which he played an FBI agent and martial arts expert. As young men of African descent navigating the crosscurrents of race and national identity in Japan, the characters voiced uncomfortable truths about their struggles to belong in the same language as the viewers who faithfully tuned in to watch.

Even though it was a career close to what Kim, as a young boy full of dreams, had imagined for himself, it was nonetheless set in motion thanks to two fateful bus trips during his childhood. The first came on a spring evening in 1963, when he was around six and a half years old. Kim's paternal grandfather stopped by his apartment in Utica, New York, to take him on an outing. Decades later, Kim told me: "I only did basically two things with my grandfather: go to church and go fishing." It was already late in the day, which meant it was too late to catch any fish. If that wasn't the reason for the visit, then it had to be for church. His grandfather, Kim noticed, was dressed in nice slacks and a crisp, button-up shirt. Still, he wondered, weren't services already over?

Kim was not inclined to ask questions of his grandfather and instead followed along like a dutiful grandson. On that day, "Papa Bass," as he was known, seemed to be guided by an even deeper sense of purpose. Kim simply did what he was told and put on some nice clothes. After a round of goodbyes to his parents and siblings, he followed his grandfather out the door, down the stairs, and across the street to the local bus stop. This, too, was unusual; the family usually walked or drove everywhere they needed to go. Once the city bus pulled up and opened its doors, the pair climbed up the steps.

Along the way, they passed a neighborhood filled with large stone houses fronted by manicured lawns and neatly trimmed hedges. "That's where your grandma cleans house for the white folks," his grandfather said, pointing out the window. After a few miles, they got off on a busy corner of Genesee Street, the city's main drag. They walked for a bit and then came to a stop in front of an imposing stone building.

When Utica's Uptown Theatre was built in 1927, the city was home to hundreds of foundries, mills, and factories that produced iron, textiles, and metal goods, all of which contributed to the theater's construction, including the ornaments on the façade and the plush seat covers in the fifteen-hundred-person amphitheater. Once complete, the theater provided a place for everyone—from factory workers to their bosses—to take in live music, vaudeville performances, and the latest picture shows.

The Uptown's popularity helped it survive Utica's industrial decline in the second half of the twentieth century. When Kim visited that day in 1963, it had lost some of its early luster, but still served as a place for locals to enjoy a bit of leisure. And to his young eyes, it was nothing short of majestic. Taking his seat, he thought to himself: "This must be the fancy church where the white people go. Maybe God's here and behind the curtain."

When the lights went down, the theater filled with the sound of heralding trumpets and the curtains opened to reveal a lush pastoral setting on the large projector screen. "In the alpine country of Austria," the narrator intoned, before introducing the village that was home to the Lipizzaner horses that American troops helped evacuate from Austria during World War II. This was no church sermon. It was Walt Disney's *Miracle of the White Stallions*.

Kim was enthralled. He didn't know why his grandfather took him, of all his siblings, to see his first movie that
day, or why he picked that film. All Kim knew was how he
felt by the end of it. "I came home so excited that night that
I asked my mom, 'Who makes movies? The same people
who make TV shows?' She said, 'Yeah, it's made in this
place called Hollywood.' I said, 'You know what? I think
they're the magic people. And when I grow up, I'm going to
be one of the magic people.'"

Kim didn't have a clear path from Utica to Hollywood or
anywhere else beyond the city's confines. During a time
when public and physical education were on the national
agenda thanks to President John F. Kennedy, who argued
that "our progress as a nation can be no swifter than our
progress in education" while advocating for building "a
strong and better America through physical effort," the
Bleecker Street Elementary School that Kim attended had
no library or gymnasium. Kim and his classmates were
largely left to their own devices when it came to nurturing
their interests and abilities. The school turned the low-
ceilinged lunchroom in the basement into a basketball
court, with a pair of wastepaper bins placed at opposite
ends to serve as makeshift baskets.

Like so many schools in the Northeast, where de facto
segregation prevailed thanks to segregation in the housing
sector, the Bleecker Street Elementary School's mostly
Black student body was helmed by an all-white administrative and teaching staff. Kim remembers the day his second-
grade class took a trip to the Utica Public Library and his
teacher told the students to pick out a book focused on

what they wanted to be when they grew up. It was 1962, and John Glenn had just become the first American to circle the earth. Kim picked up a book about astronauts and excitedly walked over to show his teacher. "Little colored boys can't grow up to be astronauts," she remarked, before telling him to find a different book.

Fortunately, Kim came from a long line of people who'd achieved extraordinary things: His maternal great-great-grandfather, Toliver Holmes, had escaped his enslavement on a Virginia plantation during the Civil War, headed north to join the Union army, went back down south to fight, survived the war, and headed north once again, this time to establish a life for himself in upstate New York. Years later, Toliver's grandson, Kim's grandfather, would grow up to become the first African American mayor of any city or town in the state of New York. After all that, no dream of Kim's was impossible as far as his family was concerned.

Kim might have followed a straight line from Utica to Hollywood had it not been for a second bus trip. This one was with his Cub Scout troop, to the 1967 International and Universal Exposition in Montreal. Expo 67 attracted millions of visitors from around the world: Pavilions represented the United Nations and more than sixty countries, including Canada, the United States, the Soviet Union, and several newly independent African nations, while exhibits like Man the Creator, Man the Explorer, and Man the Provider showcased humanity's feats in the arts, sciences, industrial development, and agricultural production. Then there was Montreal itself. With its cobblestone streets,

Gothic architecture, and French-speaking population, "the Paris of North America" was an easy draw.

For African American visitors, attending the Expo was more complicated. Civil rights organizations in the United States were concerned about Canada's history of prejudice against Black Canadians and West Indian immigrants, which—as in the United States—often took the form of restrictive housing covenants and residential segregation. This persisted despite the 1960 passage of the Canadian Bill of Rights, prohibiting discrimination on the basis of national origin, race, color, religion, or sex. They were also worried about being turned away from restaurants and lodgings in the country, and the New York Urban League urged President Lyndon B. Johnson to get assurances that Black visitors would be welcomed, or to cancel the United States' participation in the Expo. Johnson, who seemed to take the matter of the unsullied U.S. presence during this high-profile global event seriously, worked with Canadian officials to make sure African Americans would be welcome. *Ebony* further assured its readers in a multipage spread about the Expo that "officials say their province's anti-discrimination laws cover hotels, restaurants and camp grounds and they will be enforced rigorously by Quebec police authorities."

To eleven-year-old Kim, the only non-white Cub Scout in his troop, the experience of the Expo in Montreal was nothing but pure, innocent fun. "I had never even been in New York City at that point, so Montreal was exciting. The Expo was exciting. And I thought, 'This place is cool. All kinds of people from all kinds of places. People are speaking French; they've got some English.'"

DURING HIS JUNIOR YEAR of high school, Kim decided he was going to skip his senior year, graduate early, and go to college. He set his sights on Hawaii, mostly because it felt like an exciting next step. The problem was that Kim had not shared his plans with his parents. Needless to say, college in Hawaii never happened for the seventeen-year-old, whose parents quickly shut down a plan that would have sent him so far away at such a young age. After completing his senior year, Kim regrouped. He set his sights on returning to Montreal; unlike Hawaii, it was only a couple hundred miles from home, which made his mother happy, while still feeling like he was really going somewhere exotic, which made him happy. Without knowing how, exactly, to apply to college in Canada, he picked up the phone, dialed the operator, and got a number for Sir George Williams University (which later merged with nearby Loyola College to form Concordia University). He eventually got an admissions officer on the line and told him about that 1967 Cub Scout trip, how much he loved Montreal, and how drawn he was to Canada. They talked for an hour. "You're really interesting," the man told him. "We'd love to have you here at George Williams University." Kim had talked his way into a college acceptance.

Within a few months, he found an apartment and drove north with his parents. "Next thing you know, I'm in Montreal, Canada, for school."

In 1968, Sir George Williams University was embroiled in what came to be known as the Sir George Williams Affair: A group of six West Indian students accused Perry Anderson, their biology professor, of racist grading practices and asked the university to hold the instructor accountable. After ten months of stonewalling from the administration, the Black Students' Association put out a special issue of the student newspaper, *The Georgian,* which exposed the administration's failings and detailed their experiences of racism both on campus and in Montreal. "Racism for blacks neither began nor shall end with Prof. Anderson," wrote Philip J. Griffin, a research chemist at the university, who cited the poor handling of the Anderson case, police harassment, exclusion from student government, and "the 'sleepwalk' ignorance of black problems even here among SGWU students" as problems plaguing the school.

The issue galvanized the campus. By early 1969, there were protests involving hundreds of students, followed by a two-week sit-in at the building housing the Computer Centre. Instead of responding to student concerns, the administration handed the matter over to Montreal's police.

Nearly one hundred students were arrested. Among them were Roosevelt "Rosie" Douglas, from the Caribbean island of Dominica, and Anne Cools of Barbados. They were found guilty by all-white juries of obstructing the Computer Centre and sentenced to prison. Douglas was even deported after his eighteen-month term. When he returned to Montreal in 2000 as prime minister of Dominica, his first visit back since his deportation, he reflected on the events of his youth. "It was a fight for Black people to have an equal stake in the nation," he said. "We had no malice in our heads—we just wanted justice."

The Sir George Williams Affair reverberated into the next decade. In 1971, as a kind of concession to ongoing student concerns, the school created an Ombuds office and established an Office of Intercultural Affairs. This was followed by the creation of a dorm for students of color, a Black student union called Harambee Weuse ("Let's pull together" in Swahili), and Eric Fontaine's 1973 election as the first African American president of the Student Association.

Kim arrived on campus shortly thereafter, in the fall of 1974, stepping into an environment where Black students from Canada, the United States, and the West Indies all understood both the challenges they were up against and the opportunities that lay before them. They were advocating for new curricula, building coalitions among their fellow students, and—above all else—figuring out their life paths. For some students those paths were heading toward careers that had been out of reach of most of their ancestors. They were going to become doctors, lawyers, and scientists, breaking barriers that had been erected centuries before they were even born. For other students, like Kim, their paths meandered in less straightforward directions. He enjoyed attending his classes, making friends, and exploring Montreal, and in general the opportunity to be young and unencumbered. This was a new era of Black freedom, which did not need to be defined purely in terms of achieving conventional professional success or adhering to lofty missions around racial uplift through service and sacrifice. It was a time to just be young and free.

While playing in a pickup basketball game at the university gym, unbeknownst to Kim, he was being observed by the coach of the men's basketball team. After the game, the coach approached Kim and tried recruiting him. But the conversation was a short one. Once the coach realized Kim was an American, all he could offer was a practice-only position until next season, because there was a rule that allowed for only two non-Canadian players on the team at a time, and the slots were already filled (coincidentally, by two other African Americans). Though Kim enjoyed playing basketball and was pretty good at it owing to having grown up in a family of amateur players, his preference was for martial arts. Soon, he found his way to the school's Kung Fu club.

After his first year at the university, Kim decided to study overseas. He enrolled in a program in Japan sponsored by the Experiment in International Living (EIL). The organization was founded in 1932 to provide high school and college students with immersive international experiences. Founder Donald B. Watt, who pioneered the homestay model as integral to these experiences, spoke of his work as a kind of peace-building enterprise: "We call it an experiment because no one knows until he tries whether he has the intelligence, energy, and tact to make a trusted friend of a foreigner." (If this sounds familiar, it's because one of the organization's alumni was Sargent Shriver, who went to Germany as an "experimenter" in 1934 before leading a trip to Germany and Austria in 1936, and another to France in 1939. Shriver drew upon these experiences when he became director of the Peace Corps and enlisted Watt and the EIL to provide the formal training that volunteers like Herman De Bose underwent before they entered the field.)

Japan represented an important setting for the EIL's work. The events of the 1940s—the Japanese attack on Pearl Harbor, World War II, and the U.S. nuclear bombing of Hiroshima and Nagasaki—meant even the idea of friendship between the two countries and their citizens seemed preposterous. But Japan's acceptance of the Potsdam Declaration and effective surrender to the United States–led Allies helped to usher in a new era. The relationship was still fraught, of course: Losing the war was painful to the Japanese, who were now living under a U.S. occupation and beholden to military personnel who dictated the terms of their future. At the same time, under the leadership of Douglas MacArthur, general of the army, Japan transitioned from empire to democracy: Women gained the right to vote and entered the workforce in greater numbers, trade unionism flourished, young people were schooled in democratic ideals, and pacifism became the prevailing ethos.

Whether the U.S. occupation was, on balance, baneful or benign depended on both the attitudes of individual Japanese and the behavior of individual American soldiers. As one Japanese man put it, "I used to hate the Americans because we lost." Some saw the American presence as a colonial enterprise and despaired at witnessing criminal activities among soldiers, including sexual assaults of local women and the selling of black-market goods to criminal gangs. The soldiers, to their minds, were living up to the worst stereotypes of wartime propaganda.

Others were fascinated with the soldiers, "who came in all colors," and appreciated getting chocolates and cigarettes from them, playing baseball and football, and practicing their English. They were also drawn to the music and films they brought with them, which started a love affair with U.S. popular culture that would last for decades. Some even had love affairs with soldiers.

By the time the occupation ended in 1952, the two countries not only shared a complicated relationship but were entering into a future in which the United States would maintain a strong military presence on bases scattered throughout Japan, under the terms of a military alliance that still exists today. The EIL program of the 1950s was keenly aware of matters of the past, present, and future, and in 1956, Watt led a group of five American women to Kanazawa. It was no accident that the organization's first program in the country following the departure of U.S. soldiers would be exclusively for (white) women, but over time the programs came to include men. Years later, they would also start to reflect the racial diversity of the United States.

Kim arrived in Tokyo two decades after that first program, in the summer of 1976. Like many Americans Kim's age, who were born after the end of the U.S. occupation, his first real introduction to the country came during the 1964 Summer Olympics, which marked Japan's modern debut on the world stage. It showcased a vast infrastructure complete with skyscrapers, public transit, shopping districts, and enough venues to comfortably host athletes and spectators from around the world. When Kim landed at Tokyo International Airport during the summer of 1976, he felt an instant sense of recognition. "I was just in love with Japan the minute I stepped off the airplane. I thought, 'Wow, yup. This is what I thought.' "

He and his fellow students spent a few days in an EIL orientation session during which, Kim said, "they tried to teach us some words and a few basic phrases in Japanese so we could get to the bathroom and find some food, or what have you." They worked from a little red book filled with vocabulary and common phrases, doing drills and practicing bits of dialogue. "And out we went."

Over the course of the summer, he stayed with two host families outside of Tokyo. For someone accustomed, like most Americans in the 1970s, to a breakfast of eggs, sugary cereals, and pancakes, it was strange to wake up the first morning of his homestay to a tray of fish, miso soup, rice, and pickled vegetables. "Hm," he thought to himself. "Didn't we have this last night?" But he'd dutifully eat, thank his host family, and head out for a day of calligraphy workshops and martial arts classes. The latter turned out to be just the thing to reorient his thinking about the most important meal of the day. "After a couple of days of training hard, you're so hungry, you couldn't wait to get that fish and miso soup for breakfast. . . . It was terrific."

The martial arts training also awoke in him an appreciation for traditional, disciplined study. Both would come in handy over the years, but he didn't realize it at the time. His focus at that point was extending the experience of that summer for as long as possible, even after it had come to an end and it was time to head back to the United States, where he would spend the rest of the summer with his family before heading back to school. Kim thought to himself: "Okay, what I want to do is see more of the world. I still want to become a filmmaker." He told me, "I made the decision not to go back to school and the East Coast." Instead, he aimed for California. "I got off the plane in San Francisco, broke, completely broke, but I had left a hundred dollars in the bank back in Utica, New York. And I had my mom send me that . . . and I thought, 'Okay, I'm going to be in San Francisco. And then I'm going to eventually make my way to Los Angeles.'"

Kim needed a job and a place to stay while he figured out how to get to Hollywood. He pounded the pavement until he got hired to wash dishes at Fisherman's Wharf and found a bed in a boardinghouse a fifteen-minute bus ride away. For reasons that felt more nostalgic than mission driven, the little red phrasebook from his summer in Tokyo proved a constant companion. Night after night, with a kind of religious devotion, he'd study the words and phrases on its pages.

With mounting confidence, Kim eventually took his skills to Japantown. Located in San Francisco's Western Addition neighborhood, it was one of the first communities in the United States that was settled by Japanese immigrants. There was a pedestrian walkway lined with cherry blossom trees, teahouses, a bookstore, and a noodle shop where Kim could order the cheapest thing on the menu and spend hours speaking Japanese to the staff.

One day, his roommate at the boarding house told Kim about an international charter airline that was hiring flight attendants. Among the many countries it serviced was Japan, and one of the qualifications was the ability to speak a second language. Kim took his chance at applying. When he got a call back to schedule a language test, he enlisted his favorite server at the noodle shop to help him learn how to say, "Welcome aboard," "Fasten your seatbelts," and "Please place your carry-on items beneath the seats or in the overhead bins." Looking back, Kim marveled at the coup. "I actually passed the test."

Kim loved working for the airline. In addition to getting to fly in and out of Japan every once in a while, he took advantage of employee privileges on flights to different corners of the globe. After two and a half years, though, he was ready to spend more time on solid ground. Armed with the confidence of his language skills, he boarded a Tokyo-bound Japan Airlines flight with a 99-dollar round-trip ticket that would expire in one year.

AS SERVICEABLE AS KIM'S Japanese was when he returned to Tokyo in 1980, with so much local competition, he still had a lot to learn before getting hired doing anything in the language. In contrast, there was plenty of work for English speakers to help train the country's workforce to connect to the world beyond Japan's borders. He quickly found a job teaching English-language conversation to undergraduates at Sunshine Language College in Otsuka, on Tokyo's north end.

A job was no guarantee of finding housing, however, since local landlords were hesitant to rent to him. As Kim saw it, this was not so much a result of lingering anti-American sentiment from the occupation, or even racism.

Instead, it reflected a concern that foreign renters might not embrace their norms. "Starting with, you don't wear shoes inside, right? And are you going to be quiet? They don't want their other residents to be disturbed or to feel uncomfortable," he said.

Still, these kinds of challenges spoke to the insularity of Japanese society in the 1980s, when foreigners still made up a minuscule percentage of the population and had few paths to citizenship (even Koreans whose families had lived in Japan for more than one generation could not attain citizenship). Unsurprisingly, one landlord after another hung up on Kim before he could even properly ask about the units he saw advertised for rent. Finally, he learned from another English teacher about a wealthy landlady who owned a couple of apartment buildings around Otsuka. She was an open-minded woman who was curious about the West and even sent her daughter to Europe on shopping trips. On occasion she was amenable to renting a unit or two out to foreigners.

His colleague brokered an introduction. Right away, the landlady appreciated Kim's diffidence and language skills and agreed to let him a unit. When it was time to pay rent each month, he would join the other tenants in the ritual of ringing her front gate and respectfully handing over their payments, in envelopes, while she recorded the transactions in her notebook. But over the course of these visits Kim made an impression on the landlady, and soon enough she invited him to step through the gates, past the lush garden, and into her living room, which she decorated with Western furnishings and where she served biscuits and cake and tea over conversation about their lives and the greater world.

He developed a similar bond with an *obaachan,* or grandmother, he'd see on his early morning walks to the neighborhood dojo before school. *"Gaijin,"* she said one day, using the local word for "foreigner," "walk with me." She peppered him with questions: "You're an American, right?" followed by "And you're a *kokujin* [literally, person with black skin]?" Then they traded comments about the weather before parting ways. With that, the unusual pair established the broad outlines of the daily walks and conversations that would follow, which covered Japan, the United States, race, and more quotidian topics like the weather and their favorite foods.

Kim's experiences with the landlady and grandmother were a product of both who he was—respectful of the culture, fluent in the language, curious about his hosts, and open to meaningful exchanges with them—and who he was *not.* When he would join his co-workers and students from Sunshine Language College at bars and clubs in Roppongi, the nightlife district, he couldn't help but notice the English-language signs posted outside: "No Military Allowed."

These signs reflected a combination of locals' attitudes and soldiers' behaviors (both real and imagined). Taking in Kim's brown skin and short-cut Afro, bouncers or bartenders would assume he was a soldier, since unlike the white Americans who arrived as students and teachers and tourists and businessmen and soldiers alike, the majority of African Americans who were in the country were there as part of the military. It was only once he started speaking in Japanese that he would be treated to the kind of hospitality to which he'd grown accustomed.

Kim's arrival in Japan coincided with the moment when Black musical acts from the United States were becoming global superstars. The Jackson Five and Stevie Wonder were making concert stops in Tokyo, and the city hosted its own music festival where it awarded prizes to top acts. One publication described Japan as "jazz crazed," although the same could be said for the country's relationship to R&B, disco, and pop music. But there was no denying the appreciation young Japanese people had for Black music, which could sometimes lead down uglier paths. The 1970s and '80s saw the rise of Japanese "doo-wop" groups like the Chanels and Gosperats. Their members wore blackface and Afro wigs, touring the country in front of sold-out crowds of adoring fans. It was a time when African American culture was finding sources of emulation in Japan, but those emulations were often disconnected from the realities and reactions of ordinary people like Kim, since the exposure of most Japanese people to African Americans would be through either the U.S. military or mass media. The latter, in fact, was how many would come to know Kim himself.

A new teacher at Sunshine Language College needed help. She was the daughter of a Chinese actress who'd spent time in Japan making movies, but not even her mom's connections to the film industry could help her find a place to live. Kim returned the favor paid to him when he was looking for an apartment by helping her get an in with his landlady.

By this point, his round-trip ticket had expired, and he'd made the decision not to buy a return ticket to the United States. He was happy with this life in Japan, from his apartment and daily walks with the *obaachan* to his teaching job and nights on the town.

One afternoon, the colleague from his teaching job—now his neighbor—stopped by with a family friend, Junichi Takahashi. Takahashi and the colleague's mother went way back, and he'd stopped by to see how the young woman was getting along so he could report back to his old friend. He also seemed curious about the American who'd helped her get an apartment.

Standing in his doorway, Kim gamely chatted with Takahashi, first in English then in Japanese. Takahashi was impressed. "What are your plans?" he asked. Kim hadn't surrendered his childhood vision; his reply was prompt and confident: "I'm going to be an actor and filmmaker." It turned out that Takahashi was a producer and casting director. "Give me your contact information," he said to Kim. "You know, sometimes things come up; maybe I'll have something for you."

Takahashi called a couple of months later. He did have something for Kim: a small part in a TV movie about a Japanese heiress named Miki Sawada, who in 1948 founded the Elizabeth Saunders Home to house abandoned *konketsuji*. The term had its roots in the U.S. occupation, referring to children (primarily but not exclusively) born to Japanese women and American soldiers. So many of them had been orphaned because of prejudice on the part of both the United States and Japan. The U.S. Army did not permit marriages between soldiers and Japanese women unless they could take their wives home, which was a convenient way of prohibiting marriages without doing so outright, since Asians had been barred from entering the United States as of 1924. There was a brief exception to this rule in 1947 and with the 1952 McCarran-Walter Act, which permitted soldiers to marry and take their wives to the United States. But the law was not the only obstacle to long-term relationships: Japanese families often steered their daughters away from American soldiers or rejected the young women who defied their wishes. This was especially true when those relationships produced children, which they often did.

The existence of the term *konketsuji* belied the fact that there was no meaningful place for them in Japanese society, where citizenship was determined by the father. The *konketsuji* who were unclaimed or left behind by their fathers when the occupation ended in 1952 faced heartbreaking social exclusion: They could be refused admission to nursery school, kept from attending high school or college, and faced with high unemployment. The discrimination was even more pronounced for those with Black fathers. Even the mothers who fought hard to raise their children despite familial rejection struggled against these long odds. Landlords would refuse to rent to them, and other men would reject them as marriage partners.

The Elizabeth Saunders Home was meant to provide a refuge. In the 1980s, when Kim was set to play one of these (older) children in the onscreen retelling of the true story about the Elizabeth Saunders Home and its founder, Miki

Sawada, both enjoyed a glowing reputation for creating a refuge where *konketsuji* could be among their own kind. The message, as far as the broader Japanese culture was concerned, was clear: Their kind were not their mothers, or any family members on their mothers' sides. They only had one another.

Where were they supposed to go when they aged out of the orphanage? The TV movie had one answer: They would reunite with their fathers. The happy ending for Kim's character came on the eve of his eighteenth birthday, when his long-lost father came back to Japan to reclaim him and take him to his "real" home.

This was in keeping with prevailing political ideologies. In 1952, the leader of the Japan Socialist Party had a message for the departing Americans: "Take them and go home to [America]. Take responsibility and take them with you." Sawada had other answers. She worked hard to convince African American families in the United States to adopt the children, and seemed to delight in reporting having placed one in a "trash-ridden black ghetto" in Little Rock, Arkansas. That she somehow embraced the vernacular of the era's white conservatives in the United States was thanks, perhaps, to the same circulation of U.S. mass media that exposed the Japanese to African American music. "The happiest fate for a black *konketsuji*," Sawada once said, "is to be adopted by black people." With a missionary-like zeal, she played an active role in separating these children from their mothers, including founding a labor colony in Brazil that would be worked by *konketsuji*.

As far as many Japanese were concerned, the *konketsuji*

looked like their fathers, even if their faces—and their mothers—told a different story. The country's Ministry of Welfare codified this way of thinking, classifying 84 percent of *konketsuji* in a nationwide survey as white and 14 percent as Black (a term that referred to Americans with African ancestry), while leaving the other 2 percent unlabeled. Given all this, it's not surprising that Kim was cast despite not being *konketsuji* or even looking Amerasian.

That first role was relatively small, requiring Kim for just a few scenes. But it quickly led to others, from stage plays around Tokyo to a part in the nighttime soap *Chotto Kamisama* (in English, *A Little Like God*), in which he played an American design student married to a Japanese woman whose family frowns upon the union and the baby they have together. When the woman dies suddenly, Kim's character is bereft. He's also broke and moves in with his wife's family. Kim's character and his brother-in-law attempt to forge peace with each other and secure a future for the child in the family, but Kim's character eventually decides to make the choice to return to the United States and leave his son behind in Japan, promising to return someday once he is financially stable.

The title of the show refers to the brother-in-law character, a kind of martyr who, Kim said, "always sacrificed his own happiness, his own love interest, in order to keep his family whole. He had a father who had gone off the rails, so he kept his mother and his sister safe and secure in their home. He kept the house. He was trying to take care of his sister." And since he couldn't do that, he resolves to take care of his nephew. Before Kim's character leaves, he asks his brother-in-law what will happen if a woman refuses to marry him because of the color of his nephew's skin. "I wouldn't marry a woman like that who wouldn't accept this child," the man replies.

The episodes of *Chotto Kamisama* made an immediate impact when they aired. The real-life mother of the baby who played his character's son had spent time on the set, and Kim stayed in touch with her after filming. The baby was actually a little girl whose father, the Japanese woman's husband, was an African American GI stationed in Japan. The Japanese woman's parents had disowned her for marrying a Black man and refused to even meet the little girl.

One night, the young mother called home to ask her parents if they watched the show. Who didn't? Like millions of others, they had. "That's your grandchild," she told them before quickly hanging up. Later, the Japanese woman called Kim to tell him the news: "My parents called me, and they told me to come home and to bring their grandchild."

Things changed for Kim after his role on *Chotto Kamisama,* and whenever he left his apartment to go on auditions, attend script meetings, take martial arts classes, and head to Sunshine Language College, where he continued teaching English, fans would stop him to ask for a photo or an autograph or to strike up a conversation with him in Japanese. Taking all this in during a visit to profile him in 1982, a writer from *Ebony* magazine referred to Kim as "one of Tokyo's favorite sons."

The locals' enthusiasm was only partly explained by the fact of Kim's frequent presence on television, where he spoke in the fluent Japanese he'd been studying and practic-

ing for several years. The other, more meaningful explanation lay in what his characters reflected back at the people
who were watching. The orphaned boy, the widowed father, and the sophisticated detective each served in different
ways to help Japanese audiences see their own country's
history, culture, and fraught connections to the United
States in all their complex dimensions.

His newfound fame also allowed for a bit of fun. When
the disco at Tokyo Disneyland had its grand opening in
April 1983 and was off to a slow start, it was Kim's job to get
things moving. On a typical workday, customers stood
around stirring their drinks, idly listening to music, and def-
initely not dancing. Then Kim would emerge on a lift that
rose from the basement, resplendent in a halo of fog and
disco lights. "You have to picture me in this silver suit, silver
boots, and Afro," he later told me. The effect produced by
this spectacle was almost immediate: A jolt of energy would
pass through the crowd; Kim would ask, in fluent Japanese,
"Are you ready to party?" before doing the moonwalk on his
platform; two DJs on either side of him would turn up the
music; and then, finally, there would be a stampede to the
dance floor where everyone threw arms in the air, tossed
their heads back, and surrendered to the beat. After that,
Kim would go to his dressing room (it had his name on a
star over the door), change clothes, and ride home in the
back of a chauffeured town car.

Then came his biggest break: a part in *The Protector,* a
movie starring Jackie Chan and Danny Aiello as a pair of
cops from New York out to rescue a kidnapped girl. It was

a supporting role, but one that would allow him to put his martial arts training to the test alongside one of the world's greats, since his character helps Chan and Aiello fight off some local toughs. The film was slated for distribution via Warner Bros., meaning that Kim's family, friends, and, more important, casting directors back home would see it.

It filmed on location in Hong Kong. After years of being able to work around his Sunshine Language College teaching schedule, Kim took some time off, packed his bags, and hopped on a plane. Back in Tokyo after filming, Kim felt like he was on the brink of U.S. stardom, or at least a break in Hollywood. And he wanted to be there for it, so after five years in Japan, he finally moved to Los Angeles.

It was early 1985 and the movie was slated to come out in the summer. To tide himself over between auditions and until his big moment, he found work in an office where they needed a Japanese speaker. He was there, in fact, the day *The Protector* came out. "It was only in one theater, downtown in L.A., not even in a great theater anywhere." The early buzz was not good, but it was still a Jackie Chan vehicle, which meant that his mom was able to take a train from Utica to see it in New York City. "My picture was even on the marquee, along with all the other actors. And while she's doing that, I'm literally at my minimum-wage job. . . . After my job was over at the end of the day, then with a friend, I could go to the movie theater and see a movie that I was in." He parked at a metered spot, just like everyone else.

The movie was ultimately a box-office disappointment, both in the United States and in Asia, though it did better in the latter. Kim was disappointed but undeterred. He bought a book on screenplay writing, borrowed a friend's computer, and got to work on a screenplay. It was a high-concept story about Vietnam War–era soldiers who were part of a government experiment that put them in a cryogenic sleep for thirty years before sending them out to fight another war. He wrote a part for himself, as one of the soldiers who slowly comes to the realization that he's being used— again—by his own government.

The script sold quickly, and even though it never made it to screens it kick-started Kim's career as a screenwriter. A few meetings led him to Keenen Ivory Wayans, who was starting a new sketch comedy show called *In Living Color* and hired Kim as a writer. Other jobs followed, which helped him to think about having a show of his own. He created *Sister, Sister,* which was loosely based on his own sisters, and *Kenan & Kel.* Both shows helped usher in a new era of television, introducing diverse Black people and families to mainstream U.S. audiences. Kim has gone on to become a successful independent writer-director of such films as *Kill Speed, Junkyard Dog, Tyson's Run,* and *A Snowy Day in Oakland.*

Kim's years in Japan are never far from his thoughts. His latest inspiration comes from the sixteenth century, when an enslaved African man named Yasuke arrived in Japan in 1579 in the service of a Jesuit missionary and became a successful samurai warrior in service to Oda Nobunaga, perhaps the most consequential warlord in Japanese history. Like Kim, Yasuke was born into circumstances that overly constrained his present and future until an opportunity came along for him to carefully study the ways of a new world, developing an understanding of their language and martial arts until his talents and drive helped him reach heights that were never meant for him.

Walking
the Spirit

STANDING NEAR THE ENTRANCE of L'église de la Madeleine, his back to the grand neoclassical church that looms over rue Royale in Paris's eighth arrondissement, our tour guide faced a small crowd assembled on the steps below. He slid a printout from the laminated sleeve of a binder he'd been carrying around in the crook of his arm all day. It yielded a copy of an old black-and-white photo of a little girl who looked to be around three years old. "Does anyone know who this is?"

I thought back to a few hours earlier when our tour group sat in a café near the Arc de Triomphe. While we sipped coffee and pulled at croissants, our guide passed around a small stack of papers. I expected an itinerary outlining the sites and stops that lay ahead for our daylong tour. But instead, it was a quiz. At the top was a question: "Which of these notable African Americans, past and present, has lived in or spent significant time in Paris?" It was followed by four columns of more than fifty names.

A consummate teacher's pet, I immediately dug a pen out of my purse and got to work. As I set about circling names that I'd come across in my own research for this book, the point of the exercise started to dawn on me. If I'd kept it up, I would have circled every single name on the page, from Sally Hemings to Ta-Nehisi Coates.

Hours later, outside at the church, I climbed up a couple of steps to get a closer angle on the photo. It looked like an albumen silver print, the kind that was popular in landscape and portrait photography in the late nineteenth and early twentieth centuries. The chubby-cheeked girl sits in an adult-sized wooden chair, wearing a billowy white poplin dress. She looks intently into a distance just to the left of where the photographer would have stood, as though mesmerized by a parent or studio assistant trying to keep her calm and steady during the long sitting process.

The little girl was named Freda Josephine McDonald. After marrying as a teenager and setting out for a career in entertainment, she started going by the more stage-friendly moniker of Josephine Baker. Following her death at age sixty-eight on April 12, 1975, the church was the site of her funeral Mass, which made her the first woman, and the first African American, in its history to receive such an honor. As she lay in state in a space typically reserved for royals and statesmen, tens of thousands of mourners—including her former husband Jo Bouillon and their twelve adopted children—came out to pay their final respects.

The proceedings were captured by reporters and photographers from around the world. Charles L. Sanders detailed the ceremony that greeted the occasion for *Ebony* magazine. The multipage, photo-heavy spread titled "A Farewell to Josephine: France Pays a Final Tribute to One of

Its Greatest Stars" captured flag-bearers dipping their colors in honor of Baker's service to the French Resistance during World War II, and the military decorations that adorned her casket. The article noted that Baker, who "always had a great appreciation for the grandeur, flair and style with which the French do almost everything," would have loved the farewell she received in her adopted homeland.

Nearly forty-five years after that moment, on a brisk afternoon in November 2019, I joined a small group of my family, friends, and fellow travelers who'd flown in from Washington, D.C., Philadelphia, New York, and Toronto to pay our own respects, not just to Josephine Baker but to the other African Americans who at various points had called the city home. All of this was made possible thanks to Black Paris Tours, a Black-owned company that helps visitors retrace the steps of African Americans who've made their mark on the City of Light.

For a city that remains a premier destination for Americans, and for which travel influencers, magazines, and agencies jockey to spotlight unique, off-the-beaten-path experiences, Black Paris seems to belong almost exclusively to Black travelers. I admit: After seeing so much imagery of Paris that featured white tourists and white Parisians, it felt nice being centered and catered to.

Ricki Stevenson's company is not the only one to recognize the interest in Black Paris. There's also Walking the Spirit Tours, which was founded by Julia Browne. A Black woman who was born in England and raised in Canada, Browne was bringing up her daughters in Paris with her

French husband when she decided to take a class at the Sorbonne. In it, she learned about "the jazz musicians, entertainers, writers and artists who had found personal and professional fulfillment in Paris," and in 1994 she started offering tours covering the who, where, and why of the African American experience in the city. In the beginning, she offered a kind of kitchen-sink tour that spanned the eighteenth century to the present, covering Alexandre Dumas, Josephine Baker, and two centuries' worth of names in between, all while crisscrossing the city's Left and Right Banks. In the decades since, Browne has expanded her operation to include a wider and more focused range of tour types, including a Colonialism, Slavery & Anti-Slavery Walk, an Africa in Paris tour, and an Entertainers in 1920s Lower Montmartre tour, which I took in February 2020.

This time I was with Anna, my (white) best friend from high school. We'd both visited Paris for the first time on a school trip in 1995, just a year after Walking the Spirit was founded. We hadn't heard of it then.

Our guide was Christina Maximoff, a born-and-bred Black Parisian. Anna and I were her only guests that day. One of our stops was at the top of one of Montmartre's many hilly streets, at the corner of rue Blanche and rue de Calais. We stood across the street from a vacant, nondescript building.

It was the former site of Chez Florence, which in the 1920s was one of the neighborhood's most popular nightclubs. Then-owner Louis Mitchell had named it in honor of the American cabaret singer Florence Emery "Embry"

Jones, who regularly took the stage there.* Maximoff told a story about one of the nightclub's most notorious incidents.

It involved New Orleans–born jazz clarinetist and saxophone player Sidney Bechet, who'd come to Paris with Josephine Baker as part of the *Revue nègre,* stayed on a couple of years, and ended up in an alcohol-fueled dispute at Chez Florence. A gun went off and Bechet was arrested; eventually he was deported to the United States. After an outcry from local friends, his deportation was ultimately reversed and Bechet returned to great fanfare a few years later, hosting a New Orleans–style wedding reception for himself and his new bride a few blocks away from where we stood.

A thirty-something Black man hung on the fringes of our small, loose assemblage. When Maximoff paused to let us take in the scene, he asked her, in French, if she was a tour guide. Then he turned to me and Anna and asked, in the English he'd overheard us speaking, where we were from. It turned out that he had lived for some time in the United States, back when he first left Senegal. He had family there, but Paris ultimately seemed more welcoming to him. And so there we all stood, on this street of this neighborhood that flowed with so much Black history in multiple directions, up and down the hill like rivulets of rain, forming our own points on a diasporic journey.

---

* "Embry" was the way Langston Hughes spelled "Emery," and the spelling stuck through the years.

CHAPTER 8

THE TOUR GUIDE

Ricki Stevenson,

PARIS, 1990S

WHEN RICKI STEVENSON LANDED in Paris for the first time in 1992, on a trip paid for by her employer to film a series of travel segments, it was the fulfillment of a life-long dream. As a little girl in East Palo Alto, California, in the 1950s, she'd grown up hearing about the city and the home it gave to scores of African Americans, from an uncle who served there during World War I to luminaries like Josephine Baker. Ricki's mother had trained as a dancer and long admired Baker in particular, whose steps she hoped to one day retrace on a visit. Ricki recalled her mother often saying, "I wonder what the weather's like in Paris today," which infused the city with a romantic, mysterious quality. Soon, mother and daughter shared the same hope of strolling the streets of Montmartre and feeling transported to the heady days of the early twentieth century.

The seed of becoming a journalist was also planted

during Ricki's childhood. In 1959, when she was around twelve years old, Ricki watched an episode of the *Today* show. It was a segment featuring a man named Eugene Bullard, who was born in Georgia in 1895 and ended up in Europe after leaving home and stowing away on a German freighter. He traversed the continent while making a living as a vaudeville performer and boxer before ending up in Paris in 1913 for a match. As World War I got under way, he enlisted in the French Foreign Legion, becoming one of the first African American military pilots to fly in combat. He attempted to join the U.S. Army Air Service when his own country entered the war but was rejected because African Americans were mostly confined to support troops at the time.

After the war, Bullard remained in Paris, where he owned and operated Le Grand Duc club and became a fixture in the city's nightlife during the 1920s and '30s. Then came World War II. Bullard enlisted, this time serving as a machine gunner.

After World War II, he returned to the United States, and one summer evening in 1949, he was leaving a Paul Robeson concert in Westchester County, New York. Robeson had by then been labeled a Communist in the United States after expressing support for the Soviet Union's treatment of African Americans, and a white mob was forming at the gates. When Bullard and other Black attendees exited, they were brutally beaten by the men. "Go on back to Russia, you [n*****s,]" they shouted.

This was his reward for putting his life on the line for his country—which brings us back to that *Today* show appearance. Bullard was wearing a crisp uniform. "You look hand-some and dashing," host Dave Garroway told him, before pointing out the name on it: Rockefeller Center. Bullard worked as an elevator porter at 30 Rockefeller Plaza, where he would chat with his passengers on rides up and down the building's sixty-six floors, sharing enough tidbits about his past to attract the interest of someone at NBC, who understood what a remarkable life Bullard had lived and invited him to appear on the show for an extended inter-view.

"This makes no sense," Ricki recalled saying to her mother, with whom she sat and watched the segment as it aired on live television. How could this war hero, with his incredible and glamorous life story, have ended up stuck in an elevator all day? And why wasn't Garroway asking *that* question, or acknowledging *that* injustice, instead of treat-ing Bullard's past like it was a charming parlor trick to trot out and indulge before sending him back to the elevator shaft? Ricki vowed to become the kind of journalist who would ask the important questions.

Ricki's sense of outrage, or maybe injustice, was rooted in the strong sense of pride in her people and their collec-tive history that she had developed in early childhood. Her parents had met in San Francisco (her father had moved there from Oklahoma, after joining the navy, while her mother had moved there to become a dancer after growing up in Hot Springs, Arkansas, and Denver, Colorado) and raised Ricki in a home, first in Oakland and then in East Palo Alto, filled with pictures of family, friends, and famous African Americans her mother had met during her career, including the musician Louis Armstrong (who himself had spent time in Paris).

During her childhood, Ricki traveled with her parents to see Josephine Baker on tour in San Diego and hear James Baldwin give a lecture at Stanford University after her family moved to nearby East Palo Alto. After finishing high school and attending Regis University in Denver, Ricki returned to Stanford's campus, this time as a graduate student. There, she sampled from a buffet of educational experiences that included exploring the work of Richard Wright, researching the history of slavery and slave rebellion in Jamaica, and studying abroad in Haiti to explore the legacy of Toussaint-Louverture and the Haitian Revolution that he helped to lead, which resulted in the creation of the first independent Black republic. It was a truly diasporic education. "I had some friends at Stanford, a brother and sister who were from Haiti, and they were like 'come on!' That's when I learned, whenever you have friends in different places, if they say 'come go,' you go."

All of this provided the perfect background for a subsequent five-year stint as a United Nations reporter with the National Black Network, which was the first independent Black radio network in the country. She worked alongside Malvin Russell Goode, who was the first Black network correspondent in the country. (Goode's relatives John and Franke Goode had joined Oliver Golden, Joseph Roane, and many other African Americans who went to the Soviet Union in the 1930s, where the Goodes' sister Eslanda and her husband, Paul Robeson, paid a visit in 1934.)

After covering the United Nations, Ricki went on to produce the *Ossie Davis and Ruby Dee Story Hour* from 1974 to 1975, and later hosted a show of her own, *Black Issues and the Black Press*. By the 1990s, she had been married, lived with her husband and daughter in Saudi Arabia, and gotten divorced.

THEN SHE LANDED A JOB as a travel reporter for an NBC affiliate in San Francisco. Recalling her first few days, she said that the network bosses called her into a meeting. "Ricki," they said, "you're Black. And you're the only woman. We're going to be sending you around the world, and you don't know what you're going to run into."

Ricki laughed. She knew exactly what she was going to run into. "Having lived in Saudi Arabia," she told me, "and having gone to all these different places, I knew that I was treated really special in other countries, far better than the treatment I got in the United States. And that's what happened working for them: The only time I ever had challenges would be in America. But traveling all over the world? Never a problem. *Never* a problem."

Still, she had not yet made it to Paris. By the time the network sent her on that first trip, she was in her late forties. The network had put her up at a hotel in the eleventh arrondissement, and over the course of the next several days it was a base from which to provide viewers with a survey of all the city had to offer to middle- and upper-middle-class tourists in the 1990s. Ricki covered everything, including where to check out the latest fashions. She took classes at the École de Gastronomie Française Ritz-Escoffier, a cook-

ing school located in the Ritz hotel on the Place Vendôme
near the iconic Tuileries Garden. Diploma-seeking students
from across the globe paid upward of $700 a week to study,
but the school also offered cooking demonstrations and
one-time workshops for visitors interested in learning how
to make traditional holiday meals, mastering the art of
French pastry, and deciphering the rules of pairing cheese
and wine.

Ricki also got to experience the high-speed Train à
Grande Vitesse, or TGV, which had opened a little more
than a decade earlier to connect Paris to other parts of
France, like Toulouse, Bordeaux, and Marseille, and other
European capitals. On her outing, Ricki went to Disneyland
Paris, which had just opened in 1992 (following the successful debut of Tokyo Disneyland in the 1980s) in Chessy, a
suburb outside of Paris that was now quickly accessible via
high-speed rail. The vast complex came complete with an
ice-skating rink modeled after Rockefeller Center's, a Davy
Crockett playground, themed rides, shops selling Little
Mermaid and Mickey Mouse merchandise, and six hotels. It
had cost the Walt Disney Company more than $4.4 billion
to build and was a magnet for controversy before it even
opened. The announcement of Disney's public offering at
the Paris Bourse (stock exchange) was met with protest
signs reading "Mickey Go Home," and one French intellectual characterized the park's arrival as "a cultural Chernobyl." But the lure of Mickey was strong. Thanks to
coverage in the travel press, from Ricki and other Americans as well as European visitors, Disneyland Paris would
become a juggernaut for French tourism.

In addition to being an enjoyable visit filled with fashion, food, and American-style fun, Ricki's trip checked the most important box of all: She had finally made it to Paris, with her mother, who had passed, joining her in spirit. Her mother's absence added to a more generalized sense that something was missing from the experience. After spending more than half her life associating the city with people like Josephine Baker, Eugene Bullard, James Baldwin, and Louis Armstrong, African Americans who had made their way to and left their marks on the city, Ricki found hardly any signs of them anywhere. Sure, you could go to Montmartre to try to conjure up Baker and Bullard while experiencing the district's modern nightlife, or to Les Deux Magots, the Left Bank café where Richard Wright and Baldwin spent their time, to try to recapture the energy of their first thrilling visits, but you had to know where to look. No guidebook or travel segment would be much help.

Still, Ricki soaked up as much as she could of Paris, for herself and for her mother. She even nurtured a growing fantasy to move there someday and was prepared to let this one thrilling visit sustain her for the foreseeable future until a toothache changed everything. The pain was so overwhelming that Ricki couldn't wait until she got home to attend to it, so she found a dentist near the hotel, worrying the whole time about how much it would all cost her. When she braced herself for the office receptionist to hand over the bill, she was stunned to learn that the treatment had cost her nothing. Here was a moment that put the practical features of living in Paris into relief, making a burgeoning fantasy seem like a conceivable reality.

She went back to the network and put in for a leave of absence. Her plan was for her and her eleven-year-old daughter, Dede, to live in Paris for one year. Almost as soon as Ricki had settled in the city and enrolled her daughter in fifth grade, her friends and family wanted to visit. Within weeks, she was leading guests around her new hometown.

Having Ricki as a host meant more than simply stopping by her favorite cafés, restaurants, and parks—it meant getting the lessons she'd spent a lifetime preparing to give. She pointed out the streets where men like her uncle and his fellow soldiers congregated during World War I, the venues where Josephine Baker performed, the site of Bullard's nightclub, the bookstore Richard Wright opened, and the monument to Alexandre Dumas, author of *The Three Musketeers* and *The Count of Monte Cristo*, whose father was born to an enslaved woman in the French colony of Saint-Domingue (now Haiti). At each stop she provided stories fleshed out with details from her sessions poring over books at the American Library in Paris while she waited for Dede to finish school.

The timing of Ricki's move and hosting duties turned out to be providential. France was the number one travel destination for Americans in the 1990s, and African Americans were starting to make up a large share of the tourist market there. Word spread among her family and friends, and friends of her family and friends, to get on her informal schedule. They were mostly baby boomers like herself, who had the time and disposable income to make the journey and who, just like her, wanted to see the Paris they'd heard about in their own families and collective cultural lore. With that, inspiration struck, and in 1993, barely a year after her first life-altering visit, she started Black Paris Tours. She touted the company as "a richly unique cultural experience, providing travelers with information, insight, and little-known facts about the wealth of Black history in Paris."

I SPOKE TO RICKI a few days after taking one of her company's tours in November 2019. We were sitting in (the now-closed) Cafe Fauve in the eleventh arrondissement, near the hotel where she'd first stayed back in 1992. Afrobeat played softly in the background, providing a fitting soundtrack to a conversation that was ultimately about our—hers, mine, and the Ivory Coast–born owners'—place in, and movements through, the African Diaspora.

Ricki was intentional in saying "Black history" and not just "African American history." It was in keeping with her own intellectual and cultural formation in the United States and now in Paris, where the Black presence goes back to the French Empire. Black people from African and West Indian colonies began making their way to and remaining in Paris and other parts of France as early as the seventeenth century, arriving as human property and free persons, and, later, as immigrants, students, and professionals. Their multigenerational presence in the country runs on a parallel track to the xenophobic racism that in the 1990s primarily took the form of opposing immigration from the Middle East and the Maghreb (but targeted West Africans and Asians as well), supporting the far-right National Front's calls for the eviction of non-white immigrants from France, and treating French-born Arabs and Blacks as noncitizens.

It didn't take long after moving to Paris for Ricki to notice that her experience of the city was not universal. "The Afro-French have a very different experience here," she told me. Janet McDonald, a lawyer, told *This American Life* host Ira Glass about having a similar realization after she moved to Paris from Brooklyn in the 1990s: "For African Americans, we're in a very bizarre position. It's almost like being an honorary white in apartheid South Africa. And I noticed that, as my French got better and better, sometimes I wasn't as well received as I would be if I played up my American accent."

To her Black Paris Tours guests, Ricki and her growing staff of tour guides point out the past and present forms of xenophobia, hostility, and economic exclusion faced by African and West Indian immigrants and Black French people alike. It's a guardrail against overly romanticizing the city and a reminder that, however alienated African Americans have felt from their Americanness in their home country, it offered undeniable protections in Paris.

At the same time, Ricki wants visitors to see the vibrant layers of Black Paris, and this remains a feature of the tour experience. On the day of my tour, our guide steered us through the neighborhood in the eighteenth arrondissement that makes up "Little Africa," where he told us that paper euro bills circulate, on average, ten times before they ever leave. We stopped for a late lunch of Senegalese *thieboudienne* (a fish and rice dish) and *yassa poulet* (stewed chicken with onions). Afterward, we had time to walk around, passing hair-braiding shops and travel agencies advertising flights to Dakar and Bamako, to ogle jewelry store counters lined with wooden bangles and gold necklaces, browse clothing boutiques filled with racks of colorfully printed dresses and skirts, and peek inside the windows of local nightspots.

Not for the first time that day, I wondered if Paris was home to a modern crop of Josephine Bakers, James Baldwins, and Richard Wrights, or if another place was beckoning. After all, the city had the lure of history and the push of the American present. Beyond the enduring struggle for freedom and justice, Black people in the United States were facing police violence and confronting the terrifying years of a presidency that was intent on rolling back the progress of the Obama administration and rejecting its promise of a true multiracial democracy. The message of "Make America Great Again" had loomed like a threat to Black Americans and anyone familiar with the country's dark history of slavery, Jim Crow, imperialism, nativism, and other past sins it had never apologized for. Was that what was so great? If so, as before, it might be time to say goodbye.

There Are Places in This World

SHE WAS ONLY THREE YEARS OLD the last time she made the journey to Salzburg more than sixty years ago. A child in the company of her mother and slightly older brother as they made their journey over land, across the ocean, and over land again for the children to reunite with their father and the mother with her husband, and together start a new life after the war. Now, as the only one of them who was still alive, she had to take the lead.

This time there were more of us. Joining my aunt Juanita (whose name is a feminized diminutive of her father's—my grandpa's—name, John) were her husband and two adult children; her tween granddaughter; her younger sister, the fourth youngest of nine; and the sister's two adult children, including me. We all stepped off the train from Munich, our first stop on this European tour and our home base for a day trip to Salzburg, into a sunny and warm but not hot July afternoon. I'd gotten us all this far in my role as our family's in-house travel agent, having made the lodging arrangements for Munich, scheduled a bus tour the morning we landed to occupy us until check-in, planned a couple of days' worth of visits to beer gardens and market stalls, and booked the train tickets for this pilgrimage to Salzburg. My plan was to hand over the reins to Aunt Juanita as soon as we arrived, so she could steer us around town and eventually to the yellow stone building at 17 Reichenhaller Straße, where she'd once lived as a girl.

We stepped out onto Südtiroler Platz, the busy square outside of the station. One by one we turned to look at her expectantly, waiting for some flash of recognition to cross her face and for the memories to start downloading, as if from an old internal hard drive magically unlocked by the sight of the grand castle and alpine mountains in the distance. When it didn't immediately come, when she couldn't suddenly steer us around town like a local, we figured she just needed more sensory input. As we shuffled behind her, our excited impatience almost pushing her in front of us and toward baroque churches, public squares, parklets, and street corners, the same questions would spill from our lips: Do you remember this? Do you have any stories for us?

It occurred to me after a few more of these stops and mental frisks that we were doing something familiar. In pressing her into the role of our tour guide, we were doing what so many of us do when we sign up for experiences like Walking the Spirit and Black Paris Tours. We're asking for someone to serve as a medium between past and present, a conjurer of our shared history who can take us along the same streets our forebears walked and help us travel back in time. To help us see what they saw, smell what they smelled, hear what they heard, and tap into how it all felt to get at what it all meant. We're all just trying to remember.

Something unlocked for me, too. I think it was because of an incident in Munich, at the hotel where I'd reserved us a block of serviced apartments. My cousin had missed his flight from the United States, so he and his daughter were going to be arriving at the hotel while the rest of us were sightseeing and day drinking. The front desk staff had been friendly and accommodating since the first morning of our arrivals, so before heading out for the day we left instructions to make sure they gave my cousin a key to one of our rooms. It wouldn't be a problem, the staff assured us. These things happen all the time.

As we sat down to lunch a few hours later, we received a confused text from my cousin saying that the receptionist and manager told him there was no one with our names at the hotel. Was he in the right place? A flurry of messages assured us all that while he may have been jet-lagged, he and his daughter were indeed where they were supposed to be. Finally, after I made an expensive call on my cellphone to the front desk, we cleared up what they vaguely described as "a confusion." It was difficult to imagine what could have been so confusing, considering that we were staying at a popular tourist hotel where the staff spoke impeccable English, and we had written out my cousin's full name on a sheet of paper so they could match it to his passport. Instead, it seemed that the receptionist took one look at him, a youngish man with dark skin and waist-length locs, and decided that he had no business being there.

We had come across plenty of Black people around Munich, especially in the multicultural neighborhood surrounding our aparthotel, with its Turkish, Vietnamese,

Ethiopian, Eritrean, Indian, and Chinese restaurants accessible within a few blocks, all serving customers hailing from the same regions as the food on the menus. That was the appeal of the location, to make sure we could minimize the ways we, a Black family of eight, might stand out and draw unwanted attention. What we hadn't realized was that there was an invisible, impenetrable line separating our aparthotel from the surrounding community. Or that our family would, however briefly, end up on two different sides of it.

Until recently, Germany made it hard to track instances of racism, in part because it made it so hard to track race itself. Since the end of World War II, the country had tried to officially distance itself from Nazi-like preoccupations with race, which meant that it rejected statistical measures of any sort, even when it came to tracking racial differences in job, education, and housing opportunities. The idea was "If you don't want to create racism, you have to avoid using categories." Everyone was simply German. But that also led to narrow definitions of what it meant to be German. The country's interior minister proposed an exclusive vision of German culture that did not include immigrants or any of their languages and cultures. "We don't do [the] burqa," he insisted.

A 2017 United Nations report on racism in Germany also drew attention to all the ways native Afro-Germans, Black students, tourists, and—especially—migrants arriving from economically depressed and conflict regions in Africa have experienced racism in the country. From the classroom to courtrooms, they encounter unequal treatment, racist stereotypes, and outright hostility. In other words, not only had the hotel staff come across Black people in Munich, it seemed they had a narrow sense of who among them was welcome to cross their threshold: the ones, like myself, the women in my family, and my uncle (who would take offense to being called a senior citizen but who benefited from his age and the company he arrived in), who were just passing through. We weren't trying to make Germany our home, to change it in any way, or to ask anything of it other than the opportunity to pay for the privilege of its hospitality. As far as my cousin was concerned, he was a youngish man who looked to the hotel staff like the people trying to get jobs, education, housing, and a sense of cultural inclusion—the same people who were asking for too much.

I had purposely avoided Airbnb to keep this kind of situation from casting a pall over our plans. Before the trip, I had read about incidents, in the United States and abroad, in which neighbors harassed Black guests trying to use keys and door codes to enter the homes and apartments they'd rented, sometimes even escalating the situation by calling the police. And that was in cases where Black guests were sufficiently lucky to get far enough in the process to even try to open the door. There were also reports of hosts canceling reservations when they found out the prospective guests were Black, or claiming that the selected dates were no longer available, nor were any others, unfortunately. The flaws in the company's "Belong Anywhere" argument were obvious: Only certain people could truly belong. I didn't want to be reminded of that on this trip, and yet here we were. No matter the pre-planning or precautions or passports, someone was always going to have a problem with us being Black.

The incident had been lingering in the back of our minds for days, and while we were walking through the streets of Salzburg I remembered and started to reframe a story Aunt Juanita used to tell us about the teacher at her school, the one who wouldn't let her or her brother, my Uncle Buddy, use the bathroom until they figured out how to ask to be excused in German. Hearing the story as a kid, I ascribed the teacher's behavior to the strictness of all teachers, dialed up to an extreme because it was the olden days. Wasn't every teacher stricter then? Later, when I heard it after having become a teacher myself, I compared it to my own Spanish teacher's effective habit of putting tape over the English subtitles when we watched movies like *El Norte* in class, which forced us to make sense of the dialogue on our own rather than rely on the translations. "I bet it helped them learn faster," I thought. But did it? And was that all there was to it, a teacher's pedagogical rigor? Or was there something else going on, some combination of resentment of the Americans' presence in Austria and anti-Blackness on the part of the teacher?

As if a mental trapdoor had opened, I thought back to something I'd read by a Black writer, podcaster, and TV personality named Ernest White a few years before, after the Florida man who shot and killed teenager Trayvon Martin in cold blood was acquitted by a jury in 2013. White issued an impassioned call to action. "Brothers and sisters," he wrote on his blog, *Fly Brother*, "if you don't have one already, you need to get yourself a passport." He urged his readers to consider that a fuller experience of equality and humanity can be found abroad rather than in the United States. "There are places in this world," he insisted, "where our presence isn't viewed as a menace, as a problem, or even as an inconvenience. There are places where we are welcomed, listened to, appreciated, and even loved."

White was not alone in thinking that a better life could be had elsewhere. The run-up to and outcome of the 2016 presidential election had brought an uptick in news coverage of African Americans, Jamaican Americans, Nigerian Americans, and other Black people from the United States who decided to leave the country behind or were at least considering it. One site, the Salt Collective, called it #BLAXIT, or a "Black Exit" from the United States. The writer Ulysses Burley III focused on "21 things we're taking with us if we leave," in a July 2016 post: "Where we will go, I don't know, but it's clear black lives don't matter here, and it's even more apparent that the powers that be are doing everything possible to make America white again (except America was never white to begin with)." The list itself was a mostly cheeky catalog of Black cultural influences on the United States, from basketball and Beyoncé to soul food and Shondaland, with inventors, Oprah, and the Obama family filling the spaces in between. But the sentiment behind it was serious: The country has always benefited from Black people's creativity while simultaneously denigrating our humanity.

More recently, the murders of George Floyd and Breonna Taylor, both at the hands of white police officers, exposed the enduring, relentless nature of the concerns that led Ernest White to pen his call to get out of the United States back in 2013. During the summer of 2020, Tiffanie Drayton wrote an op-ed in *The New York Times* explaining her and her mother's reasons for relocating to Trinidad and Tobago, where both were born and had left for the United States when the author was a little girl. She acknowledges the specificity of her experience: "The privilege of dual citizenship afforded me sanctuary in Trinidad and Tobago." This is not a privilege available to Ernest White or African Americans for whom the United States is the only country they can lay claim to as citizens. It doesn't mean that they cannot pursue lives beyond their native shores, of course, but it does suggest a different framework of possibilities.

That's why it's been so important for me to distinguish in this book between African Americans and first- and second-generation Black Americans who descend from African and Caribbean immigrants. Not to create hierarchies or competitions, but to signal relevant differences when it comes to moving and traveling abroad. As my friend Chinyere Osuji, a Nigerian American sociologist, put it: "Travel means something different if you're going to a place where your parents used to hang out or where you used to hang out when you were young." Where does someone who knows only the United States, whose family has only ever known it for as long as anyone can remember, even start to look for a new, more welcoming home? And does such a place even exist?

A similar set of questions seemed to drive the Blaxit coverage at *The Root,* a Black-oriented online magazine that has published a series of articles on logistical issues related to getting work visas and setting up foreign bank accounts, and others exploring what it might be like to live in places like New Zealand, Sweden, and Japan, as narrated by the expat writer Jennifer Neal and told from the perspectives of long-term émigrés as well as more recent arrivals. The variety of featured locales calls to mind a passage from *I Wonder as I Wander*, Langston Hughes's memoir of a journey that took him from the United States, the Caribbean, and Europe to places as far-flung as Tashkent and Tokyo. "Having since been around the world," he wrote of looking back on his initial shock at encountering Black people during his travels, "I have learned that there is at least one Negro everywhere."

That said, the diversity of their destinations belies a common thread running through Black people's experiences of them. Joelle Wells, who moved to Melbourne, Australia, from Kansas City, Missouri, told *The Root* that she was shocked by how white her new home city was, despite its reputation within Australia as a multicultural haven. "It is not diverse here. It's diverse for *Australia*." From the very beginning of her time there, being the only Black person as far as her or anyone's eyes could see made her a target. "Within the first two months of moving here, someone threw a rock at me and called me a monkey." Similarly, Reggie Robinson-Whaley, who moved to Seoul, South Korea, from Dallas for a teaching job, spoke of his students' regular attempts at "gorilla joke[s]" at his and other Black people's expense. And George Abasiute, Jr., a Nigerian Hungarian, shared typical encounters with Budapest locals who assume he cannot speak the language due to his race: "They use vulgar words like 'monkey,' but then I ask them in Hungarian why they do that and they apologize and [walk away] . . . man, it happens all the time."

Yet when it comes to living abroad, there is an undeniable privilege in being a Black American, no matter one's family origins. A Black woman from Chicago who moved to New Zealand (and asked *The Root* to use a pseudonym for her) spoke of being held up as a kind of "model minority" compared to Indigenous Maori and African New Zealanders (many of whom had arrived as refugees), which protected her from the kinds of discrimination those groups experienced when trying to find jobs, places to live, and a sense of inclusion in the dominant culture. Even so, she found that people had a narrow conception of what being a Black American meant. "At first it was really strange," she told the publication. "A lot of people approached me as being 'authentically black,' thinking that I would want to talk about hip-hop, and know how to sing. . . . I thought they were joking, but then their faces were dead serious."

As Stephanie Stew, who lives in Thailand with her husband and young daughter, told *The Root* (in an article unrelated to the site's Blaxit coverage), she knows that she gets more respect than her Ghanaian and Nigerian counterparts who live in the country. Locals dismiss them as public nuisances but defer to her Americanness as an entitlement to respect and kindness. "We're treated better. . . . We're treated better," she insisted, before describing an instance where a hair braider, an African woman, was turned away from the hotel where Stew's visiting sister-in-law was staying and hoped to use the woman's services. The staff

thought she was a sex worker. Africans in the country recognize the imbalance, which Stew said made it difficult to
form cross-cultural bonds.

This tendency to favor Black Americans at the apparent
expense of others even happens in Africa. In 2019, the Ghana
Tourism Authority launched "Year of Return," which marked
the four-hundred-year anniversary of the arrival of the first
Africans in Jamestown, Virginia. It was a year to honor the
struggles of those early arrivals, to celebrate the fact of their
descendants' survival in the face of long odds, and to position
Ghana as "a key travel destination for African Americans and
the African diaspora." The initiative added around 300,000
tourists to the country's average annual total and a record 126
new citizens. It also came with its share of controversy for
catering its message to Black populations in the United States
and the United Kingdom. One commentator asked, "Where
are the African descendants outside of the US, the Jamaicans,
Cubans and Brazilians?"

All those thoughts were swirling in my head on that
summer day in Salzburg. I looked up at the sunny skies,
around at the pastel-colored buildings, and over at my cousin's daughter, the little girl who was jetlagged and wanting
to sleep the day she and her dad arrived in Munich, but instead had to watch and wait as he—they—got denied entry
at our hotel. All this, on the very first day of her very first
trip abroad. I wonder what she'll remember of the experience, what kind of story she'll write one day.

ACKNOWLEDGMENTS

THE IDEA FOR THIS BOOK began on a boat ride to Europe in 1952, twenty-six years before I was born, which is to say that I feel like my purpose when I came along was to piece together its core elements, push the narrative in new directions, and—most important—find the people (or allow myself to be found by the people) who would help usher the idea into its final form.

I am forever grateful to Jenny Herrera of the David Black Agency for her early and enduring enthusiasm for the project, her keen sense of the shape it needed to take to find the right publishing home, and her confident, convivial guidance throughout.

From my very first conversation with Emma Berry, I knew that I'd found an editor who understood that I was trying to write the book I wished I'd been able to read as a young college student embarking on my junior-year semester abroad. She was crucial to the character-driven focus I developed for the book, and I did not know how I would move forward without her when she left Crown. And then Libby Burton and I came together, as if through providence.

Libby saw possibilities for the book I'd never considered, pointed out ways to stitch together what felt for a long time like a collection of disconnected essays, and always made me feel capable of rising to the challenge of digging deeper and thinking bigger. Working on this book with her was a true gift that made me a better historian and writer in the process.

I have had so many careful readers of different chapters and sections of the book, who advised me on matters of both style and substance. My earliest and most devoted were the members of two writing groups with fellow historians: Surekha Davies, with whom I established a lovely duo devoted to spending countless weekends discussing ways to balance rigor and readability; and my colleagues in the Creative Nonfiction Group at the University of Toronto (U of T)—Joshua Arthurs, Julie MacArthur, Sean Mills, William Nelson, Lilia Topuzova, Nhung Tran, and Rebecca Woods—who waded through messy, disjointed scraps of prose to help me define my structure and chart my next directions.

Early on in this process I knew I wanted to approach it as an opportunity to evolve as a storyteller, and for help I looked to Alex Marzano-Lesnevich, who assigned readings during a workshop at U of T that emboldened me to try new modes of storytelling. I also absorbed the infinite witchy wisdom of Carrie Frye, who always had the right question, analogy, suggested reading, or prompt to send me in the most generative directions. Not only did Nadia Owusu lead my 2021 Tin House Workshop in nonfiction and encourage me to think about moods, facial expressions, affect, and more, but her own book, *Aftershocks,* provided a beautiful model of the expansive possibilities of the form. I'm also grateful to my fellow workshop members—Gaar Adams, Dinika Amaral, Lauren Celenza, Hope Del Carlo, Jennie Malika Evenson, Olga Mikolaivna, Amna Naseer, Anthony Christian Ocampo, and Maya Osman-Krinsky—for their generous, incisive feedback.

One of the wonderful things about being a professional historian is knowing the exact sorts of experts and sages to approach for subject-matter feedback, and I thank Paulina Alberto, Herman Bennet, Gillian McGillivray, Rebekah Pite, Leslie Taliaferro, and Nhung Tran for the generosity of their suggestions and critiques.

Of course, there would have been no content for this book were it not for the people who lived the kinds of big, daring lives I chose to write about, and for that I am indebted to my grandparents John and Willie Mae Walker, Florence Mills, Oliver Golden, Joseph Roane, Richard Wright, Mabel Grammer, Philippa Schuyler, Herman De Bose, Kim Bass, and Ricki Stevenson for their time on and perambulations through this earth. I also thank Herman De Bose, Kim Bass, and Ricki Stevenson for their willingness to sit with me, answer my questions, and trust me to do their stories justice, and Kenneth Walker (not related) for sharing his memories of Ulysses Thompson.

I give thanks and love to my grandparents John and Willie Mae, my aunts and uncles, Juanita, Buddy, John, Joyce, Angelo, Gabriel, Alonzo, and Gail, my mom, Phyllis, my sister Tanisha, and all my cousins, for their examples, memories, love, and support. As grandpa always said: "WGAGF."

Finally, but also back to the beginning, my husband, Aaron, planted the first seed that what I had in me was a book on this topic, which came via a suggestion to read another book: Langston Hughes's *I Wonder as I Wander.* Reading it introduced me to many of the people who fill these pages and gave me the confidence to think I had something meaningful to say about them. I hope this book does the same for someone else.

NOTES

PROLOGUE

4   "Is the kind of America" James G. Thompson, "Should I Sacrifice to Live 'Half-American'?," *Pittsburgh Courier*, January 31, 1942.

5   "respond to the warmth" Richard Wright, *Black Boy* (New York: Harper & Brothers, 1945), 420.

6   "to live beyond the shores" Xabaka, "'I Choose Exile,' by Richard Wright," The Art of Sunday, August 2019, https://www.artofsunday.com/logs/i-choose-exile.

7   "There is more freedom" Xabaka, "'I Choose Exile,' by Richard Wright."

I. THE TRANSATLANTIC SENSATION

14 "Une artiste véritable" "Les oiseaux noirs—1926," *La Fronde*, May 30, 1926.

14 "Here is Florence Mills" "La revue des Ambassadeurs," *Le plaisir de vivre*, June 5, 1926.

15 "The Negroes Are Conquering Europe" Ivan Goll, "The Negroes Are Conquering Europe," in *The Weimar Republic Sourcebook*, ed. Anton Kaes, Martin Jay, and Edward Dimendberg (Berkeley: University of California Press, 1994), 559–60.

16 A notoriously poor "Shaw Historic District," District of Columbia Historic Preservation Office, 2008, http://dcpreservation-wpengine.netdna-ssl.com/wp-content/uploads/2014/12/Shaw-Brochure.pdf.

16 "leaky roofs, broken and filthy ceilings" James Borchert, "The

Rise and Fall of Washington's Inhabited Alleys: 1852–1972," *Records of the Columbia Historical Society, Washington, D.C.* 71/72 (1971): 276.

17 **"vice, crime, and immorality"** Borchert, "Rise and Fall of Washington's Inhabited Alleys," 279.

17 **Before they became marquee names** Bill Egan, *Florence Mills: Harlem Jazz Queen* (Lanham, Md.: Scarecrow Press, 2004), 8.

17 **Growing up on Goat Alley** Egan, *Florence Mills*, 2.

19 **"the cleverest dancing and singing three"** "James Vaughan with Us," *Chicago Defender*, June 3, 1916.

23 **"there is no complexion"** "Miss Kathleen Walker Gets Most Amazing Results from Dr. Fred Palmer's Skin Whitener," *Afro-American*, April 24, 1926.

24 **"saw that the Negro"** Ernest Howard Culbertson, *Goat Alley: A Tragedy of Negro Life* (Cincinnati: Stewart Kidd Company, 1922), 7.

24 **"an old coal-black Negress"** Culbertson, *Goat Alley*, 12.

24 **"Go 'long"** Culbertson, *Goat Alley*, 19.

25 **It would also mark** Ken Bloom and Richard Carlin, "10 Little-Known Facts About Sissle and Blake's Shuffle Along," *OUPblog*, December 8, 2020, https://blog.oup.com/2020/12/10-little-known-facts-about-sissle-and-blakes-shuffle-along/.

26 **"sandwiched between garages and other establishments"** Egan, *Florence Mills*, 60.

26 **"the Medical Review of Reviews"** "Goat Alley Is Dim as to 'Negro Problem,'" *New York Times*, June 21, 1921.

27 **"Dresden china"** Egan, *Florence Mills*, 60.

28 **"I don't like to think of that"** Egan, *Florence Mills*, 60.

28 **"the most skilful [*sic*] individual player"** Egan, *Florence Mills*, 62.

29 **"a spontaneous outburst"** "'Plantation Revue' Lively," *New York Times*, July 22, 1922.

29 *Dixie to Broadway* http://memory.loc.gov/diglib/ihas/loc.music.tda.3226/default.html#:~:text=A%20musical%20revue%20in%20two,appearance%20before%20her%20untimely%20death.

29 *Lew Leslie's Blackbirds of 1926* **opened** "The Darktown Strutters on Broadway: A Reassuring Word About the Alleged Menace of the Negro Show," *Vanity Fair*, November 1922, 67.

29 **"from the center"** "Florence Mills' 'Blackbirds' Fly," *Afro-American*, April 10, 1926.

31 **"gave just the proper push"** Langston Hughes, "When the Negro Was in Vogue," in *The Collected Works of Langston Hughes*, vol. 13,

ed. Joseph McLaren (Columbia: University of Missouri Press, 2002), 175.

32 **In one group were** "On the Water—Ocean Crossings, 1870–1969: Comfort, Courtesy, Safety, Speed," https://americanhistory.si .edu/onthewater/exhibition/5_3.html.

33 **"no attention to comfort or decency"** "In a Cunarder's Steerage; How the Poor Cross the Ocean," *New York Times*, August 23, 1879.

34 **"Here you will find contestants"** "In the Steerage of a Cunard Steamer," in *The Pall Mall Budget: Being a Weekly Collection of Articles Printed in "The Pall Mall Gazette" from Day to Day with a Summary of News*, vol. 22 (London, 1879), 9–12 (August 16, 1879).

35 **"every day was filled with sunshine"** Ethelene Whitmire, "Traveling While Black Across the Atlantic Ocean," Longreads, January 2019, https://longreads.com/2019/01/22/traveling-while -black-across-the-atlantic-ocean/.

36 **"the sensation of Paris"** Ivan H. Browning, "Across the Pond," *Chicago Defender*, July 17, 1926.

36 **"would stand out among"** "Les Ambassadeurs vont renaître," *Le Gaulois*, April 30, 1926.

37 **"Colored Artists Holding Sway"** "French Nation Carried Away by Entertainers in Paris Palaces," *New York Amsterdam News*, December 22, 1926.

38 **"French Harlem"** Thabiti Asukile, "J.A. Rogers' 'Jazz at Home': Afro-American Jazz in Paris During the Jazz Age," *Black Scholar* 40, no. 3 (2010): 27.

39 **"Go to her cabaret any night"** J. A. Rogers, "Paris Pepper Pot," *New York Amsterdam News*, June 22, 1929.

40 **"the little [n****r] thing"** Edward Burns, ed., *The Letters of Gertrude Stein and Carl Van Vechten* (New York: Columbia University Press, 2013), 162.

40 **"I am looking forward"** Edward Burns, ed., *The Letters of Gertrude Stein and Carl Van Vechten,* 119.

40 **"French women can always find"** "Race Artists Are Dominating Paris's Great White Way," *Afro-American*, February 5, 1927.

41 **"When I heard an American accent"** Henry Louis Gates, Jr., *The Henry Louis Gates, Jr. Reader* (New York: Basic Civitas, 2012), 560.

42 **"nationality of the husband and wife"** "Americans Protest at Negro Dancing with White Woman," *Variety*, June 9, 1926.

43 **"One of the big lessons"** "South America Gets Prejudice from the South," *Chicago Defender*, June 2, 1923.

44 In one article, a reporter described Ivan H. Browning, "Across the Pond," *Chicago Defender,* May 28, 1927.

44 "Miss Maitland declared" "Colored Team Home After 22 Mos. Abroad," *Variety,* October 9, 1929.

45 "Sensation of the Season" Caroline Bressey and Gemma Romain, "Staging Race," *Women's History Review* 28, no. 3 (2019): 381.

46 "difficult even for the worst cracker" Robert S. Abbott, "My Trip Abroad," *Chicago Defender,* January 4, 1930.

47 "what the negro has made" Bressey and Romain, "Staging Race," 384.

47 "There were indeed" Bressey and Romain, "Staging Race," 384.

47 "the quickest way" Bressey and Romain, "Staging Race," 385.

48 "We've had a great loss to us" Herbert Feinstein, "Lena Horne Speaks Freely: On Race, Marriage, Stage," *Ebony,* May 1963, 63.

48 "the largest, most impressive and tearful" "World Weeps as Florence Goes to Rest," *New York Amsterdam News,* November 9, 1927.

49 *The New York Times* put the crowd "Scores Collapse at Mills Funeral," *New York Times,* November 7, 1927.

DUSHA V DUSHU

53 "When I was growing up" Yelena Khanga, *Soul to Soul: The Story of a Black Russian American Family, 1865–1992* (New York: W. W. Norton, 1992), 20.

2. THE NEGRO COMRADES

57 "thunder of horses' hooves" "Moscow Celebrates Fourteenth Year," *Moscow News,* November 11, 1931.

57 "happy, smiling faces" "Epic of Working Class Strength," *Moscow News,* November 11, 1931.

57 "I asked Fort-Whiteman" Gwendolyn Midlo Hall, ed., *A Black Communist in the Freedom Struggle* (Minneapolis: University of Minnesota Press, 2012), 129–32.

58 "struggle by all available means" "Communist International," Google Arts & Culture, https://artsandculture.google.com /entity/communist-international/m01jr72?hl=en.

59 "But unlike schooling we had known" Hall, *Black Communist in the Freedom Struggle,* 129.

60 "the greatest pro-Communist influences" "Lynchings Food for Soviets," *Chicago Defender,* October 4, 1930.

62 "Tuskegee is nationally" Yelena Khanga, *Soul to Soul: The Story of a Black Russian American Family, 1865–1992* (New York: W. W. Norton, 1992), 73–76.

65 "the fatherland of all workers" "Americans Take Color Prejudice to Soviet Russia," *Norfolk Journal and Guide,* August 16, 1930.

66 "condemn severely this savage" "Americans Take Color Prejudice to Soviet Russia."

67 "intolerable that the chief character" "Russia May Prohibit 'Uncle Tom's Cabin,'" *Chicago Defender,* March 29, 1930.

67 "Negroes are urged" "New Uncle Tom Draws Pistol and Kills Legree," *Afro-American,* May 24, 1930.

67 "Russians Need No Prodding" "Russians Need No Prodding Where Justice and Fair Play to Negroes Are Concerned," *Afro-American,* September 20, 1930.

67 "I yearned" Homer Smith, *Black Man in Red Russia* (Chicago: Johnson Publishing Company, 1964), 77–83.

68 "I was young" Khanga, *Soul to Soul,* 77.

68 "I'll be back" Hall, *Black Communist in the Freedom Struggle,* 185.

69 "The first stop was London" Khanga, *Soul to Soul,* 78.

70 "What are you" Khanga, *Soul to Soul,* 79.

71 "its heroes and heroines were Negro" Langston Hughes, *I Wonder as I Wander* (New York: Hill and Wang, 1993), loc. 1470, Kindle.

72 "enormous rooms" Hughes, *I Wonder as I Wander,* loc. 1397, Kindle.

73 "ran into a Russian embrace" Hall, *Black Communist in the Freedom Struggle,* 129–32.

74 "Free the Scottsboro Boys!" Hall, *Black Communist in the Freedom Struggle,* 185.

74 "Negrochanski tovarish" Hughes, *I Wonder as I Wander,* loc. 1412, Kindle.

75 "She had no desire to flaunt" Khanga, *Soul to Soul,* 73.

77 But even as their mosques Marianne Kamp, "Where Did the Mullahs Go? Oral Histories from Rural Uzbekistan," *Die Welt des Islams* 50, no. 3/4 (2010), 503–31.

80 "The people looked" Julia L. Mickenberg, *American Girls in Red Russia* (Chicago: University of Chicago Press, 2017), 283.

82 "As a convenience" Hughes, *I Wonder as I Wander,* loc. 3177, Kindle.

83 "Christmas day was wonderful" Hughes, *I Wonder as I Wander*, loc. 3191, Kindle.

85 "I beg you never to come" Joshua Yaffa, "Exiled: Why Did a Black Activist Disappear in Stalin's Russia?," *New Yorker*, October 25, 2021, https://www.newyorker.com/magazine/2021/10/25/a-black-communists-disappearance-in-stalins-russia-lovett-fort-whiteman-gulag.

85 "he died of starvation" Yaffa, "Exiled."

87 "it has become almost impossible" "Farm Specialist in Russia's Employ Here with Family," *Norfolk Journal and Guide*, September 11, 1937.

87 "If you have dependents" "College Grads Rave About Soviet Jobs," *New York Amsterdam News*, September 4, 1937.

88 "GLAD TO READ FRESH news" "College Grads Rave About Soviet Jobs."

89 "Arrest me" Khanga, *Soul to Soul*, 91.

90 "In just a few years" Khanga, *Soul to Soul*, 79.

90 "remembers Russia very distinctly" "The Roanes, Who Spent Six Years in Russia, Guests Here," *Norfolk Journal and Guide*, January 2, 1943.

90 "As far as I know" Carl Schreck, "Meet Yosif Stalin, the Soviet-Born Black American from Kremlin, Virginia," Radio Free Europe/Radio Liberty, April 8, 2016, https://www.rferl.org/a/soviet-union-yosif-stalin-black-american-kremlin-virginia/27663044.html.

3. THE *HIJO NATIVO*

98 "He stared at her dim face" Richard Wright, *Native Son* (New York: Harper & Brothers, 1940), 84.

100 The production was put on "Negritud, invasión y peligro en la Buenos Aires de 1945: un análisis de las representaciones raciales a través de la publicidad de la obra teatral Sangre negra," http://www.publicacions.ub.edu/refs/indices/08302.pdf.

100 "The plans are to change" Constance Webb, *Richard Wright: A Biography* (New York: Putnam, 1968), 293.

102 "Oh no" Webb, *Richard Wright*, 295.

104 "I desired to stay" Richard Wright, "The Shame of Chicago," *Ebony*, January 1951.

105 "Hell, man, this damn hotel" Wright, "Shame of Chicago."

106 "To make the screen version" Jeanine Delpech, "An Interview with Native Son," *Crisis* 57, no. 10 (November 1950): 625–27.

108 "a small, unpretentious, midtown hotel" Virginia Lee Warren, "Argentina Doubles as Chicago Locale for 'Native Son,'" *New York Times,* May 21, 1950.

108 "I've never been able" Hazel Rowley, *Richard Wright: The Life and Times* (New York: Henry Holt, 2001), 359.

111 "[Richard's] personal manners" Rowley, *Richard Wright*, 384.

112 "Everywhere I look, Lord" Richard Wright, "The FB Eye Blues," Brown Digital Repository, https://repository.library.brown.edu /studio/item/bdr:294360/.

112 "communal idea and undertaking" Webb, *Richard Wright*, 297.

114 Back in the real Paris Simone de Beauvoir, *A Transatlantic Love Affair: Letters to Nelson Algren*, trans. Ellen Gordon Reeves (New York: The New Press, 1998).

116 "to be in trouble" Webb, *Richard Wright*, 302.

116 "Eastside housewife and actress" "Mrs. Willa Curtis Gets Role in 'Native Son'; Shooting to Be Done in South America," *Los Angeles Sentinel,* January 19, 1950.

116 "believed to be the first" "Mrs. Willa Curtis Gets Role in 'Native Son.'"

117 "fundamental human rights" E. Perón, *Mensaje a las mujeres de america* (1950).

117 There was also Raúl Grigera Paulina Alberto, *Black Legend: The Many Lives of Raúl Grigera and the Power of Racial Storytelling in Argentina* (Cambridge: Cambridge University Press, 2022).

120 "Oh, Dick" Warren, "Argentina Doubles as Chicago Locale for 'Native Son.'"

121 "they [did not] try you" Webb, *Richard Wright*, 300.

121 "Dick is still in South America" Beauvoir, *Transatlantic Love Affair*, 360.

122 "It's your life against mine" Beauvoir, *Transatlantic Love Affair*, 360.

123 It wasn't even the kiss Thy Phu, "Bigger at the Movies: *Sangre Negra* and the Cinematic Projection of *Native Son*," *Black Camera* 2, no. 1 (2010): 36–57.

123 "we stuck pretty close" Delpech, "Interview with Native Son," 626.

124 "With a certain modicum of subtlety" "Film Reviews: Native Son," *Variety,* April 25, 1951.

124 **"I think it stinks"** SWIG, "'Native Son' Has One Encouraging Feature!," *New York Amsterdam News,* June 23, 1951.

125 **"could have been the quintessential"** Ellen Scott, "Blacker Than Noir: The Making and Unmaking of Richard Wright's 'Ugly' *Native Son* (1951)," *Adaptation* 6, no. 1 (February 2013): 93–119.

125 **"So now he had a taste"** John Alfred Williams, *The Most Native of Sons: A Biography of Richard Wright,* 90.

125 **"What the writer actually sees"** "Richard Wright Explains Ideas About Movie Making," *Ebony,* January 1951, 85.

126 **"I had been born"** Richard Wright, *Pagan Spain* (New York: Harper & Brothers, 1957), 1.

4. THE MOTHER OF (RE)INVENTION

131 **"You're just feeling sorry"** Ralph Martin and Tom Mathews, "The Remarkable Mission of Mabel Grammer," *Good Housekeeping,* January 1969, 40.

132 **There may have been** American Bar Association, "Birth Certificates," November 20, 2018, https://www.americanbar.org /groups/public_education/publications/teaching-legal-docs /birth-certificates/.

133 **"It isn't how much you make"** Martin and Mathews, "Remarkable Mission of Mabel Grammer," 44.

134 **The Pythian was owned** National Park Service, "African Americans and the Hot Springs Baths," http://npshistory.com/bro chures/hosp/african-americans.pdf.

135 **The school had enrolled** Pamela Pritchard, "The Negro Experience at the Ohio State University in the First Sixty-Five Years, 1873–1938: With Special Emphasis on Negroes in the College of Education" (PhD diss., Ohio State University, 1982), https:// library.osu.edu/sites/default/files/collection_files/subject_files /African%20American%20Graduates%20and%20Former%20 Students.pdf.

136 **"Beautiful Beautician"** "Beautiful Beautician," *Afro-American,* October 29, 1938.

137 **"A woman lends to the comfort"** Mabel Alston, "Your Face Is Your Fortune," *Afro-American,* November 12, 1938.

138 **"had a reputation"** Ralph Matthews, "Mabel Switched from Minks to Orphans," *Cleveland Call and Post,* January 22, 1955.

138 "associating with swarthy diplomats" Matthews, "Mabel Switched from Minks to Orphans."

139 "The eyes of the nations" Mabel Alston, "Mrs. Roosevelt Urges Unity in U.S. Living," *Afro-American*, January 2, 1943.

139 "Miss Margaret Lewis, alias Maggie" "Little Rays of Sunshine in the D.C. Office," *Afro-American*, December 19, 1942.

141 "old proverb" Mabel Alston, "Charm School," *Afro-American*, August 18, 1945.

141 "an interim of seclusion" Matthews, "Mabel Switched from Minks to Orphans."

142 "Well, well" Toki Schalk, "TOKI Types," *Pittsburgh Courier*, January 12, 1946.

142 "What we liked best" Toki Schalk Johnson, "TOKI Types," *Pittsburgh Courier*, November 22, 1947.

144 In Mannheim, they lived in Alexis Clark, "When Jim Crow Reigned Amid the Rubble of Nazi Germany," *New York Times Magazine*, February 19, 2020.

145 Once, as he entered Clark, "When Jim Crow Reigned Amid the Rubble of Nazi Germany."

145 "It's asking too much" Ollie Stewart, "Ollie Revisits Occupied Germany," *Afro-American*, September 29, 1951.

145 Mabel, a lifelong Catholic Alexis Clark, "Overlooked No More: Mabel Grammer, Whose Brown Baby Plan Found Homes for Hundreds," *New York Times*, February 6, 2019.

146 "people coming back to Paris" Ollie Stewart, "This Week's Report from Europe," *Afro-American*, February 10, 1951.

148 The rise of Hitler United States Holocaust Memorial Museum, "Nuremberg Race Laws," Holocaust Encyclopedia, September 11, 2019, https://encyclopedia.ushmm.org/content/en/article/nuremberg-laws.

148 "We were deeply hurt" Heide Fehrenbach, *Race After Hitler: Black Occupation Children in Postwar Germany and America* (Princeton, N.J.: Princeton University Press, 2005), 32.

149 "What's wrong with adopting children?" Martin and Mathews, "Remarkable Mission of Mabel Grammer," 40.

150 "By the time I got home" Martin and Mathews, "Remarkable Mission of Mabel Grammer," 40.

150 They numbered around five thousand Fehrenbach, *Race After Hitler*.

151 **They were known by** Robbie Aitken, "Making Visible the Invisible: Germany's Black Diaspora, 1880s–1945," Sheffield Hallam University, October 10, 2019, https://www.shu.ac.uk/research/in-action/projects/being-black-in-nazi-germany.

151 **"white women, of course"** Lucy Bland, Britain's "Brown Babies" (Manchester, U.K.: Manchester University Press, 2019), 29–30.

151 **"white Southern lieutenant"** Bland, Britain's "Brown Babies," 32.

152 **"There was a group of us"** "Conceived in War, Lost in Peace: Britain's Mixed-Race GI Babies," CNN, June 4, 2019, https://www.youtube.com/watch?v=4CVIvtMOzeM.

152 **She was born in 1944** Charlie Jones, "The 'Brown Babies' Who Were Left Behind," BBC News, May 17, 2019, https://www.bbc.com/news/uk-england-48294237.

153 **"They said we wanted"** Martin and Mathews, "Remarkable Mission of Mabel Grammer," 40.

153 **"Mabel can stretch"** Martin and Mathews, "Remarkable Mission of Mabel Grammer," 42.

153 **"She has found adoptive parents"** Martin and Mathews, "Remarkable Mission of Mabel Grammer," 36.

154 **"As long as I am in Germany"** Mabel A. Grammer, "What to Do About Adopting War Babies," Afro-American, March 7, 1953.

155 **"Don't allow yourself to be kidded,"** Grammer, "What to Do About Adopting War Babies."

157 **"Before she left Washington"** Matthews, "Mabel Switched from Minks to Orphans."

158 **"Oh Lord"** Martin and Mathews, "Remarkable Mission of Mabel Grammer," 46.

159 **"was so tasty"** Mabel A. Grammer, "Americans En Route Home, Society in Germany Slows," Afro-American, May 2, 1953.

159 **"and otherwise underprivileged children"** "Whatever Became Of: Mabel Grammer," Afro-American, April 1, 1961.

160 **"About my father"** Doris McMillon, "A Double Reunion: How I Found My German Mother and GI Father," Ebony, May 1, 1982, 42.

162 **"Just be thankful"** Claudia Levy, "Mabel Grammer Dies; Arranged Adoptions," Washington Post, June 26, 2002.

5. THE BEAUTIFUL AMERICAN

173 **"the thousands of Catholic"** Press clippings, 1962–66, box 1, Philippa Schuyler Collection, New York Public Library.

173 "Nietzsche, Dostoievsky and Flaubert" Lincoln Barnett, "Negro Girl, 2½, Recites Omar and Spells 5-Syllable Words," *New York Herald Tribune*, February 8, 1934.

174 "studying Chinese philosophy" Josephine Schuyler, "An Interracial Marriage," *American Mercury*, March 1946, 273.

175 "We enjoyed with equal gusto" Schuyler, "An Interracial Marriage," 274.

175 "Philippa is not a child prodigy" Barnett, "Negro Girl, 2½, Recites Omar."

176 "Honor Roll of Race Relations" "18 Nominees for Honor Roll of Race Relations for 1940 Announced," *New York Amsterdam News*, February 15, 1941.

176 "Philippa Schuyler Day" "World's Fair to Have Philippa Schuyler Day," *Tampa Bulletin*, June 15, 1940.

176 "the Shirley Temple of America's Negroes" Magazines, 1958–64, box 2, Philippa Schuyler Collection, New York Public Library.

176 "When we're travelling" Magazines, 1958–64, box 2, Philippa Schuyler Collection.

178 "What has four wheels and flies?" Magazines, 1958–64, box 2, Philippa Schuyler Collection.

178 One widely assigned textbook Donald Yacovone, *Teaching White Supremacy: America's Democratic Ordeal and the Forging of Our National Identity* (New York: Pantheon Books, 2022).

179 "a disproportionate number" Stephen Robertson, "Schools in 1920s Harlem," *Digital Harlem Blog*, July 16, 2018, https://drstephen robertson.com/digitalharlemblog/maps/schools-in-1920s -harlem/.

179 Black parents, teachers, and Thomas Harbison, "'A Serious Pedagogical Situation': Diverging School Reform Priorities in Depression Era Harlem," in *Educating Harlem: A Century of Schooling and Resistance in a Black Community* (New York: Columbia University Press, 2019).

179 "savages, uncultured and wild" Schuyler, "An Interracial Marriage," 276.

180 "In the picture, (left to right)" "Piano Prodigy Shares Her Birthday Cake," *New York Amsterdam Star-News*, August 9, 1941.

183 "beautiful Spanish villa" Magazines, 1958–64, box 2, Philippa Schuyler Collection.

183 "In the field" "Good Neighbor Policy," Office of the Historian, https://history.state.gov/milestones/1921-1936/good-neighbor

#:~:text=In%20his%20inaugural%20address%20on,respects%20
the%20rights%20of%20others.%E2%80%9D

184   **"no state has the right"** "Good Neighbor Policy," Office of the Historian.

184   **"constantly said"** "Philippa Schuyler Returns from Mexico," *Norfolk New Journal and Guide*, June 3, 1944.

185   **"It must be fun"** Philippa Schuyler, "Friends Across the Border," *Calling All Girls*, March 1945, 15.

186   **His book *Nigger Heaven*** Kelefa Sanneh, "White Mischief: The Passions of Carl Van Vechten," *New Yorker*, February 17 and 24, 2014.

188   **"an intelligent ambassador of her country"** A. E. Illiers, "Philippa Schuyler Is Hailed in Panama City," *Chicago Defender*, August 30, 1952.

188   **"out of keeping with democratic ideals"** Leslie Crawford, "The Gentle Art of Handkissing," *Ebony*, October 1967, 96.

188   **"This is how I have lived"** Philippa Schuyler, *Adventures in Black and White* (New York: Robert Speller & Sons, 1960), 9.

189   **"a ceremony given by a group"** Schuyler, *Adventures in Black and White*, 15.

189   **"In 1954, I returned to Mexico"** Schuyler, *Adventures in Black and White*, 16.

190   **"supposedly Haiti's most eligible bachelor"** Schuyler, *Adventures in Black and White*, 43.

190   **"I didn't think the West Indies"** Schuyler, *Adventures in Black and White*, 45.

191   **"mixed couples"** Schuyler, *Adventures in Black and White*, 58.

192   **"All eyes were on me"** Schuyler, *Adventures in Black and White*, 331.

192   **"a sharp voice called to me"** Schuyler, *Adventures in Black and White*, 75–77.

193   **"I have found"** Schuyler, *Adventures in Black and White*, 342.

195   **"And on that trip"** Death and memorial papers, May 2, 1969–June 1, 1969, box 3, Philippa Schuyler Collection, New York Public Library.

196   **"Miss Schuyler had been at Hue"** United Press International, "Philippa Schuyler, Pianist, Dies in Crash of a Copter in Vietnam," *New York Times*, May 10, 1967.

197   **"She was Diana"** Death and memorial papers, May 2, 1969–June 1, 1969, box 3, Philippa Schuyler Collection.

198 "**I am killing myself**" Death and memorial papers, May 2, 1969–
     June 1, 1969, box 3, Philippa Schuyler Collection.

198 "**spoke of Blacks in America**," "Author George S. Schuyler Dies at
     82 in New York," *Jet*, September 29, 1977.

MY GRANDFATHER'S GRANDDAUGHTER

207 "**promote international cooperation**" Mutual Education and Cul-
     tural Exchange Program, 22 U.S.C. § 2451, https://uscode.house
     .gov/view.xhtml?path=/prelim@title22/chapter33&
     edition=prelim.

6. THE VOLUNTEER

212 "**I'm sitting on the library steps**" Herman De Bose, interview
     with the author, April 2020. All De Bose quotes henceforth are
     from this interview.

213 "**I want to express my thanks**" "The Founding Moment," Peace
     Corps, https://www.peacecorps.gov/about/history/founding
     -moment/.

215 "**be responsible for the training**" Executive Order 10924, Establish-
     ment and Adminstration of the Peace Corps in the Department
     of State, March 1, 1961, General Records of the United States Gov-
     ernment, Record Group 11, National Archives, https://www
     .archives.gov/historical-docs/todays-doc/?dod-date=922.

216 "**winning friends for the U.S.**" "Peace Corps: Negroes Play Vital
     Role in U.S. Quest for Friends Abroad," *Ebony*, November 1961, 39.

218 "**we had two wars to win**" "Ray Elliot—1939–1945: 'Two Wars to
     Win,'" *American Centuries*, Memorial Hall Museum, http://www
     .americancenturies.mass.edu/centapp/oh/story.do?shortName
     =elliot1939vv.

218 "**Should black Americans**" "A Costly Interlude," *Peace Corps Vol-
     unteer*, July–August 1968, 4–7.

219 "**a costly interlude**" "A Costly Interlude," *Peace Corps Volunteer*.

220 "**Howard was found a 'natural'**" "Peace Corps Training at How-
     ard," *Ebony*, November 1962, 69–77.

220 "**went to Jamaica**" "This Is Janet Sledge," *Ebony*, August 1971, 119.

220 "**has led [the] poor of Peru**" "Young Publisher with Problems,"
     Ebony, November 1965, 101–9.

221 " 'help' Black and Brown people" Jonathan Zimmerman, "Be-
     yond Double Consciousness: Black Peace Corps Volunteers in
     Africa, 1961–1971," *Journal of American History* 82, no. 3 (1995): 999–
     1028.

221 "Don't you think" Zimmerman, "Beyond Double Conscious-
     ness," 999–1028.

224 "Youth sees our civilization" Associated Press, "McGovern Criti-
     cizes Vietnam War in Commencement Address," *Daily Times-
     News,* June 2, 1969, https://www.newspapers.com/clip/9272605
     /gc-religion-supports-vietnam-protests/.

229 "all persons are equal" Mary L. Dudziak, "Working Toward De-
     mocracy: Thurgood Marshall and the Constitution of Kenya,"
     Duke Law Journal 56, no. 3 (2006): 757.

229 "unreeled against the backdrop" Lerone Bennett, "Uhuru Comes
     to Kenya," *Ebony,* February 1964, 134.

231 "gimlets were chilled" Robert Conley, "Nairobi Is Losing Its Co-
     lonial Air," *New York Times,* January 5, 1964.

231 The first time was after Nick Mafi, "The Beatles Stayed Here—
     and You Can, Too," *Condé Nast Traveler,* August 22, 2014.

231 Today, a picture of Hemingway "Our Sarova Stanley Story," The
     Sarova Stanley, https://www.sarovahotels.com/stanley-nairobi
     /stanley-heritage.html.

231 "not only the major diversion" Craig Claiborne, "The Cosmo-
     politan Cuisine in Nairobi Runs from Artichokes to Zabaglione,"
     New York Times, December 7, 1970.

232 "safari-clad Englishmen" William Strickland, "The African An-
     swer," *New York Amsterdam News,* October 9, 1971.

233 "who asked that his name" "Doctor Finds Freedom from Racism
     in Africa," *Afro-American,* November 1, 1969.

233 "Even in the African-managed hotels" Strickland, "The African
     Answer."

238 "Right now there is the male" "A Very Special Volunteer," *Ebony,*
     September 1978, 65.

238 "white black" Zimmerman, "Beyond Double Consciousness,"
     999–1028.

242 "gave me the courage" Sia Barbara Kamara, "Part of the Discus-
     sion on 'Building a Community of Black RPCVs: Recruitment
     Challenges and Opportunities," National Peace Corps Association,
     last modified January 17, 2022, https://www.peacecorpsconnect
     .org/articles/first-comes-belonging-sia-barbara-kamara.

AWAY TO CANADA

247 **"full human dignity"** Gilbert King, "What Paul Robeson Said," *Smithsonian Magazine,* September 13, 2011.

247 **"I would say that unquestionably"** "Paul Robeson: On Colonialism, African-American Rights," from *Spotlight,* ABC, 1960, YouTube video, posted August 21, 2013, https://www.youtube.com/watch?v=puOIdh944vk&ab_channel=ABCEducation.

248 **"This is our home"** "The African-American Mosaic: Abolition," Library of Congress, Exhibitions, https://www.loc.gov/exhibits/african/afam005.html.

7. THE FAVORITE SON

250 **"I only did basically"** Kim Bass, interview with the author, April 2020. All Bass quotes henceforth are from this interview.

252 **"our progress as a nation"** John F. Kennedy, Special Message to the Congress on Education, February 20, 1961, https://www.presidency.ucsb.edu/documents/special-message-the-congress-education-1.

252 **"a strong and better America"** Kasie Coccaro, "Superman's Mission for President Kennedy: Let's Move!," *Let's Move Blog,* Let's Move: America's Move to Raise a Healthier Generation of Kids, April 17, 2014, https://letsmove.obamawhitehouse.archives.gov/blog/2014/04/17/superman%E2%80%99s-mission-president-kennedy-let%E2%80%99s-move.

254 **"officials say their province's"** "Annual Vacation Guide: Expo 67," *Ebony,* June 1967, 141.

256 **"Racism for blacks"** Philip J. Griffin, "Comment: What Happens to a Dream Deferred," *Georgian,* January 28, 1969.

256 **By early 1969, there were protests** Maude-Emmanuelle Lambert, "Sir George Williams Affair," *The Canadian Encyclopedia,* December 20, 2016, https://www.thecanadianencyclopedia.ca/en/article/sir-george-williams-affair.

256 **Nearly one hundred students were arrested** Lambert, "Sir George Williams Affair."

257 **"It was a fight for Black people"** Lambert, "Sir George Williams Affair."

257 **Eric Fontaine's 1973 election** Richard M. Chapman, Tyler Kemen, and Benjamin Paul, "Eric Fontaine, c. 1974 (1952–Present)," Cor-

dopedia, http://cordopedia.concordiacollegearchives.org/content /eric-fontaine-c-1974-1952-present.

258 **"We call it an experiment"** "Watt Speaks About International Experiment, Shows Group Movies," *Vassar Miscellany News,* December 10, 1947.

258 **If this sounds familiar** Alvino E. Fantini, "An Institutional Overview," *About Our Institution: Inaugural Issue on the Occasion of SIT's 35th Anniversary,* SIT Occasional Papers Series (Brattleboro, Vt.: School for International Training, 2000), 1.

259 **"I used to hate the Americans"** Edgar A. Porter and Ran Ying Porter, *Japanese Reflections on World War II and the American Occupation,* 204–11.

260 **"who came in all colors"** Porter and Porter, *Japanese Reflections on World War II,* 204–11.

260 **Watt led a group of five** Catherine Lu, Toshihiro Menju, and Melissa Williams, "Japan and 'the Other': Reconceiving Japanese Citizenship in the Era of Globalization," *Asian Perspective* 29, no. 1, 2005, 99–134.

266 **The Jackson Five and Stevie Wonder** "Jermaine Wins Prize at Tokyo Music Festival," *Los Angeles Sentinel,* April 30, 1981.

266 **"jazz crazed"** "Jazz Crazed," *Los Angeles Sentinel,* January 7, 1982.

269 **"Take them and go home"** Kristen Roebuck, "Orphans by Design," *Japanese Studies* 36, no. 2 (2016): 191–212.

269 **"trash-ridden black ghetto"** Roebuck, "Orphans by Design," 16.

269 **"The happiest fate for a black"** Roebuck, "Orphans by Design," 16.

271 **"one of Tokyo's"** "An American Export: Young Actor Becomes TV Star in Japan," *Ebony,* September 1982, 48.

WALKING THE SPIRIT

278 **"always had a great appreciation"** Charles L. Sanders, "A Farewell to Josephine: France Pays a Final Tribute to One of Its Greatest Stars," *Ebony,* July 1975, 52.

8. THE TOUR GUIDE

281 **"I wonder what the weather's like"** Ricki Stevenson, interview with the author, November 2019. All Stevenson quotes henceforth are from this interview.

282 **"Go on back to Russia"** "The Peeksill, N.Y. Riot Occurs," African

American Registry, https://aaregistry.org/story/riot-at-peekskill
-n-y/.

283   **"You look handsome and dashing"** *Today,* December 22, 1959.

286   **"Mickey Go Home"** Steven Greenhouse, "Playing Disney in the
Parisian Fields," *New York Times,* February 17, 1991.

286   **"a cultural Chernobyl"** Greenhouse, "Playing Disney in the Parisian Fields."

289   **"a richly unique cultural experience"** https://www.blackparis
tour.com/.

289   **Their multigenerational presence** Alan Riding, "A Surge of Racism in France Brings a Search for Answers," *New York Times,*
May 27, 1990.

290   **"For African Americans"** "Americans in Paris," *This American Life,*
July 28, 2000, https://www.thisamericanlife.org/165/americans
-in-paris.

THERE ARE PLACES IN THIS WORLD

295   **"If you don't want"** Aamna Mohdin, "Statistically Speaking,
Black People in Germany Don't Exist," *Quartz,* September 23,
2017.

295   **"We don't do [the] burqa"** "German Interior Minister Speaks
Out in Favor of 'Leitkultur' for Immigrants," Deutsche Welle,
April 30, 2017, https://www.dw.com/en/german-interior-minister
-speaks-out-in-favor-of-leitkultur-for-immigrants/a-38643836.

296   **"Belong Anywhere"** "Introduction," Airbnb, July 16, 2014,
https://blog.atairbnb.com/belong-anywhere/.

298   **"There are places in this world"** Fly Brother, "Trayvon Martin,"
Fly Brother, July 17, 2013, https://flybrother.net/tag/trayvon
-martin/.

298   **"Where we will go"** Ulysses Burley III, "#BLAXIT: 21 Things
We're Taking with Us If We Leave," *The Salt Collective,* https://
thesaltcollective.org/6936-2/.

299   **"The privilege of dual citizenship"** Tiffanie Drayton, "I'm a Black
American. I Had to Get Out," *New York Times,* June 12, 2020.

299   **"Travel means something different"** Correspondence with the
author, March 18, 2022.

300   **"Having since been around the world"** Langston Hughes, *I Wonder as I Wander* (New York: Hill and Wang, 1993), loc. 1897, Kindle.

300   **"It is not diverse here"** Jennifer Neal, "For Those Considering

Blaxit, I Present to You: Melbourne (Yes, Australia)," *The Root*, July 18, 2017.

300 **"gorilla joke[s]"** Jennifer Neal, "For Those Considering Blaxit, I Present to You: Seoul, South Korea," *The Root*, December 20, 2017.

300 **"They use vulgar words"** Jennifer Neal, "For Those Considering Blaxit, I Present to You: Budapest, Hungary," *The Root*, June 24, 2017.

301 **"At first it was really strange"** Jennifer Neal, "For Those Considering Blaxit, I Present to You: New Zealand," *The Root*, September 19, 2017.

301 **"We're treated better"** Diana Ozemebhoya Eromosele, "Being Black in Thailand: We're Treated Better Than Africans, and Boy Do We Hate It," *The Root*, May 26, 2015.

302 **"a key travel destination"** Kwabena Agyare Yeboah, "We Need to Talk About Ghana's Year of Return and Its Politics of Exclusion," African Arguments, December 19, 2019, https://africanarguments.org/2019/12/ghana-year-of-return-politics-of-exclusion/.

302 **"Where are the African"** Yeboah, "We Need to Talk About Ghana's Year of Return."

INDEX

ABOUT THE AUTHOR

TAMARA J. WALKER is a historian and associate professor of Africana studies at Barnard College of Columbia University, where her research and teaching focus on the history of slavery and freedom in Latin America and their legacies in the modern era. Her first book, *Exquisite Slaves: Race, Clothing, and Status in Colonial Lima,* won the Harriet Tubman Prize awarded by the Schomburg Center for Research in Black Culture. Her writing has appeared in *Columbia Global Reports, The Guardian, Slate,* and *The Root.*

tamarajwalker.com

ABOUT THE TYPE

This book was set in Dante, a typeface designed by Giovanni Mardersteig (1892–1977). Conceived as a private type for the Officina Bodoni in Verona, Italy, Dante was originally cut only for hand composition by Charles Malin, the famous Parisian punch cutter, between 1946 and 1952. Its first use was in an edition of Boccaccio's *Trattatello in laude di Dante* that appeared in 1954. The Monotype Corporation's version of Dante followed in 1957. Though modeled on the Aldine type used for Pietro Cardinal Bembo's treatise *De Aetna* in 1495, Dante is a thoroughly modern interpretation of that venerable face.

nguin Random House LLC
5 Broadway
-NY, 10019

ps://www.penguinrandomhouse.com
00-733-3000

authorized representative in the EU for product safety and compliance is

guin Random House Ireland
rison Chambers, 32 Nassau Street
2 YH68

s://eu-contact.penguin.ie

I: 9780593139073
ase ID: 151204861

Printed in the United States
by Baker & Taylor Publisher Services